Presence

Presence

Bringing Your Boldest Self to
Your Biggest Challenges

Amy Cuddy

This edition first published in Great Britain in 2016
by Orion
an imprint of the Orion Publishing Group Ltd
Carmelite House, 50 Victoria Embankment,
London, EC4Y 0DZ
An Hachette UK Company

3 5 7 9 10 8 6 4

A CIP catalogue record for this book
is available from the British Library.

Hardback ISBN: 978 1 4091 5600 0
Trade Paperback ISBN: 978 1 4091 5601 7

The publisher is not responsible for websites (or their content)
that are not owned by the publisher.

In order to protect the privacy of some individuals,
I have changed their names and identifying details and
in some cases created composites of multiple people.

The author is grateful for permission to reprint an excerpt from
"Bright as Yellow" by Karen Peris (the innocence mission).

Illustrations in chapter 6 courtesy of Nikolaus F. Troje,
from Cuddy and Troje (in preparation).
Illustrations and graph in chapter 8 by Dailey Crafton.

Printed and bound by CPI Group (UK) Ltd, Croydon, CR0 4YY

The Orion Publishing Group's policy is to use papers that
are natural, renewable and recyclable and made
from wood grown in sustainable forests. The logging and
manufacturing processes are expected to conform to the
environmental regulations of the country of origin.

www.orionbooks.co.uk

For Jonah and Paul,

the loves of my life…

Thank you for patiently reminding me, again and again,

to "just stand up on the surfboard"

Contents

And you live life with your arms reached out,
Eye to eye when speaking.
Enter rooms with great joy shouts,
Happy to be meeting....
Bright as yellow,
Warm as yellow.

— Karen Peris (the innocence mission)

Presence

Introduction

I'm sitting at the counter in my favorite Boston bookstore-café, laptop open, writing. Ten minutes ago I ordered coffee and a muffin. The server — a young, dark-haired woman with a broad smile and glasses — paused and quietly said, "I just want to tell you how much your TED talk meant to me — how much it inspired me. A couple years ago my professor posted it for a class I was taking. Now I'm applying to medical school, and I want you to know that I stood in the bathroom like Wonder Woman before I took my MCAT, and it really helped. So even though you don't know me, you helped me figure out what I really wanted to do with my life — go to medical school — and then you helped me do what I needed to do to get there. Thank you."

Tears in my eyes, I asked, "What's your name?"

"Fetaine," she said. Then we chatted for the next ten minutes about Fetaine's challenges in the past and newfound excitement about her future.

Everyone who approaches me is unique and memorable, but this kind of interaction happens far more frequently than I'd ever have anticipated: a stranger warmly greets me, shares a personal story about how they successfully coped with a particular challenge, and then simply thanks me for my small part in it. They're women and men, old and young, timid and gregarious, struggling and wealthy. But something binds them: all have felt powerless in the face of great pressure and anxiety, and all discovered a remarkably simple way to liberate themselves from that feeling of powerlessness, at least for that moment.

For most authors, the book comes first, then the responses. For me, it was the other way around. First, I conducted a series of experiments that gave rise to a talk I delivered at the TEDGlobal conference in 2012. In that talk, I discussed some intriguing findings, from my own and others' research, about how our bodies can influence our brains and behavior. (This is where I described that Wonder-Woman-in-the-bathroom thing Fetaine mentioned, which I will explain by and by, that can quickly increase our confidence and decrease our anxiety in challenging situations.) I also shared my own struggles with impostor syndrome and how I learned to trick myself to feel — and actually to become — more confident. I referred to this phenomenon as "fake it till you become it." (By the way, in the talk, that part about my own struggles was almost entirely unplanned and unscripted, because I didn't think I had the audacity to disclose something so personal to the hundreds of people in that audience. Little did I know....) I didn't know whether these topics would resonate with people. They surely spoke to me. Immediately after the twenty-one-minute video of the talk was posted on the Internet, I began hearing from people who had seen it.

Of course, watching my talk didn't magically give Fetaine the knowledge she needed to do well on the MCAT. She didn't miraculously acquire a detailed understanding of the characteristics of smooth-strain versus rough-strain bacteria or how the work-energy theorem relates to changes in kinetic energy. But it may have released her from the fear that could have prevented her from expressing the things she knew. Powerlessness engulfs us — and all that we believe, know, and feel. It enshrouds who we are, making us invisible. It even alienates us from ourselves.

The opposite of powerlessness must be power, right? In a sense that's true, but it's not quite that simple. The research I've been doing for years now joins a large body of inquiry into a quality I call *presence*. Presence stems from believing in and trusting yourself — your real, honest feelings, values, and abilities. That's important, because if you don't trust yourself, how can others trust you? Whether we are talking in front of two people or five thousand, interviewing for a job, negotiating for a raise, or pitching a business idea to potential investors, speaking up for ourselves or speaking up for someone else, we all face daunting moments that must be met with poise if we want to feel good about ourselves and make progress in our lives. Presence gives us the power to rise to these moments.

The path that brought me to that talk and this breakthrough was roundabout, to say the least. But it's clear where it started.

What I most remember were the cartoonish sketches and sweet notes on the whiteboard, left by my friends. I'm a sophomore in college. I wake up in a hospital room. I look around — cards everywhere, and flowers. I'm exhausted. But I'm also anxious and agitated. I can barely keep my eyes open. I've never felt like this. I don't understand, but I don't have the energy to try to make sense of it. I fall asleep.

Repeat — many times.

My last clear memory before waking up in that hospital was of traveling from Missoula, Montana, to Boulder, Colorado, with two of my good friends and housemates. We'd gone up to Missoula to help organize a conference with University of Montana students and to visit with friends. We left Missoula in the early evening, around six, on a Sunday. We were trying to get back to Boulder for morning classes. In retrospect, especially as a parent,

I now see how incredibly stupid this was, given that the drive time between Missoula and Boulder is thirteen to fourteen hours. But we were nineteen.

We had what we thought was a good plan: we would each drive a third of the trip; one passenger would stay up to help the driver stay awake and alert while the other passenger would sleep in the back of the Jeep Cherokee, seats down, in a sleeping bag. I drove my shift; I think I went first. Then I was the active passenger, keeping an eye on the driver. And it's a really tender memory. So peaceful. I loved these people I was with. I loved the openness of the West. I loved the wilderness. No headlights to count on the highway. Just us. Then came my turn to sleep in the backseat.

As I learned later, here's what happened next. My friend was driving the worst shift. It was the time of night when you feel as though you might be the only person in the entire world who is awake. Not only was it the middle of the night, it was the middle of the night in the middle of Wyoming. Very dark, very open, very lonesome. Very little to keep you awake. At around four in the morning, my friend veered off the road. When she hit the rumble strip on the shoulder, she overcorrected in the opposite direction. The car rolled several times, eventually landing on its roof. My friends in the front seat were wearing their seatbelts. I, who had been sleeping in back with the seats down, was ejected from the car and thrown into the night. The right-front side of my head slammed into the highway. The rest of me remained in the sleeping bag.

I sustained a traumatic brain injury. More specifically, I suffered a diffuse axonal injury (DAI). In a DAI, the brain is subjected to "shearing forces," usually from severe rotational acceleration, which is quite common in car accidents. Imagine what happens during a high-speed car crash: with the sudden and extreme change in velocity upon impact, your body abruptly stops but your brain continues to move and sometimes even rotate within the skull, which it is not meant to do, and even bangs back and forth against your skull, which it is also not meant to do. The force of my head slamming into the highway, which fractured my skull, probably didn't help matters.

The brain is meant to exist in a safe space, protected by the skull and cushioned by several thin membranes, called meninges, and cerebrospinal fluid. The skull is the brain's friend, but the two are never intended to touch. The shearing forces of a severe head injury tear and stretch neurons and their fibers, called axons, throughout the brain. Like electrical wires, axons are insulated by a protective coating, or buffer, called the myelin sheath. Even if an axon isn't severed, damage to the myelin sheath can significantly slow the speed at which information travels from neuron to neuron.

In a DAI, the injury occurs throughout the brain, unlike a focal brain injury, such as a gunshot wound, where damage strikes a very specific location. Everything the brain does depends on neurons communicating; when neurons throughout the brain are damaged, their communication is inevitably damaged as well. So when you have a DAI, no doctor is going to tell you, "Well, the damage is to your motor area, so you're going to have trouble with movement." Or "It's your speech area; you're going to have diffi-culty producing and processing speech." They won't know *if* you'll recover, *how well* you'll recover, or *which brain functions* will be affected: Will your memory be impaired? Your emotions? Your spatial reasoning? Your small-motor skills? Given how little we understand about DAIs, the likelihood that a doctor can offer an accurate prognosis is dismal.

After a DAI, you are a different person. In many ways. How you think, how you feel, how you express yourself, respond, interact — all of these dimensions are affected. On top of that, your ability to understand yourself has probably taken a hit, so you're not really in a position to know exactly *how* you've changed. And no one — NO ONE — can tell you what to expect.

Now let me give you an explanation of what happened to my brain as I understood it *then*: (Insert the sound of chirping crickets here.)

Okay, so there I was in the hospital. Naturally, I had been withdrawn from college, and my doctors expressed serious doubts about whether I would ever be cognitively fit to return. Given the severity of my injury and statistics on people with similar injuries, they said: *Don't expect to finish college. You're going to be fine — "high functioning" — but you should consider finding something else to do.* I learned that my IQ had dropped thirty points — two standard deviations. I knew this not because a doctor had explained it to me. I knew because the IQ was part of a two-day battery of neuropsychology tests they'd given me, and I'd received a long report that included that result. The doctors didn't think it was important to explain this to me. Or did they think I wasn't smart enough to understand? I don't want to give the IQ more credit than it deserves; I'm not making any claims about its ability to predict life outcomes. But at the time it was something that I believed quantified my intelligence. So, as I understood it, according to the doctors, I was no longer smart, and I felt this acutely.

I received occupational therapy, cognitive therapy, speech therapy, physical therapy, psychological counseling. About six months after the accident, when I was home for the summer, a couple of my closest friends, who'd noticeably pulled away from me, told me, "You're just not the same anymore." How could two of the people who seemed to understand me the best tell me I was no longer myself? How was I different? They couldn't see me; I couldn't even see myself.

A head injury makes you feel confused, anxious, and frustrated. When your doctors tell you they don't know what you should expect, and your friends tell you that you're different, it certainly amplifies all that confusion, anxiety, and frustration.

I spent the next year in a fog — anxious, disoriented, making bad decisions, not sure what I would do next. After that, I went back to school. But it was too soon. I couldn't think. I couldn't adequately process spoken information. It was like listening to someone speaking half in a language I knew and half in a language I didn't know, which only made me more frustrated and anxious. I had to drop out because I was failing my classes.

Although I'd broken several bones and gained a few ugly scars in the accident, I looked physically whole. And because traumatic brain injuries are often invisible to others, people said things like, "Wow, you're so lucky! You could have broken your neck!" "Lucky?" I thought. Then I'd feel guilty and ashamed for being frustrated by their well-intentioned comments.

Our way of thinking, our intellect, our affect, our personality — these aren't things we expect will ever change. We take them for granted. We fear having an accident that will make us paralyzed, change our ability to move around, or cause us to lose our hearing or sight. But we don't think about having an accident that will cause us to lose ourselves.

For many years after the head injury, I was trying to pass as my former self…although I didn't really know who that former self was. I felt like an impostor, an impostor in my own body. I had to relearn how to learn. I kept trying to start school again because I couldn't accept people telling me that I couldn't do it.

I had to study circles around others. Slowly, eventually, and to my unspeakable relief, my mental clarity began to return. I finished college four years after my pre-accident classmates.

One of the reasons I persisted was that I'd found something I liked to study: psychology. After college, I managed to enter a profession that required a fully functioning brain. As Anatole France wrote, "All changes... have their melancholy; for what we leave behind us is a part of ourselves; we must die to one life before we can enter another." Along the way, not surprisingly, I became a person for whom all these questions of presence and power, of confidence and doubt, took on a great deal of significance.

My injury led me to study the science of presence, but it was my TED talk that made me realize just how universal the yearning for it is. Because here's the thing: *most* people are dealing with stressful challenges every day. People in every corner of the world and in all walks of life are trying to work up the nerve to speak in class, to interview for a job, to audition for a role, to confront a daily hardship, to stand up for what they believe in, or to just find peace being who they are. This is true of people who are homeless and people who are by traditional standards wildly successful. Fortune 500 executives, winning trial lawyers, gifted artists and performers, victims of bullying and prejudice and sexual assault, political refugees, people dealing with mental illness or who have suffered grave injuries — all of them face these challenges. And so do all the people working to help those people — the parents, spouses, children, counselors, doctors, colleagues, and friends of those who are struggling.

All these people — the vast majority of whom are *not* scientists — have forced me to look at my own research in a new way: they simultaneously take me away from the science and bring me closer to it. Hearing their stories, I became obliged to think about how social science findings actually play out in the real world. I started to care about doing research that changes lives in a positive way. But I also started coming up with basic questions that may never have occurred to me if I'd stayed inside the lab and steeped myself in the literature.

In the beginning I was overwhelmed by the response to the TED talk and by the sense that I might have made a big mistake in sharing my research and my personal story. I had no expectation that so many strangers would watch it and no idea how incredibly vulnerable and exposed I'd feel. It's what happens to anyone whom the Internet scoops up and then blasts all over the world all at once. Some people will recognize you in public. And that requires adjustment — whether it's a stranger asking me to stand with them like Wonder Woman for a selfie or hearing someone yell from a pedicab (as happened in Austin), "Hey! It's TED Girl!"

But mostly I feel *incredibly* lucky — lucky to have had a chance to share this research and my story with so many people, and even luckier to have so many of those people share their stories with me. I love academia, but I find much inspiration outside the lab and the classroom. One of the great things about being at Harvard Business School is that I am encouraged to cross that researcher-practitioner divide, so I had already started talking to people in organizations about how research is applied, what's working, where the kinks are, and things like that. But I didn't anticipate how this enormous world of thoughtful strangers would open up to me after the TED talk was posted.

I love these people and I feel eternally connected and loyal to them. I want to honor them, to honor their willingness to try — to keep getting back in the saddle or to help other people keep trying — and their willingness to sit down and write about their struggles in an e-mail to me, a stranger. Or to tell me about it in an airport, or a bookstore-café. Now I see how a talk can work like a song — how people personalize it, connect with it, feel validated knowing that someone else has felt as they feel. As Dave Grohl once said, "That's one of the great things about music: you can sing a song to 85,000 people and they'll sing it back for 85,000 different reasons." I was speaking at a youth homeless shelter and asked the residents to tell me about the situations they found most challenging. One teenager said, "Showing up at the doorstep of this shelter." At another shelter, a woman said, "Calling to ask for services or help or support. I know I'm going to wait a long time, and that the person on the other end will be annoyed and judgmental." To this, another woman at the shelter responded, "I used to work in a call center, and I was going to say, 'Taking calls from people who you know are going to be frustrated and angry, who've been waiting a long time while I'm trying to manage a hundred other incoming calls.'"

Thousands of people have written to tell me about a range of challenges — a range that blows my mind, contexts I'd never have considered as places where this research might apply. Here's a snapshot taken from e-mail subject lines, most of which begin with something like "How your talk helped...": Alzheimer's families, firefighters, a fellow brain injury survivor, closing the biggest deal of my life, negotiating for a house, a college interview, adults with disabilities, a WWII vet who'd "lost [his] pride," recovering from trauma, racing in the world sailing championships, kids who are bullied, self-confidence in the service industry, fifth-grade students who are afraid of mathematics, my son with autism, a professional opera singer in a tough audition, proposing a new idea to my boss, finding my voice when I had to speak up. And that's just a small sample.

All the responses I've gotten to the TED talk are gifts that helped me better understand how and why this research resonates. In short: the stories helped me understand how to write this book and motivated me to do it. They are from all around the world, from people in all walks of life, and I will be sharing many of them in these pages. Maybe among these stories you will find echoes of your own.

1

What Is Presence?

We convince by our presence.
— WALT WHITMAN

WE KNOW IT WHEN we feel it, and we know it when we see it, but presence is hard to define. On the other hand, most of us are quite good at describing the lack of it. Here's my story — one of many.

Hoping to become a professor (as all good doctoral students do), I marched into the academic job market in the fall of 2004. If a doctoral student in social psychology is lucky, her faculty adviser will "debut" her at a certain smallish annual conference that's attended by the best social psychologists in the world. It's a collective coming-out party for competitive fifth-year PhD students and marks their ascension to the status of people-maybe-to-be-taken-seriously. This stage also triggers a student's most potent form of "feeling like a fraud." The student, dressed in her best guess at academic finery, gets an opportunity to mingle with senior faculty, many from top research universities that might be hiring in the coming year. The senior faculty, dressed in whatever they wear every day, get a chance to scout new talent — but mostly they're there to catch up with each other.

In a sense, students train for this moment for the entire four or five years leading up to it. They arrive prepared. Ready to pithily summarize their research program and goals in around ninety seconds — briefly enough to hold the audience's attention without accidentally signaling disrespect by taking too much of their time. They have armed themselves with what is colloquially known — inside and outside academia — as the elevator pitch.

My anxiety about this conference defied all reasonable dimensions.

At an unremarkable midsize conference hotel in an unremarkable midsize city, the meeting commenced. Heading up to the opening dinner, I stepped from the lobby into an elevator with three people — all well-established figures in my field, people I'd idolized for years. It was as if I were the rhythm guitarist from a mediocre college-town indie rock band, carrying in my hand a CD that we had recorded in the basement of the drummer's mom's house, walking into an elevator with Jimmy Page, Carlos Santana, and Eric Clapton. I was the only one who actually needed the giant name tag.

With no introduction, one of the rock stars, from a prestigious research university where I'd have been thrilled to land a job, casually said: "Fine. We're in an elevator. Let's hear your pitch."

My face went hot; my mouth went dry. Hyperaware that not one but *three* luminary scholars were confined with me in that tiny space, I began my pitch — or, rather, words started tumbling out of my mouth. I knew by the end of the first sentence that I'd started all wrong. I heard myself saying things like "So...oh, wait, before I explain that part..." I could barely follow my own story. And as the awareness of my imminent failure closed in, the ability to think about anything other than my crushing anxiety fled. Certain that I was killing my chances at not one but three schools — oh, and also at the schools where their closest collaborators worked — I acquiesced to the panic. I qualified everything. I kept trying to restart. There was no chance in hell that I'd get through it in the time it took to ride to the twentieth floor,[1] where the dinner was being held. My eyes darted from idol to idol to idol, seeking some glimmer of understanding, some microexpression of support, approval, empathy. Something. Anything. *Please.*

The doors finally opened. Two of the passengers swiftly escaped, heads down. The third — the one who'd goaded me to give my pitch — stepped across the threshold onto firm ground, paused, turned to me, and said, "That was the worst elevator pitch I have ever heard." (And . . . was that a hint of a smirk on his face?)

The doors closed. I fell against the back of my elevator cell, crumpling into a fetal ball, descending with it, down, down, down — straight back to the lobby. Despite the unequivocal censure, I felt a dim but fleeting sensation of relief.

But then: Oh. My. God. What had I done? How had I failed to say a single clever thing about a topic I'd been studying for more than four years? How is that even *possible?*

Outside the elevator, my practiced pitch started coming back to me, pressing through a smoggy haze and resuming a recognizable shape. There it was. I had the urge to run back to the elevator, chase the professors down, and ask for a do-over.

Instead, I spent the following three days of the conference backward-projecting myself into that moment, replaying the many ways it should have gone, agonizing over the scorn, or maybe even amusement, my three elevator mates must have felt. I was mercilessly anatomizing the memory, jabbing and cutting into every possible cross section, and never once forgetting that I had not just failed to represent myself, I'd also failed to represent my adviser, who'd spent many years training me and had spent a bit of reputational capital by taking me to that conference. Looping, looping, looping, my ninety-second failure ran on repeat in my brain, haunting me. I spent those three days at the conference but was not actually present for a single one of them.

I recounted my ordeal to my good friend Elizabeth, who said, "Oh, the spirit of the stairs!"

"The what of the what?"

So she told me this story, as she remembered it from her undergraduate philosophy class.

Eighteenth-century French philosopher and writer Denis Diderot was at a dinner party, engaged in debate over a topic that he knew well. But perhaps he wasn't himself on that evening — a bit self-conscious, distracted, worried about looking foolish. When challenged on some point, Diderot found himself at a loss for words, incapable of cobbling together a clever response. Soon after, he left the party.

Once outside, on his way down the staircase, Diderot continued to replay that humiliating moment in his mind, searching in vain for the perfect retort. Just as he reached the bottom of the stairs, he found it. Should he turn around, walk back up the stairs, and return to the party to deliver his witty comeback? Of course not. It was too late. The moment — and, with it, the opportunity — had passed. Regret washed over him. If only he'd had the presence of mind to find those words when he needed them.

Reflecting on this experience in 1773, Diderot wrote, "A sensitive man, such as myself, overwhelmed by the argument leveled against him, becomes confused and can only think clearly again [when he reaches] the bottom of the stairs."[2]

And so he coined the phrase *l'esprit d'escalier* — the spirit of the stairs, or staircase wit. In Yiddish it's *trepverter*. Germans call it *treppenwitz*. It's been called elevator wit, which has a sentimental resonance for me. My personal favorite is afterwit. But the idea is the same — it's the incisive remark you come up with too late. It's the hindered comeback. The orphaned retort. And it carries with it a sense of regret, disappointment, humiliation. We all want a do-over. But we'll never get one.

Apparently everyone has had moments like my conference-elevator nightmare, even eighteenth-century French philosophers.

Rajeev, one of the first strangers to write to me after my TED talk was posted, described it like this: "In so many situations in life, I don't walk away feeling like I have given my all and put everything on the table, so to speak. And it always eats at me later, when I analyze it over and over again in my head, and [it] ultimately leads to feelings of weakness and failure."

Most of us have our own personal version of this experience. After interviewing for a job, auditioning for a role, going on a date, pitching an idea, speaking up in a meeting or in class, arguing with someone at a dinner party.

But how did we get there? We probably were worrying what others would think of us, but believing we already knew what they thought; feeling powerless, and also consenting to that feeling; clinging to the outcome and attributing far too much importance to it instead of focusing on the process. These worries coalesce into a toxic cocktail of self-defeat. That's how we got there.

Before we even show up at the doorstep of an opportunity, we are teeming with dread and anxiety, borrowing trouble from a future that hasn't yet unfolded.[3] When we walk into a high-pressure situation in that frame of mind, we're condemned to leave it feeling bad.

If only I'd remembered to say this.... If only I'd done it that way.... If only I'd shown them who I really am. We can't be fully engaged in an interaction when we're busy second-guessing our-selves and attending to the hamster wheel in our heads — the jum-bled, frenetic, self-doubting analysis of what we *think* is happening in the room. The excruciating self-awareness that we are, most definitely, in a high-pressure situation. And we're screwing it up. Exactly when we most need to be present, we are least likely to be.

As Alan Watts wrote in *The Wisdom of Insecurity*, "To under-stand music, you must listen to it. But so long as you are thinking, 'I am listening to this music,' you are not listening."[4] When you are in a job interview, thinking, "I am in a job interview," you can't understand or engage fully with the interviewer or present the self you'd like to present — your truest, sharpest, boldest, most relaxed self.

Watts described the anxiety-laced anticipation of these future moments as the pursuit of "a constantly retreating phantom, and the faster you chase it, the faster it runs ahead."[5] These moments become apparitions. And we endow them with the power to haunt us — before, during, and after.

Next time you're faced with one of these tense moments, imagine approaching it with confidence and excitement instead of doubt and dread. Imagine feeling energized and at ease while you're there, liberated from your fears about how others might be judging you. And imagine leaving it without regret, satisfied that you did your best, regardless of the measurable outcome. No phantom to be chased; no spirit under the stairs.

Tina, a New Orleans native, wrote to tell me how being a high-school dropout had impeded her — not only by limiting her access to stable, well-paying work but also by undermining her feeling that she deserved to have those things. She worked many jobs, many hours a day, for many years, and at thirty-four, she graduated from college. She then slowly taught herself, through small, incremental changes, to treat "even the most difficult interactions as opportunities for me to reveal what I'm capable of and to express my worthiness."

Imagine that. That sounds like presence.

The Elements of Presence

Several years ago, during a lab meeting in my department, I had an aha moment that acutely piqued my interest in cracking open the psychology of presence.

On that day, a visiting student, Lakshmi Balachandra, was soliciting feedback about some new data. She'd been investigating the way entrepreneurs make pitches to potential investors and the way investors respond. After meticulously analyzing videos of 185 venture capital presentations — looking at both verbal and nonverbal behavior — Lakshmi ended up with results that surprised her: the strongest predictor of who got the money was not the person's credentials or the content of the pitch. The strongest predictors of who got the money were these traits: *confidence, comfort level, and passionate enthusiasm.* Those who succeeded did not spend their precious moments in the spotlight worrying about how they were doing or what others thought of them. No spirit under the stairs awaited them, because they knew they were doing their best. In other words, those who succeeded were fully present, and their presence was palpable. It came through mostly in nonverbal ways — vocal qualities, gestures, facial expressions, and so on.[6]

The findings puzzled quite a few people in the room. Are huge investment decisions really being made based solely on

19

impressions of the person making the pitch? Is it just about charisma?

I was having a starkly different reaction as I listened to Lakshmi at the lab meeting: I suspected that these qualities — confidence, comfort, passion, and enthusiasm — were signaling something more powerful than words about the entrepreneur's investment worthiness. They were signaling how much that person truly believed in the value and integrity of her idea and her ability to bring it to fruition, which may in turn have signaled something about the quality of the proposition itself.

Sometimes we easily project poised, enthusiastic confidence. As Lakshmi's study and other research suggests, this counts for a lot. It predicts which entrepreneurs get funding from investors. It predicts job interviewers' evaluations of applicants, whether the applicants will get called back, and final hiring decisions.[7] Are we right to value this trait so highly? Is it just a superficial preference? The success of these hiring and investment decisions suggests that it isn't. In fact, self-assured enthusiasm is an impressively useful indicator of success. In studies of entrepreneurs, this quality predicts drive, willingness to work hard, initiative, persistence in the face of obstacles, enhanced mental activity, creativity, and the ability to identify good opportunities and novel ideas.[8]

It doesn't stop there. Entrepreneurs' grounded enthusiasm is contagious, stimulating a high level of commitment, confidence, passion, and performance in the people who work for and with them. On the other hand, entrepreneurs and job candidates who don't convey these qualities are usually judged to be less confident and believable, less effective communicators, and, ultimately, poorer performers.[9]

There's another reason we tend to put our faith in people who project passion, confidence, and enthusiasm: these traits can't easily be faked. When we're feeling brave and confident, our vocal pitch and amplitude are significantly more varied, allowing us to sound expressive and relaxed. When we fearfully hold back — activating the sympathetic nervous system's fight-or-flight response — our vocal cords and diaphragms constrict, strangling our genuine enthusiasm.[10] If you've ever had to sing through stage fright, you'll know this feeling: the muscles that produce sound seize, causing your voice to come out thin and tight — nothing like what you are imagining in your head.

When we try to fake confidence or enthusiasm, other people can tell that something is off, even if they can't precisely articulate what that thing is. In fact, when job applicants try too hard to make a good impression through nonverbal tactics such as forced smiles, it can backfire — interviewers dismiss them as phony and manipulative.[11]

A disclaimer: my field, social psychology, has amassed a great deal of evidence that humans persistently make biased decisions based on minimal, misleading, and misunderstood first impressions. We've clearly demonstrated that first impressions are often flimsy and dangerous, and I'm not challenging that. In fact, much of my own research has focused on identifying and understanding these destructive biases.[12] What I'm saying here is that first impressions based on the qualities of enthusiasm, passion, and confidence *might* actually be quite sound — precisely because they're so hard to fake. When you are not present, people can tell. When you are, people respond.

Let's pause here, because I want to make sure I haven't lost you. This is not yet another book of advice exclusively for entrepreneurs and executives. The presence you need to persuade a roomful of investors to fund your project is the same as the presence you need to convince yourself that it's okay to speak up in a meeting. Or ask for a better salary. Or demand more respectful treatment.

As I sit here writing, I am thinking of so many of you who have shared your stories with me: Nimanthi from Sri Lanka, who's struggling to feel confident as a first-generation college student; Cedric, in Alabama, who's working hard to maintain his independence after losing his wife to cancer and while managing his own health problems; Katharina from Germany, who's reassembling herself after leaving an unhealthy relationship; Udofoyo from Nigeria, who's trying to overcome a physical disability that keeps him from participating in his classes; Nicole from California, who's looking for powerful ways to engage her adult students with Down syndrome; Fariha from Karachi, who's trying to embrace her new education opportunities, ones she never expected to have; Marcos from Brazil, who's gathering the courage to start a small family business; Aleta from Rochester, who's recovering her identity following a traumatic brain injury; Kamesh from India, who's working to get his life back on track after losing a young family member. This book is for them and for you.[13]

The stories that have most inspired me are from people whose biggest challenge is to face each new day with a bit more optimism and dignity than the day before — people with limited resources and very little formal power or status, many of whom have experienced intense hardships and who still find it within themselves to *try*. Try to feel present and powerful, not only for themselves but also for the people they love and respect. They're not striving to land a fancy job or big venture capital deal. They're trying to find a way to embrace their own power and to use that power to be present when they face life's ordinary challenges.

So now we've established that being present is an incredibly powerful state. But we still haven't answered the bigger question: What exactly *is* it? And how do we get it?

Presence Is the Next Five Minutes

Presence is removing judgment, walls, and masks so as to create a true and deep connection with people or experiences.
— Pam, Washington State, USA

Presence is loving people around you and enjoying what you do for them.
— Anonymous, Croatia

Presence is being myself and keeping confident, whatever happens.
— Abdelghani, Morocco

These are just a few of the many responses I've received to the question "How do you define presence?" which I've posed online and which has been answered by people all around the world. I'm struck by both the differences and the similarities across this diverse set of responses.

Presence may still seem like a nebulous concept. Clearly it means different things to different people. Is it about the physical, the psychological, or the spiritual? Is it about the individual alone or in relation to others? Is it a fixed characteristic or a momentary experience?

The idea of a permanent, transcendent form of presence grew in philosophical and spiritual soil. As the blogger Maria Popova has written, "This concept of presence is rooted in Eastern notions of mindfulness — the ability to go through life with crystalline awareness and [to] fully inhabit our experience."[14] It was popularized in the West in the mid-twentieth century by British philosopher Alan Watts, who, Popova explains, "argues that the root of our human frustration and daily anxiety is our tendency to live for the future, which is an abstraction," and that "our primary mode of relinquishing presence is by leaving the body and retreating into the mind — that ever-calculating, self-evaluating, seething cauldron of thoughts, predictions, anxieties, judgments, and incessant meta-experiences about experience itself."

Although achieving an enduring state of philosophical in-the-momentness is a venerable goal, it's not the kind of presence I study or write about, for reasons grounded in the reality of... well, reality. The pursuit of a lasting "crystalline awareness" requires us to have the means and the freedom to decide exactly how we spend our time, our energy — our lives. I wish we could all have that freedom, but most of us can't, not only because we have mouths to feed, people to look after, jobs to do, and bills to pay but also because no human mind is capable of shutting out all distracting thoughts all the time. It's hard to read an entire page of a book or sit through a five-minute conversation without a few distracting thoughts poking through. And that means we have to find other ways to feel present and powerful.

Presence, as I mean it throughout these pages, is the state of being attuned to and able to comfortably express our true thoughts, feelings, values, and potential. That's it. It is *not* a permanent, transcendent mode of being. It comes and goes. It is a moment-to-moment phenomenon.

Presence emerges when we feel personally powerful, which allows us to be acutely attuned to our most sincere selves. In this psychological state, we are able to maintain presence even in the very stressful situations that typically make us feel distracted and powerless. When we feel present, our speech, facial expressions, postures, and movements align. They synchronize and focus. And that internal convergence, that harmony, is palpable and resonant — because it's real. It's what makes us compelling. We are no longer fighting ourselves; we are being ourselves. Our search for presence isn't about finding charisma or extraversion or carefully managing the impression we're making on other people. It's about the honest, powerful connection that we create internally, with ourselves.

The kind of presence I'm talking about comes through incremental change. You don't need to embark on a long pilgrimage, experience a spiritual epiphany, or work on a complete inner transformation. There's nothing wrong with these things. But they're daunting; they're "big." To a lot of us, they're elusive, abstract, idealistic. Instead, let's focus on moments — achieving a state of psychological presence that lasts just long enough to get us through our most challenging, high-stakes, a-lot-is-on-the-line situations, such as job interviews, difficult conversations, idea pitches, asking for help, public speeches, performances, and the like.

Presence is about the everyday. It's even, dare I say, ordinary. We can all do it; most of us just don't yet know how to summon that presence when it temporarily escapes us at life's most critical moments.

A significant body of scientific research offers insight into the psychological and physiological mechanics of this sort of transitory presence. And here's the best thing: we can adjust these mechanics. Through self-nudges, small tweaks in our body language and mind-sets, we can achieve presence. We can self-induce presence. To some extent, this is about allowing your body to lead your mind — but we'll get to that later.

Can this kind of presence help you become more successful in the traditional sense? Quite possibly. But what matters more is that it will allow you to approach stressful situations without anxiety, fear, and dread, and leave them without regret, doubt, and frustration. Instead, you will go forth with the knowledge that you did everything you could do. That you accurately and fully represented yourself and your abilities. That you showed them who you really are. That you showed *yourself* who you really are.

There will always be new challenges, new uncomfortable situations, new roles — things that push us off balance and stoke our anxiety, forcing us to reexamine who we are and how we can connect with others. To be present, we have to treat these challenges as moments. Presence is not all or nothing. Sometimes we lose it and have to start again, and that's okay.

So let's consider these ideas, see how they fit with science, and apply them not to our big-picture lives but to the moment five minutes from now when we walk into that job or college interview, when we step up to make that penalty kick, when we raise that thorny issue with a coworker or friend, when we present a new idea that we're excited but nervous about. That's where the rubber meets the road. It's where we benefit most from learning to be present.

What Does Presence Look and Feel Like?

Presence is confidence without arrogance.
— Rohan, Australia

Presence manifests itself in two ways. First, when we are present, we communicate the kinds of traits Lakshmi Balachandra identified in her research on venture capital pitches — passion, confidence, and comfortable enthusiasm. Or, as Rohan from Australia described it —

confidence without arrogance. Second, presence comes through in something I'll call synchrony, which we'll get to in a little bit.

Let's return to the venture capitalists, who are especially fascinating on the subject of how presence looks and sounds. They must swiftly decide whether an idea and, more important, its owner are investment worthy. So what *are* successful venture capitalists looking for? If they're comparing multiple good business proposals, which tiny cues tilt them away from one entrepreneur seeking funding toward another?

I'm going to summarize the observations I've collected from many successful venture capitalists over the years:

> I'm watching out for clues that let me know they don't completely buy what they're selling. If they don't buy what they're selling, I don't buy what they're selling.
>
> They're trying too hard to make a good impression on me when they should be showing me how much they care about this idea that they're pitching.
>
> They're too high energy and aggressive, maybe a little pushy. It seems defensive. I don't expect them to have all the answers. Actually, I don't want them to have all the answers.
>
> I don't mind if they're a little bit nervous; they're doing something big, something that matters to them, so it makes sense they'd be a little bit nervous.

Let's unpack these observations.

I'm watching out for clues that let me know they don't completely buy what they're selling. If they don't buy what they're selling, I don't buy what they're selling.

If a person asking you to invest doesn't believe her own story, why would you believe it? "Meaning what you say," wrote management scholar Jonathan Haigh, "is really at the heart of presenting."[15] An idea whose owner is unfaithful will not survive.

Presence stems from believing and trusting your story — your feelings, beliefs, values, and abilities. Maybe there was a time you had to sell a product you didn't like or convince somebody of an idea you didn't believe. It feels desperate, discouraging, hard to hide. It *feels* dishonest because it *is* dishonest.

I don't think people can learn to truly sell something they don't believe in. And even if I did, I wouldn't want to teach anyone how to do it. So if that's what you're looking for, you're reading the wrong book.

Similarly, you can't sell a skill you don't have. Occasionally people mistakenly think I'm suggesting that we can learn to fake competence.[16] Presence isn't about pretending to be competent; it's about believing in and revealing the abilities you truly have. It's about shedding whatever is blocking you from expressing who you are. It's about tricking yourself into accepting that you are indeed capable.

Sometimes you have to get out of the *way* of yourself so you can *be* yourself.

Recently, along with graduate students Caroline Wilmuth and Nico Thornley, I conducted a study in which subjects had to sit through intense mock job interviews.[17] We told the subjects to imagine that they were interviewing for their dream jobs and instructed them to prepare a five-minute speech to answer what might be the most frequently asked (and certainly the most bewildering) job interview question: Why should we hire you? They were told they could not misrepresent themselves — they had to be honest. Then, in front of two hard-nosed interviewers, they delivered their speeches, explaining why they should be hired. To increase the stress, the interviewers were trained to not respond to, encourage, or prompt the interviewees at any time during the speeches. No feedback whatsoever. For five whole minutes. This may not sound too daunting, but imagine trying to convince two people to hire you as they silently watch, take notes, and judge you — while holding completely neutral facial expressions for the entire time. In addition, the subjects were told that their interviews would be videotaped and evaluated later by another set of trained judges.

Six judges evaluated the videos. Two rated the interviewees on a five-point scale measuring how much presence they exhibited — how captivating, comfortable, confident, and enthusiastic they were. A second pair of judges rated the interviewees on a five-point believability scale — how authentic, believable, and genuine they were. And a third pair of judges rated the interviewees on their overall performance and hireability — how well they did and whether they should be hired.

Consistent with the findings from entrepreneurial pitches, the more presence our job interviewees displayed, the better they were evaluated and more strongly they were recommended for hire by the judges — and this effect of presence was substantial. But here's the catch. Presence mattered to the judges because it signaled authenticity, believability, and genuineness; it told the judges that they could trust the person, that what they were observing was real... that they knew what they were getting. In short: the manifest qualities of presence — confidence, enthusiasm, comfort, being captivating — are taken as signs of authenticity, and for good reason: the more we are able to be ourselves, the more we are able to be present. And that makes us convincing.

In addition, we asked the participants, after the interviews, if they felt they had done their best. Interviewees who showed more presence felt much better about how they did. They seemed to feel that they had represented themselves as well as possible. They left the interview with a sense of satisfaction, not regret, regardless of the outcome.

Before moving on, I want to clear up a widespread misunderstanding about presence — the belief that it's reserved for extroverts. Let me clearly say: presence has nothing to do with extroversion. Not only are introverts every bit as likely as extroverts to demonstrate resonant presence, but research conducted in the last decade has also overwhelmingly shown us that introverts tend to have qualities that very effectively facilitate leadership and entrepreneurship, such as the capacity to focus for long periods of time; a greater resistance to the kinds of decision-making biases that can doom entire organizations; less need for external validation of their self-concepts; and stronger listening, observing, and synthesizing skills. Susan Cain, Harvard Law School graduate and author of the culture-shifting bestseller *Quiet: The Power of Introverts in a World That Can't Stop Talking,* explains, "By their nature, introverts tend to get passionate about one, two or three things in their life... [a]nd in the service of their passion for an idea they will go out and build alliances and networks and acquire expertise and do whatever it takes to make it happen." One need not be loud or gregarious to be passionate and effective. In fact, a bit of quiet seems to go a long way toward being present.[18]

They're trying too hard to make a good impression on me when they should be showing me how much they care about this idea that they're pitching.

When we are trying to manage the impression we're making on others, we're choreographing ourselves in an unnatural way. This is hard work, and we don't have the cognitive and emotional bandwidth to do it well. The result is that we come across as fake.

Nonetheless, many people attempt to manage the impression

they're making on others by scripting and choreographing both their verbal and nonverbal communication. This approa assumes we have quite a bit more control over any given situation than we actually do. But does impression management work?

Science has addressed this question, mostly in the context of job interview performance and hiring decisions. For example, people might try to enforce a positive image of themselves on interviewers by pouncing on every opportunity to recite a story about their accomplishments or by smiling and making frequent eye contact. The net return on these impression-management approaches is generally poor, especially in long or structured interviews and with well-trained interviewers. The harder candidates work to manage the impression they make — the more tactics they deploy — the more the interviewers start to see the candidates as insincere and manipulative, which ultimately bodes poorly for landing the job.[19]

But this doesn't apply only to the person who's there to be judged. Keep in mind that in all interactions, both parties are judging and both are being judged. In job interviews, most of us think of the candidate as the one who's being evaluated, but candidates are also taking the measure of their interviewers. This is partly because we automatically form an impression of every person with whom we interact. But there's also a practical reason: the interviewer represents the organization, so the candidate studies her or him, searching for usable information.

As a result, interviewers often "sell" themselves and their organization in an effort to adapt to what they think candidates want to hear. In a recent study, organizational behavior professors Jennifer Carson Marr and Dan Cable wanted to know whether interviewers' desire to make themselves and their companies attractive to job candidates — as opposed to the desire to accurately evaluate and hire candidates — would affect the quality of their evaluations and selections. In a combination of lab and field studies, they found that the more the interviewers were focused on attracting candidates (i.e., the more they wanted to be "liked"), the less accurate they were at selecting candidates who would do well after being hired, in terms of performance, good citizenship, and core-values fit.[20]

The takeaway is this: *focus less on the impression you're making on others and more on the impression you're making on yourself.* The latter serves the former, a phenomenon that should become clearer and clearer throughout this book.

They're too high energy and aggressive, maybe a little pushy. It seems defensive. I don't expect them to have all the answers. Actually, I don't want them to have all the answers.

Sadly, confidence is often confused with cockiness. As the investors I spoke with made clear, real confidence does not equal blind faith in an idea. If people truly believe in the value and potential of a project, they're going to want to fix its flaws and make it even better. They see it accurately — acknowledging its strengths and its weaknesses. Their goal is not to force it on anyone; it's to help others see it accurately so that they, too, can nourish it. True confidence stems from real love and leads to long-term commitment to growth. False confidence comes from desperate passion and leads to dysfunctional relationships, disappointment, and frustration.

The maddeningly complicated literature on self-esteem might shed more light on this idea. Once considered the antidote to all society's ills, interventions geared toward improving self-esteem have fallen out of favor in recent years. One reason is that it's difficult to accurately measure self-esteem. Some people who claim to have a positive self-image do indeed have one. But others are expressing something known as fragile high self-esteem — their seemingly positive view of themselves depends on continuous external validation, a self-view that's based less in reality than it is on wishful thinking. They are intolerant of people and feedback that might challenge their brittle high opinion of themselves. While they may appear confident in some ways, people with fragile high self-esteem quickly become defensive and dismissive of situations and people they perceive as threatening.[21]

On the other hand, the source of secure high self-esteem is internal. It doesn't need external validation to thrive, and it doesn't crumble at the first sign of a threat. People who have a solid sense of self-worth reflect that feeling through healthy, effective ways of dealing with challenges and relationships, making them both more resilient and more open.

While self-esteem and self-confidence are not synonymous, they certainly share features. A truly confident person does not require arrogance, which is nothing more than a smoke screen for insecurity. A confident person — knowing and believing in her identity — carries tools, not weapons. A confident person does not need to one-up anyone else. A confident person can be present to others, hear their perspectives, and integrate those views in ways that create value for everyone.

True belief — in oneself, in one's ideas — is grounding; it defuses threat.

I don't mind if they're a little bit nervous; they're doing something big, something that matters to them, so it makes sense they'd be a little bit nervous.

When we care deeply about something, presenting it to a person whose feedback we value might make us nervous. We can be both confident and a bit anxious at the same time. In challenging situations, a moderate and controllable amount of nervousness can actually be adaptive, in the evolutionary sense: it keeps us alert to real danger and sometimes signals respect. A bit of worry keeps us attuned to real things that are going wrong and focuses us on preventing disaster. Some nervousness can even signal passion to others. After all, you wouldn't be nervous if it didn't matter to you, and you can't easily persuade an investor or potential client to buy into your idea if it's not clear that you care deeply about whether or not it succeeds.[22]

So don't get caught up in the idea that you have to somehow magically erase all traces of nervousness. Trying to force yourself to feel calm is not going to help you become present. That said, anxiety that sticks around can wear us down and interfere with concentration. What you want to do is avoid clinging to your nervousness; notice it and move on. Anxiety gets sticky and destructive when we start becoming anxious about being anxious. Paradoxically, anxiety also makes us more self-centered, since when we're acutely anxious, we obsess over ourselves and what others think of us.[23]

Presence manifests as confidence without arrogance.

The Synchronous Self

Presence is when all your senses agree on one thing
at the same time.
— Majid, United Arab Emirates

Virtually all theories about the authentic self, and, by extension, about presence, require some degree of alignment — synchrony, as I will call it. In order for you to feel truly present, the various elements of the self — emotions, thoughts, physical and facial expressions, behaviors — must be in harmony. If our actions aren't consistent with our values, we won't feel that we're being true to ourselves. If our emotions aren't reflected in our physical expressions, we don't feel real.

Carl Jung believed that the most important process in human development was integrating the different parts of the self — the conscious with the unconscious, the dispositional with the experiential, the congruous with the incongruous. He called this lifelong process *individuation*. Ultimately, Jung argued, individuation could bring you face-to-face with your "true personality," a process he believed had "a profound healing effect," both psychologically and physically. Through individuation, he said, "People become harmonious, calm, mature and responsible."[24] In Jungian analytical psychotherapy, individuation is the goal. As for our goal: when we achieve this internal psychological alignment, we get closer to being present.

When we are truly present in a challenging moment, our verbal and nonverbal communication flows. We are no longer occupying a discombobulated mental state — as I was on that ill-fated elevator ride — simultaneously analyzing what we think others think of us, what we said a minute earlier, and what we think they will think of us after we leave, all while frantically trying to adjust what we're saying and doing to create the impression we think they want to see.

Usually our words are relatively easy to control. We can summon up the phrases and terms we've studied and rehearsed in the mirror. It's a lot harder, and maybe impossible, to manage the rest of our communication machinery — what our faces, bodies, and our overall demeanor tell the outside world. And those other things — the nonwords — matter. A lot.

"I am convinced that it was not the word that came first but gesture," explained the great ballerina Maya Plisetskaya. "A gesture is understood by everyone . . . you need nothing else, no words."

Although some gestures are idiosyncratic to their cultural habitats, Plisetskaya was right: a great many are indeed universally recognized, regardless of the spoken language of the actor or the observer. When we are authentically expressing a genuine emotion, our nonverbal displays tend to follow predictable patterns.

The seminal tests of the universality of emotion expressions were conducted by pioneering researcher Paul Ekman, who has been studying emotions for well over fifty years, along with psychologists Carroll Izard and Wallace Friesen. Traveling around the world, to places such as Borneo and Papua New Guinea, they found that people everywhere, in literate and preliterate cultures alike, showed a high degree of recognition of facial expressions. In other words (no pun intended), we don't need verbal language to read each other's faces.

In fact, there's now strong cross-cultural support for the universality of at least nine emotions: anger, fear, disgust, happiness, sadness, surprise, contempt, shame, and pride. Our facial expressions, vocalizations, and even posture and movements tend to harmonize, which communicates important social information about whom and what we should trust, avoid, and so on. These emotional expressions are universal; in virtually every society in the world, they look the same.

Imagine that you ask a friend how work was on a certain day, and she tells you about something that really made her angry. Her body will tell the same story as her words. Her brows will pull together, her eyes may glare, her lips will tighten and narrow, her voice will lower in pitch and might increase in intensity, her upper body is likely to tilt forward, and her movement becomes rapid and tense.

Someone who is singing a lullaby should look and sound quite a bit different. If not, then she's inadvertently signaling some kind of internal conflict (i.e., chances are she's not terribly happy to be singing that song). Negative or positive, emotion is authentic, and so its manifestations across nonverbal and verbal channels are synchronized.

Another way to understand the synchrony that occurs when we are being authentic is to look at the *asynchrony* that shows up when we're not. Deception has the potential to tell us a lot about why presence leads to synchronous behavior.

Let me start with a question: How do you know if a person is lying? If you're like most people, your first response will be something like "Liars don't make eye contact." In a survey of 2,520 adults in sixty-three countries, 70 percent of respondents gave that answer.[25] People also tend to list other allegedly telltale signs of lying, such as fidgeting, nervousness, and rambling. In an interview with the *New York Times*, psychologist Charles Bond, who studies deception, said the stereotype of what liars do "would be less puzzling if we had more reason to imagine that it was true."[26] It turns out that there's no "Pinocchio effect,"[27] no single nonverbal cue that will betray a liar. Judging a person's honesty is not about identifying one stereotypical "reveal," such as fidgeting or averted eyes. Rather, it's about how well or poorly our multiple channels of communication — facial expressions, posture, movement, vocal qualities, speech — cooperate.

When we are being inauthentic — projecting a false emotion or covering a real one — our nonverbal and verbal behaviors begin to misalign. Our facial expressions don't match the words we're saying. Our postures are out of sync with our voices. They no longer move in harmony with each other; they disintegrate into cacophony.

This idea is not exactly new. In fact, Darwin proposed it: "A man when moderately angry, or even when enraged, may command the movements of his body, but... those muscles of the face which are least obedient to the will, will sometimes alone betray a slight and passing emotion."[28]

When people lie, they are juggling multiple narratives: what they know to be true, what they want to be true, what they are presenting as true, and all the emotions that go along with each — fear, anger, guilt, hope. All the while, they are trying to project a credible image of themselves, which suddenly becomes very, very difficult. Their beliefs and feelings are in conflict with themselves and each other.[29] Managing all this conflict — conscious and unconscious, psychological and physiological — removes people from the moment.

Simply put, lying — or being inauthentic — is hard work. We're telling one story while suppressing another, and as if that's not complicated enough, most of us are experiencing psychological guilt about doing this, which we're also trying to suppress. We just don't have the brainpower to manage it all without letting something go — without "leaking." Lying and leaking go hand in hand. In fact one way to understand the classic telltale signs of lying is that they're simply common signs of leakage. As social psychologist and deception expert Leanne ten Brinke explains:

> Deceptive individuals must maintain their duplicity by falsifying emotional expressions concordant with the lie, and suppressing "leakage" of their true emotions. For example, a deceptive employee must convincingly express sadness as he explains to his boss that he will need to miss work to attend his aunt's funeral out of town, simultaneously suppressing excitement about his real plans to extend a vacation with friends.[30]

In his popular book *Telling Lies*, emotions expert Paul Ekman proposes that lies inevitably leak out and that one can learn, through extensive training, how to spot these leaks by watching facial expressions and other nonverbal behaviors. He argues that we should specifically look for incongruities between what people are doing and what they're saying.[31]

To study this, ten Brinke and her colleagues analyzed nearly three hundred thousand frames of video showing people who were expressing true versus false remorse for real transgressions. People expressing true remorse presented fluid emotional displays through their nonverbal and verbal behaviors. Phony remorse, on the other hand, came across as choppy and chaotic: people expressed a greater range of conflicting emotions and far more unnatural breaks and hesitations. The researchers describe these inauthentic displays as "emotionally turbulent."[32]

One of the most fascinating studies on the psychology of deception was conducted by Harvard psychologist Nancy Etcoff and her colleagues. It turns out that we are not much better than chance at accurately detecting lies, although most of us think we excel at it.[33] Etcoff hypothesized that this might be because when we are trying to spot deception, we pay too much attention to language — to the content of what a person is saying. Etcoff decided to look at a population of people who *can't* attend to language: people with aphasia, a language-processing disorder that profoundly impairs the brain's ability to comprehend words.[34]

In this particular study, all the aphasics had sustained damage to the left cerebral hemisphere, an area of the brain strongly associated with language and speech comprehension and production. Etcoff compared these people to others who'd sustained damage to the right cerebral hemisphere (not associated with language and speech comprehension and production) and with healthy participants who'd experienced no damage.

All participants watched a videotape of ten strangers speaking. The strangers spoke twice: in one clip, they lied, and in the other they told the truth. The aphasics, who could not effectively process the words spoken in the confessions, were significantly better than the two other groups at picking out the liars, suggesting that attending to words might, paradoxically, undermine our ability to spot lies.

Consistent with these findings, in a pair of recent experiments, ten Brinke and her colleagues showed that humans, like their nonhuman primate counterparts, are better at detecting deception through the unconscious parts of the mind.[35] The conscious parts of the mind are, understandably, homing in on language — and being fooled by lies. These findings suggest that the more consciously we focus on the verbal cues that we believe signal inauthenticity, the less likely we are to notice the nonverbal signs that actually reveal it.

Clearly it's much easier for us to lie with words than with the physical actions that accompany what we're saying. On the other hand, when we're consciously looking for signs of deception or truth, we pay too much attention to words and not enough to the nonverbal gestalt of what's going on. We do the same when we choose how to present ourselves: we overattend to the words we're saying, and we lose track of what the rest of our body is doing, which in itself throws us out of synchrony. When we stop trying to manage all the little details, the gestalt comes together. It works. It may seem paradoxical to suggest that we need to be aware of our bodies in order to act naturally, but, as we'll see, the two things actually go hand in hand.

Truth reveals itself more clearly through our actions than it does through our words. As the great American dancer Martha Graham put it, "The body says what words cannot." She also said, "The body never lies." Certainly being inauthentic is not the same as intentionally deceiving someone, but the results look similar. Presenting an inauthentic version of yourself strikes the observer the same way as intentional deception does, thanks to your asynchronous nonverbal behaviors. The less present we are, the more poorly we perform. The two are mutually reinforcing.

In fact we can even be tricked into losing confidence and performing poorly in front of an audience via the introduction of a false asynchrony, which researchers have tested in studies.[36] Musicians rely heavily on synchronous auditory feedback of their own performances — hearing the music they play as they play it. When that synchrony is artificially manipulated through earphones, musicians lose confidence in their abilities and become distracted trying to understand the asynchrony, which then impairs their performance.

So, as Majid wrote, presence is "when all your senses agree on one thing at the same time." *Presence manifests as resonant synchrony.*

What do we know so far? Presence stems from believing our own stories. When we don't believe our stories, we are inauthentic — we are deceiving, in a way, both ourselves and others. And this self-deception is, it turns out, observable to others as our confidence wanes and our verbal and nonverbal behaviors become dissonant. It's not that people are thinking, "He's a liar." It's that people are thinking, "Something feels off. I can't completely invest my confidence in this person." As Walt Whitman said, "We convince by our presence," and to convince others we need to convince ourselves.

So how do we learn to believe our own stories?

2

Believing and Owning Your Story

Presence is the inner self showing up.
— PADI, SPAIN

THE WISH TO FEEL and be seen as "authentic" seems like a basic human need, and maybe that's why the term "authentic self" is so popular these days. Actually, sometimes I feel it gets thrown around like confetti on New Year's Eve.

But here's a question: What *is* the authentic self? What exactly does it mean to be true to yourself? Is it what your friends have in mind when they encourage you to "just be yourself"? Is it the feeling we have when we're "being real"? Can we expect to be the same person, in every circumstance, at every moment? How many selves are in there, and how is it determined which one we express?

Before we answer that, let's talk briefly about a broader question: What is the self?

Scores of psychologists have tackled this question, amassing more than a hundred years' worth of theory and research — and that's on the heels of philosophers trying to answer this question for thousands of years. I can't adequately boil down all that previous work here, but the following are, in my opinion, the three most important things to understand about the self, particularly as it relates to presence.[1]

The self is:

1. Multifaceted, not singular.
2. Expressed and reflected through our thoughts, feelings, values, and behaviors.
3. Dynamic and flexible, not static and rigid. It reflects and responds to the situation — not like a chameleon, but in a way that makes us responsive and also open to growth. It doesn't mean that our core values change, but sometimes there's a process that involves fitting our true self to the situation or role that we're in by choosing which core values and traits to render visible.

If the self is multifaceted and dynamic, do we even *have* a single, static authentic self? In a bygone era, there were scholars who put forth the romantic notion that we do, but most modern-day psychologists and philosophers agree that we do not possess a fully integrated, permanent authentic self.[2]

I take a pragmatic view: the authentic self is an experience — a state, not a trait. This transitory phenomenon has been described by psychologist Alison Lenton as "the subjective sense of being one's true self"[3] and as "one's momentary sense of feeling in alignment with one's 'real self.' "[4] I think of it as the experience of *knowing* and *feeling* that you're being your most sincere and courageous self. It is autonomously and honestly expressing your values through your actions. It comes and goes, but we recognize it because it "feels right." Virtually everyone can recall a moment when they felt they were being true to themselves, but few can say they always feel that way. We hold flexible views of ourselves based on the part we're playing in any particular moment and context (e.g., parent, spouse, teacher).[5] So even when you feel that you are being true to yourself, the specifics of that self — the parts that are activated — change from situation to situation.

But is our authentic *best* self the same thing as our authentic *true* self? Naturally there are parts of ourselves that we (and the people who know us) are less than fond of — some that might even be considered destructive. Many of us are working to modify these parts — an irrational fear, a hair-trigger temper. There also are parts of ourselves that we keep private, not because they're harmful but because we're not obliged to share every personal thing with the rest of the world.

And then there are parts that are not destructive to others but that we try to change or hide because we feel undeservedly ashamed of them, as reflected in this e-mail:

> I am currently a medical student in Turkey. I have very high grades and I do love learning medicine, "thinking" about science, finding new ideas. I know my potential, I know I am carrying something big inside me. But the thing is:
>
> I am stuttering. . . .
>
> Because of this, I cannot participate in class, I cannot discuss anything, and worse, I cannot ask my questions. . . .
> For four years, I've had to hide them.

I've gotten many letters and messages from people struggling with obstacles that prevent them from fully believing, trusting, and being their boldest selves. We all have characteristics that we feel we should overcome or hide, that we don't feel are part of who we want to be.

These obstacles are real. They are painful. Are they things we'd really rather live without? Often the answer is yes. What I would like to suggest, though, is that while we may not have chosen to include such obstacles when we envision our ideal selves, they can represent an important dimension of our *authentic* best selves: they challenge us but are undeniably part of us. The brain injury I sustained in college doesn't acutely impede me today, but it will always be an essential part of who I am — not just for its physical impact on my brain and nervous system but also through its countless, rippling effects on my experiences since then: my relationships; my decisions; my ways of thinking, learning, and feeling; my worldview. For a long time, it was a part of myself that I was ashamed to share. For a long time, it waylaid and ensnared me.

Physical and psychological adversity shape us. Our challenges give us insights and experiences that only we have had. And — I don't want to be glib about this — they are things we need to not only accept but also embrace and even see as strengths. While we may not have chosen to include them in our concepts of ourselves, they are there. And what more can we do but own them?

We're getting closer, but still we haven't answered the question: Who or what exactly is our authentic best self, and how do we find it when we need it? Scholars who study what makes people happy and effective at work may be able to offer some insight. They want to know this: How can employees be their happiest, most effective selves in the workplace?

Laura Morgan Roberts, organizational behavior professor and widely recognized expert on the ways people develop positive, authentic identities on the job, explains that we all have had moments when we felt acutely alive, true to ourselves, and performing at our full potential and that our memories of these moments are particularly vivid. "Over time," she and her colleagues write, "we collect these experiences into a portrait of who we are when we are at our personal best."[6]

Roberts guides people through the process of creating this portrait by helping them to identify *enablers* and *blockers* — the attitudes, beliefs, and behaviors that help and hurt their ability to summon forth their best selves.[7] For example, I might list as an enabler "I'm good at identifying themes across widely disparate ideas"; as a blocker, I would say, "I'm exceptionally poor at estimating how much time it will take to complete a project." Here are some of the questions Roberts and other organizational scholars have developed to help us identify the best parts of ourselves. I recommend jotting down your answers now — and note that you need not limit them to the workplace.[8]

- What three words best describe you as an individual?
- What is unique about you that leads to your happiest times and best performance?
- Reflect on a specific time — at work or at home — when you were acting in a way that felt "natural" and "right." How can you repeat that behavior today?
- What are your signature strengths and how can you use them?

But it's not enough to identify the values, traits, and strengths that represent your authentic best self — you must then affirm and trust the answers. You must believe them. They tell an important part of your personal story, and if you don't believe your story, why would anyone else?

We interpret life's biggest challenges as threats to this story — or, more precisely, as questions about the adequacy of the person the story describes. Moments that threaten the self tend to hinge on feelings of social disapproval or rejection: not being admitted to a university, losing a job, a romantic breakup, making a mistake in front of an audience, opening ourselves up to someone who responds judgmentally. Our instinct, when under siege this way, is to focus completely on the threat, committing all our psychological resources to defending ourselves. The psychologists Geoffrey Cohen and David Sherman describe our response to these threats as "an inner alarm that arouses vigilance and the motive to reaffirm the self."[9]

Professor Claude Steele, well-known Stanford University social psychologist and author, defined a process by which we try to defeat the threat before it even exists: we affirm our most deeply held values — the best parts of ourselves — before entering into a potentially threatening situation. He called this *self-affirmation theory.*

An important clarification: when we read or hear the term "self-affirm," we might be reminded of the classic *Saturday Night Live* sketch about a mock self-help show, "Daily Affirmation with Stuart Smalley." While looking into a mirror, Smalley, played by Al Franken, would recite things like "I'm good enough, I'm smart enough, and, doggone it, people like me" and "I'm a worthy human being." Of course, the more Smalley repeated these affirmations, the worse he felt, leading him to say things like, "I am in a shame spiral" and "I don't know what I'm doing. They're gonna cancel the show. I'm gonna die homeless and penniless and twenty pounds overweight and no one will ever love me." We laughed because we knew — through intuition or experience — that this kind of self-affirmation usually backfires.

The kind of self-affirmation I'm talking about — the kind whose effects Steele and others have studied — doesn't have anything to do with reciting generic one-liners in the mirror, nor does it involve boasting or self-aggrandizement. Instead it's about reminding ourselves what matters most to us and, by extension, who we are. In effect, it's a way of grounding ourselves in the truth of our own stories. It makes us feel less dependent on the approval of others and even comfortable with their disapproval, if that's what we get.

Hundreds of studies have examined the effects of performing self-affirmations, many through the use of simple exercises. In one, people examine a list of common core values — for example, family, friends, health and fitness, creativity, working hard, professional success, religion, kindness, serving others, and so on. They choose the one or two that are most central to their identities — those closest to the core of who they are. Then they write a short essay about why those values are important to them and a particular time when they proved to be important.[10]

For instance, a person who deeply values service might write, "Serving others is the most important thing to me. I am passionate about it, and I believe we all would be better off if we focused on taking care of each other. It also deeply satisfies me and fills me up. I enjoy doing it and feel that it comes easily to me. When I was in high school, I spent a lot of time at a local retirement home where most of the residents were alone because they had lost their spouses. I would spend time sitting with them, listening to them, and maybe holding their hands. Those days were the most satisfying for me because I was doing what I really believed in."

To see how self-affirmation really works, let's look at a study led by David Creswell, David Sherman, and their collaborators in which participants were asked to deliver an impromptu speech before a panel of judges.[11] As if public speaking weren't stressful enough, the judges were told to seem stern and unapproachable, and after delivering their speeches the participants were instructed to spend the following five minutes counting aloud backwards from 2,083, in intervals of thirteen, while the judges repeatedly barked at them, "Go faster!"

If you're anything like I am, just picturing being in this situation gets your heart rate up, and that's precisely the point. This particular task — known as the Trier Social Stress Test (TSST)[12] — was designed to maximize stress so that psychologists can study how people respond to it. It is a social-anxiety nightmare.

But what does this have to do with self-affirmation? Well, before the speeches, the experimenters randomly assigned participants to do one of two things: either write about a personal core value (the exercise I described a moment ago) or write about a value that is not particularly important to them — that doesn't contribute to their self-definition.

After the speeches and the counting backwards ordeal, the researchers measured the subjects' emotional state. They did this by testing their saliva for cortisol, a hormone we release when we're under stress, especially stress involving social judgment.[13] The TSST experience in general, across many, many studies, has been shown to cause a cortisol spike. But in Creswell and Sherman's study, the people who had written about personal values that matter to them had significantly lower levels of the hormone than the other group. In fact, the self-affirmation group experienced no increase in cortisol at all. Affirming what we might call their authentic best selves — reminding themselves of their most valued strengths — protected them from anxiety.

Several years later, Creswell and Sherman's team replicated these results with a real-world source of stress — university midterm exams. This time they measured the students' before-and-after levels of epinephrine, also known as adrenaline, a hormone that signals stimulation of the sympathetic nervous system (the fight-or-flight response).[14] Students who had done self-affirmation exercises weeks before the exams showed no change in their epinephrine levels, but the other students weren't so fortunate. Their levels rose significantly over the weeks leading up to exams.

In addition, at the start of the experiment all the students were surveyed to see how much they worried about negative social judgments (rating their degree of agreement with statements such as "In college, I worry that people will think I'm unintelligent if I do poorly" and "I often worry that people will dislike me"). Students who were most worried benefited most from affirming their core values.

Scores of other experiments have looked at self-affirmation inside and outside the lab, showing that it helps with raising grades and reducing bullying in schools, with quitting smoking and increasing healthful eating, with decreasing stress and improving the effectiveness of couples therapy outcomes, with sharpening negotiation skill and performance, among many other things. In fact, self-affirmation seems to work best when the pressure is on and the stakes are high.[15]

Together these studies make an important point: before heading into a situation where we may be challenged, we can reduce our anxiety by reaffirming the parts of our authentic best selves we value most. When we feel safe with ourselves, we become significantly less defensive and more open to feedback, making us better problem solvers, too.[16]

Notice what is surprising about these findings: the participants affirmed their personal *core* values — not values or abilities that were relevant to the stressful tasks at hand. People didn't need to convince themselves that they were good public speakers in order to be confident about giving a speech; they just needed to have shored up an important part of their best selves — such as "I value being creative and making art." Beyond improving confidence and performance on specific tasks, knowing who we are can also elevate our sense of meaning in life.[17] In one set of studies, people viewed traits they'd previously selected as representative of their "true" selves or of the selves they present to others (e.g., witty, good-natured, self-disciplined, intelligent, patient, adventurous) and then were asked to quickly judge them as "me" or "not me." The faster they judged true-self traits as "me" — presumably, the more in touch they were with their authentic selves — the higher they rated their own lives' meaning and purpose.

In companion studies, subconsciously exposing people to words they felt described their true inner selves versus their public selves — which differ somewhat for most of us — led to their feeling a greater sense of meaning and purpose as well.

All these studies suggest that you can make your deepest self accessible just by spending a little time reflecting on — and perhaps writing about — who you think you are. The key to effective self-affirmation is that it is grounded in the truth. Your authentic best self — your boldest self — is not about psyching yourself up or saying, "I am the best at this task" or "I'm a winner." Your boldest self emerges through the experience of having full access to your values, traits, and strengths and knowing that you can autonomously and sincerely express them through your actions and interactions. That is what it means to believe in your own story. In essence, self-affirmation is the practice of clarifying your story to yourself, allowing you to trust that who you are will come through naturally in what you say and do.

And the *way* you tell your story to yourself matters. In a recent study on narrative identity — how we make sense of the events of our lives — researchers interviewed people in their fifties and sixties, a period of life that tends to be marked by family, work, and health transitions and a time when we reflect deeply on our lives. In addition to interviewing the participants, the researchers tracked the subjects' psychological and physical health over a period of four years.

In these interviews, four narrative themes emerged from the way people told their life stories: agency (people felt they were in control of their lives), communion (people described their lives as being about relationships), redemption (people felt that challenges had improved their attitudes or conferred wisdom in some way), and contamination (people felt that positive beginnings had turned toward negative endings).

Those whose narratives fell into the three positive categories — agency, communion, and redemption — experienced significant positive mental health trajectories in the following years. But people who described their lives in terms of contamination experienced poorer mental health. And the relationships between the narratives and the health outcomes were even stronger for people who were facing significant challenges, such as major illness, divorce, or losing a loved one.[18]

Becoming present is not just about knowing and affirming your story — it's also about how you narrate your story. Telling yourself what matters to you is one thing, but equally important is taking control of how you tell your story — to yourself and to others.

Expressing Your Authentic Best Self

Finding and believing in our authentic best selves can help us overcome threats that might otherwise undermine us during big challenges. But alone, it's still not enough to make us present during those challenges. After finding your authentic best self, you must figure out how to express it.

Mariko, a young Japanese woman who was working for a large company, was preparing to give a talk at a United Nations–sponsored conference. She described herself as "so stressed out and my heart was beating so hard, which was unusual for me," explaining that she usually feels quite confident. She figured she must need to practice her speech more. So she practiced. And practiced and practiced and practiced. But it was no antidote for her anxiety surge. Desperate, she went to a trusted adviser, who told her, "Why do you keep preparing for this presentation? You must know that the most important thing at a presentation is your presence." She realized she'd maxed out on preparing; not only was it no longer helping, it was also diverting psychological resources away from the task of being present.

"I realized that I was preparing for nothing," she said. "And I realized that *how* to be who I am is the most powerful message to other people and to myself."

To be present, it's not enough to know who you are and express it to others; you need to act on it. In 1992, psychologist William Kahn studied psychological presence in the workplace, identifying four critical dimensions: a person must be attentive, connected, integrated, and focused.[19]

"These dimensions collectively define what it means to be alive, *there* in the fullest sense, and accessible in the work role," he wrote. "The result is personal accessibility to work (in terms of contributing ideas and effort), others (in terms of being open and empathetic), and one's growth (in terms of growth and learning). Such presence is manifested as personally engaged behaviors."[20] As he says:

> Consider the example of a project manager at an architecture firm working with a draftsperson. The project manager noticed that the draftsperson was struggling with what seemed to be a relatively simple dimension of the drawing. A deadline was fast approaching and she walked over to talk with the draftsperson. As she did so she became aware of her own clenched hands, which she understood as a symptom of her annoyance and frustration not just with

the draftsperson but with the difficult deadline and the vice president who had set it up. She asked the draftsperson about the work and heard him relate his struggles and frustrations with what he perceived as a lack of information about the task. She asked further questions to clarify his experience, quipped a joke to relax him that referred to the lack of information throughout the system (modeled by the client and vice president), noted that he was correct up to a point but that he did have relevant information he had overlooked, suggested a way to frame the problem, and gave feedback about his progress thus far. Throughout the conversation, she was relaxed, direct, and concerned.[21]

When you do engage your authentic best self, it pays off, and organizations can play a critical role in making it safe for employees to do just that. In a study conducted by professors Dan Cable, Francesca Gino, and Bradley Staats, participants were encouraged to begin a series of work tasks by thinking about their individualities (for instance, by describing a time they acted as they were "born to act" and then designing a personal logo). When they did that, they felt more strongly that they could "be who [they] really [are]."[22] As a result, they gained more satisfaction from the tasks and also performed more efficiently and made fewer errors.

Some organizations socialize new employees by focusing on the group's identity and needs, failing to acknowledge those of the individuals. Workers may even be discouraged from expressing their true identities. These studies tell us that when people bring their unique qualities to their jobs, they are happier and perform better.

The benefit of feeling authentically engaged with a situation exists even beyond Western, individualistic cultures. In a companion study that Cable and his colleagues conducted in an Indian call center, all new employees went through a half-day training workshop. Some of them attended sessions that emphasized newcomers' authentic best selves — they were asked to think and write about what they could uniquely bring to the job, then spend fifteen minutes sharing their answers with the rest of the group. They were then given fleece sweatshirts and badges emblazoned with their own names. Other employees' training emphasized the pride to be gained from their new organizational affiliation — they were taught about the company's culture, asked to think and write about which parts of the company they'd be most proud of, then spend fifteen minutes sharing their answers with the rest of the group. They were then given fleece sweatshirts and badges emblazoned with the name of the company. A third group was in a control condition in which they went through a common, basic orientation.

The employees who were encouraged to express and engage their authentic best selves performed their jobs better than employees in the two other groups, as reflected in customer satisfaction ratings, and stayed at their jobs longer, a concern in an industry with high turnover.

We're getting closer to a solid, functional definition of what presence is and how it works in the real world. By finding, believing, expressing, and then engaging our authentic best selves, especially if we do it right before our biggest challenges, we reduce our anxiety about social rejection and increase our openness to others. And that allows us to be fully present.

"Acting" with Presence

At some point in your life, in the lead-up to a high-stakes encounter or situation, you've probably gotten the advice to "just be yourself." Intuitively we all know that this makes sense; we will perform better and others will respond better if we can act as we naturally are. But the key word here is *act* — after all, if others are present, "just being yourself" is still a kind of performance. We tend to associate performance with artifice, which on the surface might seem antithetical to presence. And yet there's no denying that a great artist in the midst of a performance is spectacularly present, to the extent of creating an almost electric charge. What can great performers teach us about presence?

I am a lover of live music. I'm not willing to disclose the number of hours I've spent at concerts — from the tiniest bars to the biggest stadiums, from the most obscure indie bands to rock legends — but it's a lot. And when the moment is right, it's intoxicating. I don't think there's anything I find more blissful than a moment of perfect connection at a live concert. But what makes it a moment of perfect connection? When musicians are fully immersed in playing, everything they are doing — including subtle movements of their heads and bodies — is harmonious not only with the rhythm and melody but also with the essence of the music. They are not thinking about what they're doing in a fragmentary way — "Play G, tilt head slightly left, rock weight to left foot, hold for four counts," and so on. When a musician is present, we are moved, transported, and convinced. When musicians are present, they bring us with them to the present.

A musician friend, Jason Webley, once told me that a good performance is one that doesn't feel like a movie that could be played again and again but rather like something that's unfolding for the first time in front of you. "I don't mind if the performer seems a bit anxious," he said. "I want to know that I'm watching something real from someone who loves what they're doing. That makes me believe that what I'm watching and hearing is true. It makes me believe the musician."

We see the same thing in dance performances. Technical mastery is not enough to move ballet dancers to the top position — principal dancer — in a company. One might rack up an impressive list of roles as a first or second soloist. But a principal dancer goes beyond technical perfection and becomes united with the music, her character, her partner, others on stage, and the audience. She is not just performing or entertaining. And an audience feels it — although they may not be able to articulate why and may even misattribute it to technical superiority alone. The principal dancer is the one who must *convince* everyone — including her fellow dancers and the audience.

Mikko Nissinen is artistic director of Boston Ballet. Born and raised in Finland, he has danced with many companies, including the San Francisco Ballet, where he was a principal dancer for nine years. As a former ballet dancer myself, I was especially eager to ask him about presence. "Any new experience can create questions, create doubts, and that pulls you away from the zone. When you find your true presence, it is the strength to *be* there. To be there in a state of balance, because you're not trying to protect yourself. You just are. So it's sort of *your* true state." As an example, he described watching Mikhail Baryshnikov dance a piece that had been choreographed for him by the legendary Jerome Robbins. Mikko had seen Baryshnikov perform the same Robbins piece a year earlier, when it was new to him — and it was technically perfect. But the second time, it was more than that: "I have to say it was almost like...a transformative moment. He danced the piece well, as he had the year before, but this time — because of his presence, the energy that was going between...." Mikko hunts for the words, mouth open, hands searching. Between Baryshnikov and the audience? Between Baryshnikov and the music? "He was able to connect us to…to *everything!* He built a bridge to the heavens! It was just unbelievable. My God, that was just absolute mastery of being in the present."

Recently I talked with an actor who struck me as an intuitive expert on presence. I say "intuitive," but although the particular steps to presence might have been intuitive for her, that doesn't mean they were always easy to take. Through experience, they became easier. And they're steps we all can learn.

At the time, I'd already been studying and thinking about the subject for a couple of years, and discussing it with this actor felt like a conversation with the embodiment of all the research I'd gathered. Sharp and warm, she seemed to light up as we spoke, leaning toward me, eyes heartily engaged, nodding and smiling in shared excitement. We had a common understanding, yet she was able to distill the essence of presence in a way that I could not.

We were sitting in her kitchen, with family members coming and going, dishes being washed, leftovers being eaten, a dog barking to be let out, neighbors dropping by. The scene was so utterly normal that, if not for the topic of conversation, I could have easily forgotten that I was talking with one of the greatest Hollywood actors of all time.

I'm not alone in appreciating Julianne Moore's complete mastery of presence — around two months after our conversation, she received the Academy Award for best actress in a leading role for her performance as a woman with early-onset Alzheimer's in the film *Still Alice*.[23]

In his *Time* magazine review of the film, Richard Corliss wrote of Moore, "One of America's great actresses turns this story of tragic forgetfulness into a heroic struggle.…Alice found the perfect vessel in Moore, who almost always manages to be both fearless and pitch-perfect."[24] David Siegel, who directed Julianne in the 2012 film *What Maisie Knew*, said, "She believes very much in being present in the moment of performance ... but she doesn't carry it with her when she leaves."[25] She enters without fear, performs without anxiety, and leaves without regret.

Julianne and I ended up having a four-hour conversation. I was there to talk about presence in her professional life, but it didn't take long to notice that she's found the same presence in her personal life. Wearing a flannel shirt, leggings, and wool socks — and every bit as beautiful as always — she was washing out the dozens of votive candle holders she'd used during the holiday party she hosted the night before, all while engaging in playful debate with her husband and daughter about whether or not one should eat cupcakes before breakfast — after all, are cupcakes *really* that different from pancakes? (cupcakes won) — chatting about which colleges to visit with her son, who was about to finish high school, and chuckling along with me as we swapped anecdotes about embarrassing parenting moments.

When I read through the transcript of the interview, I was horrified: we'd spent two of the four hours chatting about the most mundane things — and I had talked almost as much as she had. My first thought was, how did we manage to get so off topic? And how did I manage to waste so much of her time? But then I realized that allowing the conversation to flow naturally was yet another manifestation of Julianne's ability to be in the moment — and to bring others into that moment with her.

When we did get down to talking about presence, it was sometimes hard to tell which one of us was writing a book about it.

I asked her, "What do you think prevents us from being present with the people in our lives?"

"People feel the least present when they don't feel seen," she said. "It's impossible to be present when no one sees you. And it becomes a self-perpetuating process, because the more that people don't acknowledge you, the more you feel you don't exist. There's no space for you....Conversely, you are the most present when you are the most seen...and then people are always corroborating your sense of self." As a kid, Julianne didn't want to be the center of attention, but, like the rest of us, she longed to be seen and understood. Her family moved around a lot, and she said that in every new environment, she inevitably felt unseen — by the students, by the teachers. And in every new setting, she explained, she had to admit to herself, "I don't know who I am in this situation. I have to figure it out."

Every move presented a new challenge. And in every new challenge, Julianne had to identify and affirm her authentic best self. Until she could do that, no one *could* see her.

I asked her, "Aside from being seen, what is presence for an actor? How does an actor learn to become present?"

"The key to presence — and this is the one thing they tell you in school — the key is relaxation," she says. "But when you're eighteen and you've started drama school and they say you have to be relaxed to do this, you're like, 'But all my feeling comes from tension and anxiety — all those big bursts of anger, angst, tears...' And so you go from that place at eighteen to years later, when you realize the key to facilitating emotion and feeling and nuance and presence...is relaxation."

I also asked her about preparation. It's clear she takes that very seriously, and when getting ready for a role she works out many of her character's particular gestures and small behaviors in advance — things that, from studying psychology, she knows to be consistent with the character's personality and emotional state. "I'm prepared enough to let myself have an experience on camera," she says. "If I'm not prepared, I'm too panicked. I can't be present." But preparation, she recognizes, is only part of it. As she explained on *Inside the Actors Studio,* she leaves "ninety-five percent of the performance to be discovered on set.... I want to have a sense of who a character is, and then I want to get there and have it happen to me on camera."[26]

This is a good time to address the issue of preparation more broadly. People sometimes mistakenly think I'm suggesting that we scrap preparation altogether and instead just wing it. I'm not. We can't possibly feel safe enough to be present if we haven't given thought to the content of what we'd like to convey. In a *Harvard Business Review* piece on preparing for a job interview, Karen Dillon, coauthor of *How Will You Measure Your Life?*, tells us what we should focus on.[27] For example, Dillon suggests developing "small narratives" for the dozen or so most frequently asked (and maddeningly vague) job interview questions, such as "Why should we hire you?" and "Why do you fit this role?" She also recommends preparing answers for questions we want to avoid, just to be safe. It's not about having a memorized script; it's about having easier cognitive access to this content, which frees you to focus not on what you fear will happen but on what's actually happening.

Here's what I *am* saying: preparation is obviously important, but at some point, you must stop preparing content and start preparing mind-set. You have to shift from *what* you'll say to *how* you'll say it.

Often, though, we face big challenges for which we have little direction or knowledge of what will be expected of us, and that can be unsettling — and almost impossible to prepare for. Especially when it's something we want to do well. What then?

Julianne thought for a moment, then said, "That reminds me of when I auditioned for *Safe* for Todd Haynes. I read the script, and I could hear it so clearly, and I really, really wanted it." But she didn't know how the director, Todd Haynes, saw the character — she could not prepare a character to his preferences. "I can remember walking down Broadway, going to the audition. I wore white jeans and a white T-shirt, it was very — I just wanted to look kind of like this blank thing. And I thought, 'If he doesn't like what I'm going to do, then I'm not right — then it's not the voice that he wrote. Because this is what I hear. And if he [Haynes] hears the same thing, then he'll hire me. But if he wants something else, I know I can't do that.'" She explained this with a great sense of acceptance — no frustration. (As it turned out, and as you'll know if you've seen *Safe*, she and Haynes heard the same voice.)

So even when serving as a vessel for a character, Julianne can only do her job well when she's doing it in a way that is authentic and honest for her.

Regarding the kinds of challenges that are impossible to prepare for, she said, "That great American saying —'Just do your best' — people can find that crippling," because what the heck does that even mean? Does it mean "Just be *the* best?" And if you don't know what's expected of you, how can you be the best? "In fact," Julianne added, "I think what it's about is being your most authentic, being your most present. *Fill* it. Bring yourself."

"But what happens when you bring yourself and it doesn't go well?" I asked.

In one of the final scenes of the 1999 film *The End of the Affair*, Julianne was supposed to throw herself, sobbing, over her lover's body. "I couldn't do it. I just couldn't do it. I kept trying, kept going back, and I just couldn't do it. And we had shot most of it, and this was like my penultimate scene that we were shooting."

The director, Neil Jordan, encouraged her to go back to her

trailer to relax. He said to her, "You know, you shot the entire movie. Even if this doesn't happen, it's not going to affect the performance you've given." Julianne said she learned then "that sometimes you just hit a wall. And it's okay. Even if it feels bad, it's okay to let it feel bad. Because eventually you'll stop feeling bad, because feelings just don't last very long."

No regret, no rumination. No shame. No fear that she wouldn't be able to nail it the next time. And of course, later they got the scene.

Toward the end of our time together, Julianne said, "Sometimes you feel like you're trudging through the mud, not getting anywhere; you can't take flight with it. And then sometimes you just feel like, 'That really took flight,' you know? It makes you feel very alive.

"That's why we do it. That's why every actor does it. For those moments — because it feels — not to be hokey, but it feels transcendent."

But "If someone feels powerless and worn down, they're going to feel too nervous to be present," she said. "And they're also going to feel too protected. If you're protecting yourself against harm — emotional harm or humiliation — you can't be present, because you're too protected."

She paused a moment, then said: "It's power. It's always about power, isn't it?"

Is that it? Is *presence* really, in the end, just another word for "power"? That would explain a lot.

"What do you do," I asked, "when you're present and ready to engage but the other actor in the scene is not?"

"Some people have already figured out what they're going to do, and they're not going to do [it] with you, and so they're doing their thing... and you can't connect with them through their eyes, you can't connect with them physically. And the whole thing about acting is that it's so much of an exchange, you know?

"Where the exciting thing happens, where you don't know what's going to happen, is when two present people are connecting and bringing something, and it's like . . . That's where it's transcendent." But if the other actor isn't engaged, the power of presence can sometimes overcome even that obstacle, Julianne maintained.

"When you are present and available, people have a desire to offer you their authentic self. All you have to do is ask. No one keeps a secret. No one. And they might be resistant initially to telling you something, but eventually they'll give you their whole life story," Julianne said. "And it's because of people's desire to be seen."

I replied, "It seems that when *you* become present, you allow *others* to be present. Presence doesn't make you dominant in an alpha sense; it actually allows you to hear other people. And for them to feel heard. And for them to become present. You can help people feel more powerful even when you can't give them formal power."

She paused, and her face lit up. "Yes! And when it happens — when your presence can bring out their presence — you elevate *everything*."

3

Stop Preaching, Start Listening: How Presence Begets Presence

As we let our own light shine, we . . . give other people per-
mission to do the same. As we're liberated from our own
fear, our presence automatically liberates others.
— MARIANNE WILLIAMSON

ONE SPRING EVENING IN 1992, members of the clergy crowded
into a tiny church in Boston. They'd come together to respond to
a terrifying jump in gang violence and killing — seventy-three
young people murdered in one year, a 230-percent increase from
just three years earlier. People were exasperated, desperate. They
lived in fear of losing their children to the open warfare that had
engulfed their city. Nothing they had tried — extra after-school
programs, parent-led lockdowns, increased policing — could stop
the carnage. A week before the meeting, during a funeral service
in the same church for a slain teenager, fourteen gang members
stormed in and stabbed a young man nine times.

At the meeting sat a young Baptist minister, Reverend Jeffrey
Brown. He was a relative newcomer to the community and its

problems — born in Alaska, the son of an army officer, he had spent his childhood moving from base to base. Then he attended college in central Pennsylvania before coming to Boston for divinity school. He was there that night, one of more than three hundred clergy in attendance, because his community — like much of the city — was suffering. But he had no experience with gangs or crime or the reasons why they flourish.

I'll let him describe what happened after that meeting.

"What happened is what always happens when you get a roomful of preachers together," Jeffrey said. "They talked. And then they made a meeting to talk again next Tuesday, and the Tuesday after that...And they began bringing in members of the community — teachers, parents, police — to talk about what was going on. After two months, they wanted to break into committees, Amy! And I knew that was the end — when you break into committees because nothing's working, it's time to try something different.

"So Eugene — Reverend Eugene Rivers — said, 'You know who we haven't talked to? We haven't brought one young person in here to talk about what's happening.' They all said, 'All right, Eugene, we nominate you to be head of the street committee.' It was meant to embarrass him, but it didn't. Eugene said, 'Okay, this Friday at my house.' That Friday, thirteen people showed up. Eugene lived at Four Corners, which at the time was ground zero — one of the most violent neighborhoods in the city. We showed up, and he just said, 'Okay, let's go!' We said, 'Go where?' And he said, 'Out there!'"

"Out there" was not exactly where Jeffrey Brown had hoped to find himself at that point in his career. In college he had been a communications major, and once he became a clergyman he set his sights on being pastor of a megachurch — one of the big sub-urban congregations that were then spreading throughout the country, preaching the gospel of success and prosperity. If you'd asked him just a couple years earlier about his ambitions, he'd have said he wanted a church with thousands of members, his own television ministry — the whole shebang. Gang wars hadn't been on his radar.

Of course on Sundays, in church, he'd had to at least acknowl-edge what was going on in the streets. "I got up in my pulpit and preached against the violence," he said, "and then after the ser-mon I'd get in my car and drive right through it to my nice home in my nice neighborhood."

But the bloodshed and the despair continued to close in. Jef-frey found himself presiding at the funerals of sixteen- and seventeen-year-old kids, struggling to say something meaningful, something that would make an impact. "It went beyond my train-ing as a young minister," he said. "You take your death-and-dying courses, [learn about] the value of ritual, what to say that would be comforting. But you don't really have anything for what happens when a young person has been gunned down. And the com-pounding effect of the trauma is when you have young people sitting there and they have already been through a couple of homicides. So it was disturbing, trying to talk and connect with these young people. It just wasn't working. They weren't really hearing what was being said at the funeral. And you had some who just seemed vacant. Still reeling over what had happened. And there were others who were angry, and you could tell there was also a gathering of that anger, because they were going to retaliate."

Minister friends of his who were also struggling appealed to Jeffrey for help: he was a young man, not much older than many of the perpetrators and victims of the violence that was gutting the community. Couldn't he make a connection? Find a way of getting through to these kids? "But I couldn't," he says. "It was as foreign to me as it was to my friends."

It was around that time that Jeffrey had a dream. In it, Jesus appeared to him in church, wearing an orange suit and a red shirt and a purple tie. He showed Jeffrey his palatial office, then led him to a big Mercedes-Benz and drove him to a mansion. Then Jesus turned to Jeffrey and said, "What do you think?" Jeffrey answered, "It's a lot." And Jesus looked at Jeffrey and said, "Is this really me?" And then Jeffrey woke up.

"I dreamed it more than once," Jeffrey said, "so I thought, 'There's something not right here.' I just knew it was like a message, that this is not the right direction. But that was very daunting for me, because I thought, 'I don't know how to connect; I don't know what I'm doing.'"

Jeffrey realized he needed to try harder to address the community's problems. He built new programs in his church aiming to help at-risk youth. "I even tried a rap sermon one time," he said, chuckling. (A friendly young congregation member gave him a tip afterward: "Don't do that again.") He met with local high school kids, but the gang members and crack dealers weren't attending school, so they remained beyond his reach. He didn't know what to do next.

Not long before that first meeting of the ministers, a twenty-one-year-old named Jesse McKie was murdered in the street near Jeffrey's church. Some gang members stopped the young man to steal his leather jacket, and when he resisted they stabbed him six times and took it. Yards away from the church door, Jesse bled to death.

"I had never met Jesse," Jeffrey said. "The first time I met his parents was at the memorial service. I think they called me because I was young and I was known to work with youth and all that. They were like, 'Can you come and lead a candlelight vigil and pray?' And I said, 'Sure,' but I was really nervous."

Jeffrey thought he knew pretty much everyone in the area, but as he stood in the freezing cold, leading the vigil for Jesse, he saw all around him the faces of people he'd never met before, even though many of them lived in the subsidized housing just down the street from where he lived. "Then I went back to [Jesse's family's] house and they talked about him, and there were a lot of people who were there who were just from the 'hood. I couldn't wait to get out."

What happened next confused Jeffrey. People started coming up to him and shaking his hand, "even though I didn't *do* anything other than pray. I didn't have a program for them, I didn't provide a service for them, I just, you know, prayed and was *there*, and they shook my hand." He couldn't stop thinking about it. He thought about it in the car on the way home, and he went to bed thinking about it, and the thought that kept coming to him was, "What I did tonight was really ministry."

Soon afterward the police caught three of the guys who killed Jesse. They were in their midtwenties, just a couple years younger than Jeffrey. "I was like, man, these are stone hard-core gang members, but why, if they're around my age, why are they so far away from my thinking? I'm black, they're black; I live in the city, they live in the city; and, you know, I don't understand it. All that was just churning inside me. And I didn't have anybody to really talk to, because I did try to talk to some of my colleagues, but they were hell-bent on building their megachurches. They're like, 'How many people joined your church this month?' and I'm like, 'Who cares?! This kid was killed! Shouldn't we do something about this?' "

Jesse's murder marked a turning point for Jeffrey. He saw the inherent flaw — the paradox — of his approach to the problem. "You had these gang youth who I was treating as the 'other,'" he says, "and I was trying to build community, but I wasn't giving them any gateway into my definition of community. So I said, 'If you're going to build a community, you have to build community with everybody, which means the folks that other people don't *want* in the community, which means these kids.'"

Jeffrey showed up at Eugene's house that Friday night after the clerics' meeting because he knew that the head of the "street committee" was right. It was time to seek a solution *out there*.

"So we walked," Jeffrey recalled. "We walked from ten at night until two in the morning. And it was always poppin'." On the second Friday, fewer than half the original thirteen clergy members returned. Soon, that number dropped to four — Jeffrey, Eugene, and two others. But they were committed. "I knew that walking the streets and talking to the kids was the key to something," Jeffrey said, "but I didn't know what."

Showing Up

It took guts for Jeffrey and the ministers to go out night after night, uninvited and unprotected. And, as you might have guessed, they were not immediately welcomed as saviors. But they kept at it and eventually found a way not only to connect with the area's young men but also to partner with them to reduce youth violence in Boston dramatically.

Presence with others is first about showing up. Literally, physically, showing up. No one had come to talk to these young people on their turf and their schedule. But, more specifically, presence is about *how* we show up — how we approach the people we hope to connect with and influence.

Jeffrey knew that he was walking into the toughest neighborhood in Boston during a perilous time. The kids he encountered there were just as hardened and bold — at least on the outside — as you would imagine. The normal instinct might have been for Jeffrey to show those young men that he could be just as tough as they were — a worthy adversary. Of course that would have been the worst possible move. Those kids had been up against toughness all their lives. Toughness held no surprises for them.

Jeffrey and the other ministers did just the opposite. They met toughness with gentleness and kindness and earnest interest in what the kids thought and felt. It was a little shocking — probably the last thing any of those young men expected. It was disruptive. Jeffrey knew that at first it might make him look like a weakling in their eyes. He was okay with that. He did it because he knew it hadn't ever been tried, and he figured maybe it would work.

You may be thinking, "Well, of course approaching others with kindness, openness, and curiosity is the best strategy," but you'd be surprised how common it is for us to instinctively take a different approach, one that has more to do with demonstrating our own power and control. For more than fifteen years, psychologists Susan Fiske and Peter Glick and I have been studying how people judge each other in first encounters. In research done in more than two dozen nations, we've seen the same patterns.[1]

When we meet someone new, we quickly answer two questions: "Can I trust this person?" and "Can I respect this person?" In our research, my colleagues and I have referred to these dimensions as *warmth* and *competence* respectively.

Usually we think that a person we've just met is either more warm than competent or more competent than warm, but not both in equal measure. We like our distinctions to be clear — it's a human bias. So we classify new acquaintances into types. Tiziana Casciaro, in her research into organizations, refers to these types as lovable fools or competent jerks.[2]

Occasionally we see people as incompetent *and* cold — foolish jerks — or as warm *and* competent — lovable stars. The latter is the golden quadrant, because receiving trust and respect from other people allows you to interact well and get things done.

But we don't value the two traits equally. First we judge warmth or trustworthiness, which we consider to be the more important of the two dimensions. Oscar Ybarra and his colleagues found, for instance, that people process words related to warmth and morality (*friendly, honest,* and others) faster than words related to competence (*creative, skillful,* and others).[3]

Why do we prioritize warmth over competence? Because from an evolutionary perspective, it is more crucial to our survival to know whether a person deserves our trust. If he doesn't, we'd better keep our distance, because he's potentially dangerous, especially if he's competent. We do value people who are capable, especially in circumstances where that trait is necessary, but we only notice that *after* we've judged their trustworthiness.

Recalling those first Friday night walks when ministers and gang members circled each other on the same uneasy turf, Jeffrey said, "What we figured out is that while we were walking, they were watching us. And they wanted to make sure of a couple of things. Number one, that we were going to be consistent in our behavior — that we would keep coming out there. And second they wanted to make sure that we weren't out there to exploit them." Outsiders who come into a troubled neighborhood with big talk about "taking back the streets" might bring along a TV camera, a reporter, or just an inflated sense of self-importance.

The young people were wondering, said Jeffrey, "Is this another hustle? Is this an ego-driven thing that you're doing more for yourself than for us?" Before any dialogue could begin — before both parties could be present with each other, there had to be trust.

After establishing trust, they wanted to evaluate strength. As Jeffrey said, they wanted to know, "'Are you ready to handle what's out here?' Those initial conversations can be intimidating, because you've got young people making conversation that is aggressive and protective, and you have to wade through that. And you have to do it in a way where you also remain open."

Given all that, a funny thing happens when I ask people — students, friends, executives, artists — whether they'd rather be seen as trustworthy or competent: most choose the latter. Perfectly understandable, for two reasons. Competence is more easily measured in concrete, practical ways — it can be displayed on a résumé or performance record or test score, so we have a sense of control over how competent we seem. Also, while our trustworthiness and warmth benefit other people, we believe that our competence and strength directly benefit us.[4]

So we want others to be warm and trustworthy, but we want them to see *us* as competent and strong. While that first desire helps keep us safe, the latter can lead to costly mistakes.[5]

I've seen many MBA students learn this the hard way during their summer internships. Their goal is to get the company they're interning for to ask them to return for a real job after they graduate, and they have about ten weeks to prove they're worthy of that offer. It's like a ten-week job interview.

Often these students are so determined to show everyone that they're the smartest and most competent of the bunch that they overlook the costs of their strategy. It can make them seem cold and aloof. It can prevent them from taking part in social occasions with coworkers and managers. It can lead them to the mistaken belief that asking for help will make them look weak and incompetent, when in fact asking for feedback from a manager or from peers would give them a chance to interact, show respect, and become part of the group.

The big surprise comes at the end of the summer internship, when the overachieving students are called in to talk with their managers, only to learn that they are not getting job offers — because no one really got to know them. They didn't seem to "play well with others." Their competence wasn't in question, but they're told — indirectly or not — that they haven't established any productive collaborations or relationships of *trust*.

Not convinced? Consider a 2013 study of 51,836 leaders whose employees rated them first on a wide variety of behaviors and traits and then on their overall leadership effectiveness. Only twenty-seven were rated both in the bottom quartile (below the twenty-fifth percentile) on behaviors and traits reflecting likability *and* in the top quartile (above the seventy-fifth percentile) on general leadership effectiveness. In other words, your chance of being seen as an unlikable but effective leader is about one in two thousand.[6] Other researchers have found that the top characteristic associated with an executive's failure is an insensitive, abrasive, or bullying style — the exact opposite of warmth and trustworthiness.[7]

But before I go on, I want to check in, in case you're wondering why I'm telling you about Reverend Jeffrey Brown, about gang violence, about warmth and competence — about any of this.

The lesson is that trust is the conduit of influence, and the only way to establish real trust is by being present. Presence is the medium through which trust develops and ideas travel. If someone you're trying to influence doesn't trust you, you're not going to get very far; in fact, you might even elicit suspicion because you come across as manipulative. You might have great ideas, but without trust, those ideas are impotent. A warm, trustworthy person who is also strong elicits admiration, but only after you've established trust does your strength become a gift rather than a threat.

I'm also hoping to show you that learning to find presence in the most challenging moments isn't only good for you, it can yield great benefits for others as well. Presence gives you the power to help others in *their* most challenging moments.

Stop Being Silk

Let's return to Jeffrey. Jesse's murder was a turning point for him. It didn't automatically make it easier for him to get through to the kids he was trying to help. But it was the catalyst. Soon after came a moment when Jeffrey finally understood the reality of how he was being perceived on the street. It was also when the gang members at last got a glimpse of the real Jeffrey.

"So I'm dealing with this kid Tyler, who's like, 'What are you doing out here, man?' I remember one time I had this jacket on, and Tyler starts feeling it, and he says, 'Man, this is *silk.*' And I say, 'No, it's not,' but he's going, 'Look at this man out here with a silk jacket on,' and every time I go out there he's got something to say about this jacket, and finally I had enough, I got tired of it, and I said, 'Man, stop talking about my stuff. This ain't no silk jacket!'

"And he said, 'Yeah, *now* you're being real. You were being silk before.' And I said, 'Oh, okay, now I think I understand what's going on here.' And that's when we started to have a conversation, because what he really wanted to talk about was how difficult it was going to be to turn around the mind-set of many of the young people around him. It was like, 'You can't come out here and have one conversation and then all of a sudden everything changes.' And that's when I knew, okay, this isn't going to be a walk in the park. This is going to be a journey."

Jeffrey had to be real with those kids before the kids could be real with him. Through his actions, he had to tell his real story — the one he truly believed, not the one he wanted others to believe. He had to be his most sincere self — no facades, no barriers — in order to let them know it was okay for them to do the same. Revealing your true self frees others to reveal theirs. We have to stop being silk.

Shutting Up

When you listen to someone, it's the most profound
act of human respect.
— William Ury

William (Bill) Ury is cofounder of the Harvard Program on Negotiation and coauthor of the perennially bestselling book *Getting to Yes*. Bill is not only among the most experienced and successful negotiators I've ever met, he's also the kindest and most patient. With the gentlest touch, he helps to resolve conflicts around the world — in companies, governments, and communities — settling disagreements that others were unable to budge. During the 1980s he helped the US and Soviet governments create nuclear crisis centers designed to avert an accidental nuclear war. He's worked on ending a billion-dollar battle over control of Latin America's largest retailer, and he has advised the president of Colombia on ending a fifty-year civil war. When the parties to a dispute are hearing each other for the first time — when the issue has progressed substantially toward resolution — they truly believe that

Bill is some kind of magician. Of course, he swears that's not true. He claims that what he does is embarrassingly simple.

In 2003 Bill got a call from former president Jimmy Carter asking him to meet with Venezuelan president Hugo Chávez. With protesters crowding the streets of Caracas to demand an end to Chávez's presidency and others fiercely supporting him, the country seemed on the brink of civil war. Carter hoped Bill might be able to help find a way forward. In his book *Getting to Yes with Yourself*, he recalls the lead-up to the meeting:

> As was my habit, I went for a walk in the park to seek clarity. I suspected that I would be given only a few minutes with the president, so I was outlining in my head a clear set of recommendations to make. But what occurred to me on the walk was to do the exact *opposite* of what I had been planning: don't offer advice, unless of course requested to do so. Just listen, stay focused on the present moment, and look for openings. The risk, of course, was that the meeting would end very soon and I would lose my one chance to influence him with my recommendations, but I decided to take it.[8]

Throughout his meeting with Chávez, Bill stuck with this unusual strategy — he listened closely, "trying to understand what it was like to be in his shoes." Chávez told Bill about his life, about his experience in the military, about his outrage at the "traitors" who sought to overthrow him.

> I was just focused on the present moment, looking for an opening, and a question occurred to me: "Since you don't trust them, understandably given what happened to you,

let me ask you: What action if any could they possibly take tomorrow morning that would send you a credible signal that they were ready to change?"

"*Señales?* Signals?" he asked as he paused to consider the unexpected question.

Equally unexpected was the fact that Chávez had an answer. "Within minutes, the president agreed to designate his minister of the interior to work with [my colleague] Francisco and me to develop a list of possible practical actions that each party could take to build trust and de-escalate the crisis."

Looking back, Bill writes, "I am convinced that, if I had followed my first thought to begin the meeting by reciting my recommendations, the president would have cut the meeting short after a few minutes. . . . Instead, because I had deliberately let go of trying to give advice and instead just stayed present and attentive to possible openings, the meeting had become highly productive."

Why is it so hard for us to shut up and listen?

There's a simple answer. When we encounter someone we've never met before, we immediately fear that we won't be taken seriously. That we'll seem "less than." So we talk first, to own the moment, to take charge, to prove ourselves. We want to show what we know, what we think, what we've already accomplished. Talking first says: I know better than you, I am smarter than you, I should speak while you listen. Talking first sets the agenda: here's what we're going to do, and here's how we're going to do it.

Whereas if I let you talk first, there's no telling what you'll say. If I let you talk first, I'm giving up control over the situation, and who knows where that will leave me? Giving up control is scary. It's taking a step into the unknown. Who does that? Only the foolish. Or the brave.

Like Jeffrey on his nightly street patrol, Bill walked into that meeting with Chávez knowing he was walking into a tense situation where sides had been taken, resolutions formed, and lines drawn. Listening is difficult at such times, and eagerness to reach a quick solution often takes over. The key, says Bill, is "to look for the *present moment.*"

> In most situations, I find, there is an opening if we are attentive enough to see it. But it is all too easy for us to miss. I have been in so many negotiations where one side signals an opening or even makes a concession and the other side does not see it simply because they are not really paying attention. Whether it is a marital argument or a budget disagreement in the office, it is so easy for us to be distracted, to be thinking about the past or worrying about the future. Yet it is only in the present moment when we can intentionally change the direction of the conversation toward an agreement.

Listening is crucial to presence. And the challenges that arise when we really need to listen are the same ones that make it hard to be sufficiently present to do so.

Real listening can't happen unless we have a sincere desire to understand what we're hearing. And that's not an easy thing to manage, because it requires us to suspend judgment — even when we're feeling frustrated or scared or impatient or bored and even when we feel threatened or anxious about what we're about to hear (because we think we know it or because we don't know it). We have to give other people space and safety to be honest — and we can't respond defensively when we're listening. For some of us, it also means we need to overcome our fear of silence — of space.

The determination to listen — really listen — was at the heart of the effort by Jeffrey and the other ministers. That meant an admission that community leaders and law enforcement were powerless to stop the violence without the consent and cooperation of the perpetrators themselves. Gang members and crack dealers would have to be heard and even heeded. Their knowledge and opinions would have to be actively sought, then taken seriously. Considering the way that political leaders, law enforcement officials, and other adults usually approach gangs of young criminal offenders — i.e., *not* with an ear turned toward collaborative listening — you can see that the ministers were attempting something radical, not to mention risky.

Listening meant resisting the urge to do what they did best — preach. (Watch Jeffrey's TED talk and you'll see how at home he is in front of an audience, telling a story, sharing a message.) Preaching nonviolence would have been as ineffectual as strutting in with a tough, "I'm in control" attitude. Instead the ministers asked questions: "What is drug dealing like? What does it mean to stand on a corner slinging rocks? How do you avoid the police? How do you avoid rival gang members? How do you deal with the fact that there are no retired drug dealers? That this is a fast, short life?"

Listening meant letting go of what Jeffrey thought he knew. "There was so much for me to learn about life on the streets," Jeffrey says. "It was clear to me that my perception was shaped by the eleven o'clock news and popular culture, and the reality was very different." Because he and the other ministers listened instead of preaching, he says, "the youth stopped being the problem to be solved and started being our partners in this effort. They became invaluable.... We asked them, how do you see the church helping this situation? What can we do together?"

The paradox of listening is that by relinquishing power — the temporary power of speaking, asserting, knowing — we become more powerful. When you stop talking, stop preaching, and listen, here's what happens:

• **People can trust you.** As we've seen, if you don't have people's trust, you will find it very hard to influence them in a deep and lasting way.

• **You acquire useful information,** which makes it much easier to solve any problem you face. You may think you know the answer, but before you've listened to what another person really thinks and feels — what truly motivates her — you can't be sure.

• **You begin to see other people as individuals — and maybe even allies.** You no longer see other people as stereotypes. You move from "us versus them" to simply "us." Your goals become shared, not conflicting.[9]

• **You develop solutions that other people are willing to accept and even adopt.** When people contribute to the solutions — when they are co-owners of them — they are more likely to commit to and follow through with them. People are also much more likely to accept even a negative outcome when they feel that the procedure that got them there was fair. For something to be "procedurally just," as psychologists call it, the affected parties must believe that they've been heard, understood, and treated with dignity and that the process and its key drivers are trustworthy. And they're much more likely to feel that a procedure was fair when they were involved in developing it. For example, employees can accept not receiving a promotion if they helped develop the guidelines and expectations that led to the decision.[10]

• **When people feel heard, they are more willing to listen.** This is both stunningly intuitive and stunningly hard for us to do:

if people do not feel that you "get" them, they are not inclined to invest their time and energy in activities — such as listening — that will help them to understand you. And it's particularly important for leaders to understand, because they need to serve as models of good listening.[11]

Phew, that's a lot of listening and understanding.

As a result of what they heard, four of the clergy members, Jeffrey included, drafted a document that was part manifesto, part mission statement. It consisted of ten points: principles and actions they hoped would end the killing and improve conditions in the city's poorest neighborhoods, mostly through the involvement of clerics and churches at the street level — not from on high or at a comfortable distance — who would devise solutions alongside the gang members, with their advice and participation.

The Boston TenPoint Coalition turned into a movement whose success shocked the city and captured the attention of people in the United States and beyond: youth murders in Boston dropped from a peak of seventy-two in 1990 to an all-time low of fifteen in 1999. The change became known as the Boston Miracle, and scholars and practitioners attribute it largely to the formation of the coalition and the efforts of Jeffrey and his fellow ministers. Cities from around the world sought the advice of the clergy members in combating drugs, crime, and killings.[12]

Another of the coalition's great triumphs — one that came later, in 2006 — gives a sense of the radical strategies pioneered by its members. Still working to stop the endless cycle of gang attacks and retaliation, they decided to float the idea of a truce.

"And what the youth said in response to that was that you're not going to be able to get us to do that cold turkey," Jeffrey said. "So why don't you start with a period of time, like a cease-fire? So we created that between Thanksgiving and New Year's, and we called it season of peace. They gave us the directions for what to do, you know?

"I had them in a room, and I made the pitch for the season of peace and asked for their approval. And that's when I got my first indication that this might work, because a young guy gets up, and he says, 'All right, so do we stop shooting at midnight on Wednesday night? Or do we stop on Thanksgiving morning? And do we start shooting again on December thirty-first or on January first?'

"And it was a conflict for me," Jeffrey said, "because I was like, 'I don't want you to start shooting *at all*.' But I said, 'Okay, you stop shooting Wednesday night and you can start again after New Year's Day.' Now, you know, ethically I was like, 'I can't believe you told them they could start shooting after the first of the year.' But we were trying to get them to establish peace and give them a sense of what it's like to be able to go into a neighborhood and not have to look over your shoulder every five seconds."

As you can imagine, in Boston at that tense time, there was little confidence that a bunch of clergy members could usher in a period during which gang members would suddenly stop shooting each other.

"The first time we did that season of peace, the cops were like, 'Hey, good luck,'" almost with a wink and a snicker, Jeffrey recalled. "Because things were hot leading up to Thanksgiving 2006. And then the first twenty-two days after that there were no shootings, no shots fired, nada. Gary French, who was in charge of the Boston police gang unit, called me, and he kept calling me every day, saying, 'Nothing happened yesterday.' And he wanted to know, 'What did you do? Who did you talk to?' The police wanted all this information from us, you know? And I said, 'Well, first of all, you can't have that information. But it's nothing more than I already told you — it's looking at the youth not as the problem but as partners.'"

This is not to say that listening to another person guarantees a favorable outcome every time. In fact, part of presence is accepting the possibility of disappointment and not allowing that to knock you off course or cause you to doubt. What appears at first to be failure may actually be something else altogether — an opportunity to grow in an unanticipated way.

Letting Presence Speak for Itself

Around this time, Jeffrey was working closely with a kid named James, the leader of a gang in Roxbury and one of the architects of the truce the coalition had engineered with another major gang. Jeffrey described James as "a really special kid ... [with] a concern not just for himself but for everybody that he associated with. So he really wanted this peace to spread throughout the city."

Two days after a meeting with James, Jeffrey got a phone call. "I was at home making dinner," he said. "And I had to stop and just get in the car and go." James had been shot and killed.

Arriving at the hospital, Jeffrey did his best to comfort James's distraught family members, some hysterical with grief and others unable to believe that he could really be gone. The ER waiting room was filled with James's friends, who were already plotting to avenge the murder. "And I'm like, 'You can't do that.'" Which was not what James's angry comrades wanted to hear. "I was struggling to find the words to say, because in my mind I was thinking, I need to say *something*, right? But the more I thought about what to say, the more I couldn't find those words.

"Finally the doctors came to me and said, 'We have to get this emergency room under control. Can you just lead them all out?' And — and I was like, 'I don't know, but I can try.' So I just started walking up to people, and I said, 'Come on, we're gonna go outside and pray together. Do you want to pray?' And they were like, 'Yeah, okay.' And I got 'em all outside, and then we started praying. And the longer I prayed, the more people started crying and wailing. So I said, 'Okay, now hug somebody. Just hug somebody. Hold 'em tight.' It was one of those times where I so was flabbergasted I just didn't know what to say or do. But by not saying something it seemed to, well . . . people would start talking to me, and I'm nodding my head, saying, 'I hear you.'"

There, in that anguished and chaotic hospital waiting room, Jeffrey learned an important lesson: in some situations, there's no such thing as winning. There was nothing anyone could have said or done to ease the suffering and calm the anger of those James left behind. Jeffrey struggled, but was left with these thoughts: I have no answers. There are no words. To think, in every case, that you will be able to summon a magic phrase or an impressively bold deed is simply self-aggrandizing. At moments like these, just being there and listening may be enough. In the long run it may be better than anything else.

"People have called that a ministry of presence," Jeffrey said, "and I find that is among the most effective ways to do ministry, you know? To shut up and just be there."

Sometimes we express ourselves most eloquently by not expressing anything — by allowing our presence, unexplained and unembellished, to speak for itself.

The first meeting of the "street committee" took place more than twenty years ago. Today the result has become a case study taught at Harvard Business School. When I teach my students about Jeffrey's work, he attends and answers questions. In fact, he's visited my class every time I've taught the case — which is at least two dozen times. Many case study protagonists visit classes when their cases are taught, but surely none has a record like Jeffrey's — in terms of both frequency and impact.

By the time Jeffrey comes in, my students have read the case — they've met this man on paper, and they've developed a healthy respect and admiration for him. But nothing quite prepares them for Jeffrey in person. When he walks into the room, the class falls silent — in awe, reverence, curiosity. He doesn't arrive wearing full reverend regalia. He's in jeans, a crisp button-down shirt, and a sharp-looking blazer. He speaks in a deep, calm, resonant voice. He is honest and humble yet confident and strong. He never rushes. He does not fear pauses, and because he doesn't fear them, neither do we. That's how presence begets presence.

4

I Don't Deserve to Be Here

*Everyone wants to be Cary Grant. Even I want
to be Cary Grant.*
— CARY GRANT

WHEN PAULINE ROSE CLANCE was a doctoral student in clinical psychology, in the late 1960s, she became haunted by fears that she wasn't good enough to succeed.

Everyone else is smarter than I am. I got lucky this time, but I'll fail the next time. I'm not even supposed to be here. She was losing sleep, feeling dread before and regret after every evaluation, every test, every performance. Her friends, she knew, were tired of hearing her go on about these worries that tormented her. And no one else seemed to feel the same way. *Letting me in here must have been a mistake. I'm going to be found out.*

"I really believed it," Pauline explained to me, "and I overtly felt anxiety. I thought: I just have to learn to live with this. This is who I am."

As a child, Pauline never imagined she'd go to college. "I grew up right in the hills of Appalachia. Went to small schools until I got to high school and went for just eleven years because they didn't have a twelfth grade then. We didn't have our own books at home, but my dad always wanted us to get books from the library; my parents were interested in the world. Although I had teachers who took a real interest in me — who gave me the message that I could go to college — my schooling left a lot to be desired, so I had doubts about my education.

"My counselor in high school told me, 'You have to be ready to make Cs. Don't expect to make As. Don't be too hard on yourself.' I went to college expecting to be an average student. But I wasn't. Actually I was a very good student. I had some fears around taking tests. Can I keep succeeding? Will I be able to do this? But it was in a small enough college, so my fears felt manageable."

Pauline's doubts caught up with her when she started graduate school. She wanted to go to a well-known, prestigious university, but, she says, "I was told in no uncertain terms by their psychology department that as a woman I had to be about three times as good as any of the men. The interviewer said, 'We do have a secretarial job open.' So I ended up going to the University of Kentucky, where the admissions committee for the doctoral program in clinical psychology, which was quite competitive, accepted more people than they intended to keep. We were explicitly told, 'Look around you. Lots of you will not make it.' Then they had tests every year to eliminate underperforming students." Despite doing well on those exams, Pauline continued to feel at risk, sure that she'd be the next unfortunate soul to be kicked out of the program.

While the details of Pauline's story are uniquely hers, the general feeling that we don't belong — that we've fooled people into thinking we're more competent and talented than we actually are — is not so unusual. Most of us have experienced it, at least to some degree. It's not simple stage fright or performance anxiety; rather, it's the deep and sometimes paralyzing belief that we have been given something we didn't earn and don't deserve and that at some point we'll be exposed. Psychologists refer to it as *impostor syndrome, the impostor phenomenon, impostor fears,* and *impostorism.*

If achieving presence requires us to be totally in tune with our truest feelings, beliefs, abilities, and values, then we certainly cannot be present when we feel like a fraud. Instead, we are discordant, frazzled, utterly unconvincing. And just as presence is self-reinforcing, so, too, is feeling fake.

Impostorism causes us to overthink and second-guess. It makes us fixate on how we think others are judging us (in these fixations, we're usually wrong), then fixate some more on how those judgments might poison our interactions. We're scattered — worrying that we underprepared, obsessing about what we *should* be doing, mentally reviewing what we said five seconds earlier, fretting about what people think of us and what that will mean for us tomorrow.

Impostorism steals our power and suffocates our presence. If even *you* don't believe you should be here, how will you convince anybody else?

Presence and impostorism are opposing sides of the same coin — and we are the coin.

Feeling Like an Impostor

Despite her self-doubts, Pauline pushed through and completed her doctoral program. In fact, because she did quite well, after she earned her degree she accepted an offer to join the faculty of

Oberlin College, the highly competitive private liberal arts school in Ohio.

At Oberlin, Pauline spent half her time teaching in the psychology department and the other half working in the counseling center. "When I did counseling," she recalled, "I saw these people who had gone to the best schools, often private schools, had highly educated parents and excellent standardized test scores, grades, and letters of recommendation. But here they were, saying things like, 'I'm afraid I'm going to flunk this exam.' 'Somehow the admissions committee made an error.' 'It was because my English teacher wrote me such a fantastic letter.' 'I'm an Oberlin mistake.' They were discounting all the things they had done."

She described one particularly memorable encounter with a student named Lisa, who had been planning to do honors work and was having second thoughts. "I'm not going to do the honors," she announced. Pauline was surprised. Lisa was such a strong student. Why had she changed her mind? Pauline wanted to know. What was she afraid of?

Lisa responded, "They'll *really* find out that I don't deserve to be here."

The fear sounded familiar to Pauline, but Lisa and her fellow students were all so outstanding. How could they feel this way? It was clear that for some reason they held distorted views of themselves. In fact, she noticed, this feeling appeared to be prevalent among high-performing women: despite their external achievements, they feared they were fooling people. They believed that their accomplishments were attributable not to their own abilities but to luck or "people skills." Each one of these outstanding students felt she *didn't deserve to be there*. And each one felt alone in her experience.

Pauline wondered, could this particular anxiety be shared by others? Were she and the handful of students she'd seen the only ones who suffered from it? Could it be measured?

She decided to turn her research toward answering these questions. Pauline and a collaborator, Suzanne Imes, began to systematically investigate what they were by then calling the impostor phenomenon (IP), which they defined as "an internal experience of intellectual phoniness,"[1] in which women fear having what they believe to be their true abilities (or lack thereof) exposed. As Academy Award winner and Harvard graduate Natalie Portman said in her 2015 Harvard Class Day speech, "Today I feel much like I did when I came to Harvard Yard as a freshman in 1999. I felt like there had been some mistake, that I wasn't smart enough to be in this company, and that every time I opened my mouth I would have to prove that I wasn't just a dumb actress."[2]

Pauline, with input from mathematician Nancy Zumoff, developed a scale to measure the extent to which a person did or did not feel this way. The scale asks subjects to rate as true or false a series of statements, such as:

> I'm afraid people important to me may find out that I'm not as capable as they think I am.
> Sometimes I feel or believe that my success in my life or in my job has been the result of some kind of error.
> When I've succeeded at something and received recognition for my accomplishments, I have doubts that I can keep repeating that success.
> I often compare my ability to those around me and think they may be more intelligent than I am.
> If I receive a great deal of praise and recognition for something I've accomplished, I tend to discount the importance of what I've done.[3]

In 1978, Pauline and Suzanne published the first academic paper on the impostor phenomenon. The article described the general concept of IP, focusing on the experiences of women who seemed to be suffering from it, and discussed possible treatments. IP, as they saw it at the time, was a mental health issue, a neurosis that was "particularly prevalent and intense among a select sample of high achieving women."[4] The subjects in that first study were 178 high-achieving women, including college students and doctoral candidates, and women from a range of professions, including law, medicine, and academia. Most were white, middle-to-upper-class, and between the ages of twenty and forty-five. As Clance and Imes say in the article:

> Despite outstanding academic and professional accom-
> plishments, women who experience the impostor phe-
> nomenon persist in believing that they are really not bright
> and have fooled anyone who thinks otherwise. Numerous
> achievements, which one might expect to provide ample
> objective evidence of superior intellectual functioning, do
> not appear to affect the impostor belief.[5]

This Is Much Bigger Than We Thought...

Pauline and many others studying impostorism initially believed that the condition was unique to high-achieving women, reasoning that "since success for women is contraindicated by societal expectations and their own internalized self-evaluations, it is not surprising that women in our sample need to find [an] explanation for their accomplishments other than their own intelligence."[6] But it wasn't long before Pauline began to wonder whether IP might be more widespread. "After talks," she said during our discussion, "men would come up to me and say, 'You know, I've felt that, too.' By 1985, I definitely saw this as an experience that men were having also. And I have certainly worked with men [in my clinical practice] who experience it excruciatingly."

In recent years, there's been a swell of popular interest in impostorism. It gets shout-outs in the business world from leaders such as Sheryl Sandberg and publications such as *Slate* and *Fast Company*. But most of this has been in the context of female self-improvement: What can women do to achieve their greatest ambitions? Aside from well-documented sexism,[7] what other factors might be holding them back? I, too, believed this was a women's problem — and then, after my TED talk was posted online, I started receiving e-mails about impostorism, and lots of those e-mails were from men. In fact, of the thousands of e-mails I've received, about half of those with stories about feeling like a fraud were from men.

Pauline and other researchers soon found the same thing: women and men were experiencing impostorism to an equal degree.[8]

Why, then, did it initially appear to be a women's problem?

First, some people have trouble recognizing it in themselves, something Pauline and Suzanne noticed right from the start. Other studies have since produced similar findings. Perhaps the men in the studies just weren't identifying their feelings as clearly as the women did.[9]

But there was a more troubling and likely possibility. "In private practice, it wasn't as common for men to talk about it," explained Pauline. "But when [the survey] was anonymous, men were expressing it to the same degree as women." They weren't discussing it with their friends or family members or seeking emotional support because they were too ashamed.

Men who deviate from the strong-assertive stereotype — in other words, men who are able to express self-doubt — risk experiencing what psychologists call "stereotype backlash": punishment, which often takes the form of harassment or even ostracism, for failing to conform to societal expectations.[10] (Stereotype backlash is not limited to men — it can happen to anyone who deviates from culturally prescribed stereotypes about race, sex, and the various other social "categories" to which they belong. For example, women frequently experience stereotype backlash in the workplace for being "too masculine."[11]) Although men experience impostorism to the same extent women do, they may be even more burdened by it because they can't admit it. They carry it around quietly, secretly, painfully.

So impostorism afflicts men and women equally. But is it limited to certain demographic groups — professional, racial, cultural? After Pauline and Suzanne's groundbreaking work, the following few decades of inquiry provided a clear answer. Researchers have found impostorism in dozens of demographic groups, including but not limited to teachers, accountants, physicians, physician assistants, nurses, engineering students, dental students, medical students, nursing students, pharmacy students, law students, doctoral students, undergraduate entrepreneurs, high school students, people new to the Internet, African Americans, Koreans, Japanese, Canadians, disturbed adolescents, "normal" adolescents, preadolescents, old people, adult children of alcoholics, adult children of high achievers, people with eating disorders, people without eating disorders, people who have recently experienced failure, people who have recently experienced success...and so on.[12]

In 1985, Pauline and a collaborator, Gail Matthews, published a survey of their clinical psychology clients, noting that among forty-one men and women, around 70 percent had experienced impostorism.[13] At least two-thirds of Harvard Business School students experience impostorism[14] — and more than 60 percent of HBS students are men.

As I prepared to leave our meeting, Pauline said, "One more thing: if I could do it all over again, I would call it the impostor experience, because it's not a syndrome or a complex or a mental illness. It's something almost everyone experiences."

Given impostorism's prevalence, it's impossible to identify the root cause for each individual instance. In the parlance of the social sciences, it seems to be *overdetermined* — meaning there are so many possible variables that no one can figure out which to blame. Early childhood experiences have been linked to impostorism, but so have family dynamics, societal expectations, prejudices, personality, and life experiences at school and in the workplace.[15]

This doesn't mean that some people aren't more susceptible than others. Certain traits and experiences have been found to go hand in hand with the impostor experience.[16] Rates of perfectionism and performance anxiety are high among those suffering from impostorism, as are low self-acceptance and little sense of mastery over one's environment. High neuroticism has also been linked to the impostor syndrome, along with low self-esteem and introversion. But one of the most prevalent factors is a fear of failure, which has been cited as the root problem across many studies.[17]

Who fears failure most? People who have achieved something — people who are demonstrably anything *but* frauds.

One day I received the following e-mail from a man named David, who works as a university administrator:

I have suffered with impostor syndrome since college. It's like the world kept telling me I was a 90 when I knew I was just a 50. For example, I have a bunch of achievement awards over my desk at work. And every time I received another I'd think, "Oh, crap! Now they think I'm a 92! They're going to be so pissed off when they find out I'm only a 50." The awards didn't make me feel better about myself, they just exacerbated the disparity between what "they" thought and what I felt.

How can this be? Shouldn't his concrete accomplishments — winning achievement awards, earning advanced degrees, getting a desirable job — have "cured" David's impostorism? At some point, shouldn't we be able to escape the feeling by achieving exceptional things? How can people such as Denzel Washington, Tina Fey, Maya Angelou, and Mahatma Gandhi have suffered from impostor fears?

Neil Gaiman has written numerous bestselling novels, comic books, and short stories, including *The Sandman, Coraline, Anansi Boys, American Gods,* and *The Ocean at the End of the Lane,* as well as more than a dozen film and television screenplays. He has won major literary awards and was the first author to receive both the Newbery and the Carnegie Medals for a single work (*The Graveyard Book*). By virtually every imaginable professional measure, Neil is *spectacularly* successful.

Yet, famously, he has suffered from feelings of being a fraud. In fact, Wikipedia lists Neil as one of six famous people who have publicly discussed their struggles with impostor syndrome. His situation certainly gives real-world credibility to the idea that no one is immune. I asked if he'd be willing to talk with me about it, which he graciously agreed to do.

Neil Gaiman has gentle, rounded eyebrows, sad eyes, a mop of curly brown-and-silver hair, and the kind of soft-British-accent voice you'd want to listen to as you go to sleep. Even in casual conversation, he's a storyteller — not in the sense that he's making things up but that he recalls his own memories in the shape of a story. When he pauses, it doesn't make you uncomfortable and it doesn't seem scripted — it reassures you that he cares about what he's saying. At the moment he's talking to you, he is present.

Until his first two books came out, Neil said, "I was absolutely faking it, because people were giving me money to write books and there was no guarantee that I would actually turn anything around that was even publishable. I genuinely didn't know what I was doing. . . . For that first eighteen months, if someone had come along and said, 'You are a fake, sir,' I'd have said, 'Yes, you're quite right.'"

Then suddenly he was a published author, getting attention (the holy grail for any writer), "actually making enough of a living" to support himself. Soon enough he was on the bestseller list and winning major literary awards. He was being sent to see movies for free, as a film critic, getting paid to do exactly what he wanted to do, rather than getting up in the morning and feeling like he had to go to work. To him, it was all highly strange and unusual. I noticed that, as befits a self-described "impostor," Neil had trouble even describing the experience of earning money, recognition, and praise. He rushed his story; he laughed uncomfortably.

Of that first decade, Neil said,

I would have this recurring fantasy in which there would be a knock on the door, and I would go down, and there would be somebody wearing a suit — not an expensive suit, just the kind of suit that showed they had a job — and they would be holding a clipboard, and they'd have paper on the clipboard, and I'd open the door and they'd say, "Hello, excuse me, I'm afraid I am here on official business. Are you Neil Gaiman?" And I would say yes. "Well, it says here that you are a writer, and that you don't have to get up in the morning at any particular time, that you just write each day as much as you want." And I'd go, "That's right." "And that you *enjoy* writing. And it says here that all the books you want — they are just *sent* to you and that you don't have to buy them. And films: it says here that you just go to see films. If you want to see them you just call up the person who runs the films." And I say, "Yes, that's right." "And that people like what you do and they give you money for just writing things down." And I'd say yes. And he'd say, "Well, I'm afraid we are on to you. We've caught up with you. And I'm afraid you are now going to have to go out and get a proper job." At which point in my fantasy my heart would always sink, and I'd go, "Okay," and I'd go and buy a cheap suit and I'd start applying to real jobs. Because once they've caught up with you, you can't argue with this: they've caught up with you. So that was the thing in my head.

Impostorism undercuts our ability to feel good about the things we do well, particularly when we are being compensated for them. About three years ago, as I was driving my then nine-year-old son, Jonah, to school, we had the following conversation (I wrote it down, as parents often do when kids say something especially wise):

Jonah: You are the luckiest person in the world.

Me: Why do you say that?

Jonah: Because you get paid to do exactly what you'd be doing if you weren't getting paid.

Me: What's that?

Jonah: Analyzing why people do what they do, then using what you learn to try to help people be better.

And my very first thought — which I remember so well not because I wrote it down but because it was so visceral — was this: "Uh-oh. He's right. There's no *way* I can keep this up. Soon they'll be on to me." It filled me with dread.

Neil felt that the man with the clipboard was coming to take away his identity — a feeling heightened by the fact that Neil enjoyed what he was doing. We think, "Something's wrong in this situation, because I can't possibly enjoy what I'm doing *and* be rewarded for doing it." In response, we either discount what we do — it's not actually valuable — or we dismiss the reasons we are able to do it: we're frauds who somehow slipped under the radar and don't deserve our lucky fate.

And just as we understate our successes, we exaggerate our failures. One disappointment gives us all the evidence we need to support our belief that we are phonies. We assume that a single low test score reflects our overall lack of intelligence and skill.[18] We overgeneralize because we grasp at anything that reinforces our secret knowledge that we are unworthy. If we succeed, we were lucky. If we fail, we were incompetent. It's a tough way to go through life.

Here's the cruel irony: achievements don't stamp out impostor fears. In fact, success can actually make them worse. We can't reconcile a lofty vision of ourselves with our secret knowledge that we don't deserve it. Worldly success introduces us to others who will hold us to a standard we can't possibly meet, thus revealing our true weak, incompetent selves. Achievements present us with new situations and opportunities, which only exacerbate the impostor fears, since every new situation is another proving ground.

Trapped by the Impostor

Earning a PhD in physics from one of the most competitive and hard-core science programs in the world wasn't enough to make Elena feel worthy.[19] She was, in her words, "a poor Latina from the South Bronx, daughter of hardworking but uneducated parents." It was difficult for Elena to come to terms with her acceptance at an Ivy League university. She worried, she said, that they needed to fill their minority quota, and she was overwhelmed and intimidated at the prospect of going there. But, courageously, she went. Quickly her own fears and doubts were compounded by other obstacles. As she explained:

> I will never forget the day that a professor told me unequivocally that I did not belong there because of my social status and that I should consider withdrawing. I graduated, but with a total blow to my self-esteem. I went on to get my PhD and was taken in by a well-known professor at another university who said he was "doing me a favor" by allowing me to do postdoctoral research and teach his honors physics class. I was terrified that the students would find out I was a fraud, but I did it.

Although she more than competently conducted research and taught the class, in the end, she explained, the professor told her that he "merely wanted me to keep his wife company" and to do the physical work in the lab. He warned her that she would likely fail.

That was over thirty years ago, and only now do I realize that my life could have taken a completely different path. I left the world of physics totally demoralized. I never established myself with a career even though I know I have talent.

When we feel like impostors, we don't attribute our accomplishments to something internal and constant, such as talent or ability; instead we credit something beyond our control, such as luck.[20] Rather than owning our successes, we distance ourselves from them. We deny ourselves the very support we need in order to thrive. Elena's story is a heartbreaking reminder of how vulnerable we leave ourselves when we fall prey to the impostor experience. Doubting her own worthiness, she readily internalized the voices of others who doubted her.

Research has identified many of the self-defeating behaviors that "impostors" exhibit: for example, they expect to do badly on exams even when they have a record of performing well. They overestimate the number of mistakes they made when they finish the exam.[21] These behaviors reinforce the notion that we are not as good, as smart, as talented, or as able as the world thinks we are. They cause us to criticize ourselves relentlessly, spin our wheels, choke at the worst possible moments, disengage — thereby virtually ensuring that we will underperform at the very things we do best and love most. At its most extreme, impostorism can become a self-paved path to failure.[22]

Elena's teachers failed her. They fueled her worst fears about herself rather than nurturing her strengths. Inevitably, there are people out there who are going to withhold their approval from us, assert their superiority over us, even actively try to undermine us, and we have to protect ourselves from negative voices like theirs. But often we're projecting criticism and judgment where none exists, and that can undercut our performance as well. While we're agonizing over what we imagine other people are thinking, we aren't listening as they tell us what they really *do* think. And if we can't hear them, we certainly can't respond effectively. The impostor experience stops us from reacting in the moment — it keeps us from responding to the world as it truly exists. Instead we're hypervigilant for clues that we're about to be unmasked. We scrutinize the dynamics of every social situation, scrambling to decipher how other people perceive and judge us, then we attempt to adjust our behavior accordingly. With all that going on, is it any wonder that we no longer are connected to what we think or value or feel?

Research shows that in pressure-filled situations, when we are distracted by thinking about possible outcomes of our performance, our skills are measurably diminished. When we explicitly monitor ourselves, second by second, any task that requires memory and focused attention will suffer.[23] We don't have enough intellectual bandwidth to perform at our best and simultaneously critique our performance. Instead we're caught in a faulty circuit of trying to anticipate, read, interpret, and reinterpret how other people are judging us, all of which prevents us from noticing and interpreting what's actually happening in the situation. This dynamic, which psychologists refer to as *self-monitoring*, is significantly higher for people who experience impostor fears. It takes us out of ourselves. It stands in the way of our presence.

Fears that we will be unmasked as frauds can defeat us even before we begin. Jessica Collett, a sociology professor at the University of Notre Dame, became interested in studying the effects of impostorism on career and educational ambitions. In particular, she and her collaborator Jade Avelis wanted to know if impostor fears were a cause of "downshifting" — lowering one's professional ambitions. They surveyed hundreds of doctoral students, mostly in the sciences, asking if they had changed their goals from tenure-track research careers to less competitive teaching or policy positions. "We see that impostors are overrepresented in both the groups that seriously considered changing and those that actually did so," Collett said.

I Was an Impostor Myself

I don't just study impostorism, I experienced it. And I didn't just experience it, I *inhabited* it. It was like a little house I lived in. Of course, no one else knew I was there. It was my secret. It nearly always is. That's how impostorism gets such a good grip — it pays you hush money. If you don't tell anyone about those feelings, then people are less likely to think, "Hmm...maybe she really *doesn't* deserve to be here." No need to give them any ideas, right?

In my 2012 TED talk, I shared a story about my experiences as an impostor. After my brain injury I kept trying to return to school, only to drop out because I couldn't process information. I was in a fog. Nothing feels worse than losing part of your core identity.

Anything else can go and still you feel some of your old power. But I had lost my ability to think — a pretty important part of me — and I felt utterly powerless.

I fought my way back — very slowly — and eventually finished college and persuaded someone to take me on as a grad student at Princeton. But for years afterward I was haunted by impostor fears. Every achievement led me to feel more afraid, while even the smallest failure confirmed my belief that I didn't belong. "I'm not supposed to be here" ran through my head over and over.

During our first year in grad school each doctoral student in the psychology department was required to deliver a twenty-minute talk to a group of twenty or so people. The night before my talk, I was so overwhelmed by fear that I told my adviser I was going to quit — just so I didn't have to give that talk.

"No, you're not," she said. "You're going to do the talk. And keep doing it — even if you have to fake it — until you have a moment when you realize that you can do it."

I didn't exactly nail the talk the next day. I don't think I moved any part of my body other than my mouth. I felt as if I could go blank at any moment. And there was nothing I wanted more than for it to be over. At the end, when someone raised his hand to ask a question, I thought I might pass out. But I survived it, and my audience didn't seem to think it was quite as bad as I thought it was. And I kept giving talks — virtually every talk I was invited to give. I even invited myself to give talks. Anything to get more practice.

It took a while, but after grad school at Princeton, a year teaching psychology at Rutgers, two years teaching at the Kellogg School of Management at Northwestern, and a year at Harvard — a place where someone like me was definitely not supposed to be — my adviser was proved right: I did come to realize that I could do it.

Here's how that moment arrived: a student of mine at Harvard, a woman who had spoken barely a word all semester, came to my office before the final class. I had sent her a note saying that she hadn't yet participated, and it was do-or-die time. She stood there in front of me looking totally defeated, and after a long silence finally spoke: "I'm not supposed to be here," she said. She teared up as she said it.

She told me about her background — coming from a small town, not having a fancy pedigree, feeling acutely like an outsider and an admissions mistake.

She sounded just like I once had.

And at that moment, it hit me: *I no longer feel that way. I'm not a fake. I'm not going to be found out.* But I didn't realize those bad old feelings were gone until I heard the words coming out of her mouth.

My next thought was this: *She's not an impostor, either. She deserves to be here.*

When I delivered my TED talk, I never would have guessed that the story about my impostor syndrome would resonate with so many listeners. In fact, I nearly dropped it from the talk entirely, thinking it was too far a reach from my main subject — and way too personal.

In the moments after I walked off the TED stage, several strangers came up and hugged me — most with tears in their eyes. In one way or another, they all said the same thing: "I felt like you were telling my story." One smartly dressed man, probably in his early fifties, said, "I'm a successful businessman — by conventional standards — and I know you'd never know it from looking at me, but I feel like an impostor every day I walk into my office." I couldn't have imagined then that I would hear the same words from thousands more people, in e-mails I receive to this day, each one telling a new story about feeling like a fake.

I'm trained primarily as a prejudice researcher. My dissertation, in social psychology, focused on stereotypes and how they predict unique patterns of discrimination. I've always been concerned about people who feel marginalized. How do we make things better? Prejudice, sadly, is not going away overnight. That's not an excuse to ignore the problem, but we're not going to eliminate it tomorrow. I teach psychological research on sexism and racism, but I have very little hopeful news to share about remedies.

That bothered me. For example, when I talk to groups of young women who are about to apply for jobs, what do I tell them? "Yep, the research clearly documents the prevalence of sexism in the workplace. Thanks for listening. Good luck!" I still actively study the origins and effects of prejudice, but now more than half my research focuses on identifying scientifically grounded mini interventions — things people can do to perform well even when faced with negative judgments and biases. Even when the negative judgments and biases are their own.

Can We Break Up with Our Impostor Selves?

I've spent the better part of my life convinced that I don't belong, am lucky, or a fraud. Never, not once, did it ever occur to me that other people felt that way.
— Chris, a successful forty-year-old executive

In 2011, the musician and author Amanda Palmer (who is also Neil Gaiman's wife) gave a commencement speech at the New England Institute of Art (NEiA) in Brookline, Massachusetts. "She talked about the fraud police," Neil recalled, "and how she was scared that the fraud police would come along. And she asked people to put up their hands if they also worried about the fraud police. And I looked around at all these hands up — maybe a thousand. And I went, 'Oh, my God, it's... it's everybody.'"

As I review the research and talk to people like Pauline and Neil who've experienced the same fears, I see the one quality of impostorism that stands out from all the others: it makes us feel *alone* in the experience, and even when we learn that other people have similar fears, we don't take heart. Instead we say, "Fine, except your fear is unfounded, while I am *truly* a fraud." Pauline saw her lack of a fancy pedigree and glowing recommendation letters as proof of her unworthiness. Meanwhile, to her, the impostor fears of others were distortions. Neil, in his mind, didn't have the right kind of writing experience and hadn't even gone to college. But the NEIA graduates — they were exceptionally talented students who'd proved themselves.

So if most of us are walking around feeling like impostors, how is it possible that none of us knows? Because we're ashamed and afraid to talk about it. Elena, who abandoned her career as a scientist despite having a PhD in physics from one of the most competitive universities in the world, wrote: "No one, not even my husband, understands the painful loss of self that I experienced during college, going from star honor student to a 'failure.'"

If we all only knew how many people feel like impostors, we'd have to conclude that either (1) we all *are* impostors and we don't know what we're doing or (2) our self-assessments are way off. Emotionally, carrying around these secret fears while thinking that no one else feels as we do simply taxes us further. Feeling alone is, for most of us, worse than feeling harassed.[24] In fact, feeling isolated activates the same areas of the brain as physical pain does.[25]

Given that everybody seems to feel it, is there hope that any of us can entirely escape the clutches of our impostor fears? Neil said yes — he remembers the point at which he stopped having the fantasy of the man with the clipboard knocking on his door. Was it when he won the Newbery Medal, I asked, or any of the other honors that have been bestowed upon him? No, he said, and he told me this:

> My friend Gene Wolfe actually really helped me with this. I was writing a book called *American Gods*, and it was a big impostor-syndrome book because I wanted to write this giant book about America, but I'm English, and I wanted to talk about all these — you know, just gods and religions and ways of seeing the world. But I finished *American Gods* and it took me about eighteen months of writing. And I was very pleased with myself. And I ran into Gene, and I said — and bear in mind this is, like, my third or fourth novel — "I've finished the first draft of my book *American Gods*, and I think I figured out how to write a novel." And Gene looked at me with infinite pity and wisdom in his eyes and he said, "Neil, you never figure out how to write a novel; you just learn how to write the novel that you're on."

You never figure out how to write a novel; you just learn how to write the novel that you're on. Maybe that's a critical truth about impostorism. Most of us will probably never completely shed our fears of being fraudulent. We'll just work them out as they come, one by one. Just as I can't promise that learning about presence will give you a Zen master existence in the "eternal now," I can't say that you will soon shed all your impostor anxieties forever.

New situations may stoke old fears; future sensations of inadequacy might reawaken long-forgotten insecurities. But the more we are aware of our anxieties, the more we communicate about them,[26] and the smarter we are about how they operate, the easier they'll be to shrug off the next time they pop up. It's a game of whack-a-mole we can win.

5

How Powerlessness Shackles the Self
(and How Power Sets It Free)

Most powerful is he who has himself in his own power.
— LUCIUS ANNAEUS SENECA (4 BCE–65 CE)

CASSIDY, A WOMAN TRYING to break into the real estate business, sent me this e-mail:[1]

> For fifteen years, I was a national and collegiate-level track and field champion, and my whole life that is how I identified myself. Since graduating college and retiring from sports, I have been really struggling with not being able to call myself an elite athlete. I have since wondered, "Well, now that I'm retired and have joined the 'real world,' what and who am I?"
>
> I find myself embarking on new career paths and quickly becoming discouraged and unable to see myself in these new roles. I feel like I'm smart and have potential but there's not one thing anymore that I'm *really* good at, that I consider myself to be an expert on. I'm often consumed

with feelings of defeat, anxiety, and insecurity. My body language is almost 100 percent powerless — hunched over at my desk. I have no confidence. I'm too afraid to take the risks I know I need to take to gain my footing, certain that if I fail, I'll be judged as incompetent. So I avoid challenging situations, passing up opportunities because they feel sort of threatening.

I hear or read stories of personal powerlessness every single day — in e-mails from strangers, in conversations with students, and during meetings with employees of all ranks in various organizations. Although the details differ, the basic sketch is so often the same: a change is accompanied by a self-perceived loss of power and strength and followed by feelings of insecurity, anxiety, discouragement, and defeat. Then come physical manifestations of powerlessness along with loss of confidence and ambition.

This depleted state, which can result from a small setback or even just the normal life changes we all go through, convinces us that we lack the power to control the situations we're in. Then, as Cassidy said, opportunities take on the aspect of threats to be avoided, and feelings of fear further reinforce our sense of powerlessness, keeping us locked in an exhausting cycle.

Social psychologist Dacher Keltner and his colleagues shed light on how this cycle works: they propose that power activates a psychological and behavioral *approach system*. When we feel powerful, we feel free — in control, unthreatened, and safe.[2] As a result, we are attuned to opportunities more than threats. We feel positive and optimistic, and our behavior is largely unrestricted by social pressures.

On the other hand, powerlessness activates a psychological and behavioral *inhibition system*, the "equivalent to an alarm-threat system."[3] We are more attuned to threats than to opportunities. We feel generally anxious and pessimistic, and we're susceptible to social pressures that inhibit us and make our behavior unrepresentative of our sincere selves.

When we're deciding whether or not to do something — ask a person out on a date, raise a hand in class, even volunteer to help a person in need — we focus on one of two things: either the possible benefits of the action (e.g., a new relationship, expressing ourselves, or the gratification of having helped someone) or the possible costs of the action (e.g., having our hearts broken, sounding foolish, or looking foolish). If we are focused on the potential benefits, we're likely to take the action, thereby approaching the positive. If we are focused on the potential costs, we're likely not to act, thereby avoiding the possible dangers.[4]

Power makes us approach. Powerlessness makes us avoid.

Power affects our thoughts, feelings, behaviors, and even physiology in fundamental ways that directly facilitate or obstruct our presence, our performance, and the very course of our lives. When we feel powerless, we cannot be present. In a way, presence *is* power — a special kind of power that we confer on ourselves. (Recall Julianne Moore's observation when I asked her about presence: "It's power. It's always about power, isn't it?")

Should we be troubled by the presence-power connection? I mean, power corrupts, right?

Maybe so, but power can liberate, too. In fact, I'm going to make a bold claim: *powerlessness is at least as likely to corrupt as power is.*

How the lack of power distorts and disfigures us is important to understand. Equally critical is knowing how the possession of power — a certain kind of power — can reveal our truest selves. I love what Howard Thurman, the author and civil rights leader, wrote on the subject: "There is something in every one of you that waits and listens for the sound of the genuine in yourself. It is the only true guide you will ever have. And if you cannot hear it, you will all of your life spend your days on the ends of strings that somebody else pulls."[5]

Are you going to pull your own strings or are you going to let someone else pull them for you?

Personal Power versus Social Power

There are two kinds of power I'd like to discuss — social power and personal power. They're related. But they're also dramatically different.

Social power is characterized by the ability to exert dominance, to influence or control the behavior of others. Social power is earned and expressed through disproportionate control over valued resources. A person who possesses access to assets that others need — food, shelter, money, tools, information, status, attention, affection — is in a powerful position. The list of things this type of power can gain is endless, but social power itself is a limited resource. The constant is that it requires some kind of control over others.[6]

Personal power is characterized by freedom *from* the dominance of others. It is infinite, as opposed to zero-sum — it's about access to and control of limitless *inner* resources, such as our skills and abilities, our deeply held values, our true personalities, our boldest selves. Personal power — not entirely unlike social power, as I'll explain — makes us more open, optimistic, and risk tolerant and therefore more likely to notice and take advantage of opportunities.

In short, social power is power *over* — the capacity to control others' states and behaviors. Personal power is power *to* — the ability to control our own states and behaviors. This is the kind of power Holocaust survivor and Nobel Peace Prize winner Elie Wiesel was referring to when he wrote, "Ultimately, the only power to which man should aspire is that which he exercises over himself."

Ideally, we want both kinds of power, but, as Wiesel suggests, personal power — the state of being in command of our most precious and authentic inner resources — is uniquely essential. Unless and until we feel personally powerful, we cannot achieve presence, and all the social power in the world won't compensate for its absence.

Stefan is a successful financier who wields a great deal of social power — he makes decisions about whether or not to invest in companies that come to him for funding. But that's no guarantee that he will possess an equal amount of personal power.

"I am usually much younger than the CEOs I am meeting with," he says, "and I find myself lacking confidence and adopting very reserved, submissive body postures, which is strange because I am in the position of power. I am the one calling the shots. But I don't feel that I especially belong or deserve to be in the position that I'm in. I have long felt that my life and career have been nothing but a series of random chance opportunities that I was lucky enough to take advantage of."

That's what social power without personal power looks like. Not so enviable. On the other hand, if we start with personal power, we may increase our social power without even trying. As Joe Magee, a professor at New York University and an expert on power, explains, "Personal power is all about having the confidence to act based on one's own beliefs, attitudes, and values, and having the sense that one's actions will be effective." Effective, in this context, doesn't mean we will always get the result we desire; instead it means that we will come away from every interaction feeling that we fully and accurately represented who we are and what we want. We can't control the outcome, because we can't control the many other variables that determine it, like what other people will do. But we can be sure that we have presented our boldest, most sincere selves. When we do this, we are more likely to be compelling, even influential, and to produce the desired outcome — social power — precisely because that's *not* what we're focused on. Personal power allows us to shed the fears and inhibitions that prevent us from fully connecting with ourselves — with our beliefs, feelings, and skills. Feeling powerless undermines our ability to trust ourselves. And if we cannot trust ourselves, we cannot build trust with others.

In an ideal world, our feeling of personal power would be unassailable. In reality, it's apt to fluctuate, especially when the world plays rough with us. We can lose our sense of personal power, for example, as a result of a blow to our social power. I recently received an e-mail from a university student in Iran. A straight-A student and the valedictorian of his class, this young man was voted most likely to end up at Harvard or MIT during his junior year of high school. Instead he wrote, "I was rejected from both, which changed my general outlook from powerful to powerless. And with it went my self-confidence, as I thought I was not smart enough, and my pride, as I thought I was not good enough. I ended up staying at home at a local university. My grades went down. I have lost my sense of ambition."

That's a good example of how precarious and fragile personal power can be — even someone who has achieved a certain amount of success can be brought low by just a few negative verdicts from complete strangers. And notice the ripple effect that occurs: loss of power in one area of this young man's life has changed his whole orientation to the world. His sense of his own potential has contracted, and with it his motivation, his ability to meet his usual standards, and his prospects, all because he suddenly felt powerless.

What I'm getting at here is this: whether we *feel* powerful or powerless has huge consequences in our lives. And, as we're about to discover, these feelings can be triggered much more easily than we might think. "Power ... transforms individual psychology such that the powerful think and act in ways that lead to the retention and acquisition of power," wrote Magee and Columbia Business School professor Adam Galinsky.[7] Pamela Smith, a professor of management at the Rady School of Management at the University of California, San Diego, and Galinsky have demonstrated in their research that power often operates at a nonconscious level, meaning that it can be activated without our knowledge — turned on like a switch — and can affect our thoughts, feelings, and behaviors in ways we're not even aware of. That's good news. It means we don't need to wear a crown to feel powerful, and we don't have to plot and strategize ways to deploy our power in order to reap its benefits.[8]

Recall a moment when you felt *personally* powerful. A time when you felt fully in control of your own psychological state — when you had the confidence to act based on your boldest, most sincere self, with the sense that your actions would be effective. Maybe it was at work, at school, at home, or in some other part of your life. Take a few minutes right now to remember and reflect on that experience of your personal power, on how it felt.

It felt good, right? Whether you know it or not, you've just been *primed*. Thanks to that little exercise, your psychological state was, and likely still is, infused with feelings of confidence and strength. I could just as easily have asked you to remember a time when you felt powerless and stress-ridden, but of course I don't want to bring you down. Had you done that, however, it, too, would have changed your psychological state, at least temporarily — for the worse. That unhappy sensation of being at someone else's mercy would have come flooding back into the hidden recesses of your brain.

This is one of the ways that social psychologists conduct research into power: by using various devices and exercises to make subjects feel powerful or powerless. Then, once the participants have been primed, the study itself can be carried out, and in this way we can see the differences between the ways powerful and powerless people respond.

It may sound like a cheap parlor trick, but it works — a little thought exercise, such as remembering a powerful or powerless moment, briefly seeing words that connote power (*control, command, authority*) or the lack of it (*obey, yield, subordinate*), or being assigned the temporary role of boss or employee, can make a measurable difference in our mental and emotional states. Even these gentle prompts can induce genuine nonconscious feelings.[9]

I point all this out to help you understand some of the research I'm going to describe in this chapter. But it also illustrates something important: that the feeling of power or its absence can be summoned forth even by little nudges in one direction or another. We are easy beings to manipulate. That leaves us vulnerable, yes, but it can also work to our advantage, especially when we learn how to nudge ourselves.

The Paradox of Powerlessness

At the start of this chapter we met Cassidy, the former track-and-field champion who wrote to me about the profound sense of powerlessness she was feeling in her postathletic life. Anxious and insecure, she avoided trying for fear of failing and worried that failure would cause people to judge her as incompetent. No wonder she saw opportunities as threats. The same threats exist for us all, but powerlessness heightens our sense of the potential danger, setting off a chain reaction that, paradoxically, disables us all the more. A heightened sense of danger increases our social anxiety in several ways.

Feeling Powerless Impairs Thought

You know that constricted, closed-in feeling that often accompanies social anxiety — the feeling that you might "go blank" or that you're not firing on all cylinders? Well, you're not alone. One theory is that anxiety is caused by a combination of how we appraise a demanding moment — is it a threat or a challenge? — and how we then assess our ability to find the necessary resources to meet the demands of that moment. When we appraise the demanding moment as an ominous threat instead of a big challenge, and when we feel we don't have access to the resources necessary to deal with that threat, our anxiety is highest.[10] That is personal powerlessness — the feeling that we can't access our own mental resources when we most need to. Both chronic and acute anxiety impair some of our most important cognitive functions in part by interfering with activity in the prefrontal cortex (among other areas), which plays an essential role in aligning our actions and thoughts with our internal goals and feelings.[11]

It's really quite maddening: if our anxiety is rooted in the fear of making a bad impression, then the worst thing we can do is disable the exact faculties that would help us make a good impression — the tools that allow us to accurately understand and appropriately respond to other people.

But that's exactly what happens when the feeling of powerlessness takes hold of us. Lucidity abandons us, and our brains become unable to meet the demands of complicated or stressful situations. Powerlessness and the anxiety that results from it undermine what psychologists call executive functions — high-order cognitive tools such as reasoning, task flexibility, and attention control, all of which are critical to coping well in challenging situations.[12] With impaired executive functioning, we become less effective at updating mental information, inhibiting unwanted impulses, and planning future actions. Anxiety also wallops working memory — our ability to recall old information while simultaneously taking in, integrating, and responding to new data — which relies heavily on executive functions.

Consider the results of a series of studies in which subjects were primed to feel powerful or powerless and then asked to perform simple tasks — the sorts of challenges you'll be familiar with if you've ever visited popular "brain-training" sites.[13] In one study, subjects were first told they'd be a superior or a subordinate in a two-person computer-based task. Then, before the paired task (which never happened), they worked alone on a "two-back" task, in which they saw a series of letters on a screen and had to quickly judge whether each letter was the same as the letter that was shown two letters before. This measured the subjects' cognitive capacity for "updating": they had to continually update the series of letters they held in their heads. Subjects primed to feel powerless made significantly more mistakes than did those primed to feel powerful.

In a second study, subjects were exposed either to words related to having power or to words related to lacking it. Then they completed one of the most popular tests in cognitive psychology, the Stroop test. First published by psychologist John Ridley Stroop in 1935, the Stroop test essentially measures how cognitively agile we are when trying to block interfering signals.[14] The task is simple: you are presented with a series of words, many of which are the names of colors, like *red* and *blue*, but the word is written in a different color ink (e.g., the word *red* is written in blue ink and the word *blue* is written in red ink). Your job is to quickly and accurately name the color of the ink. Sounds easy, right? It's not, because we find it challenging to "inhibit" the habit of immediately reading words written in our first language: if you see the word *blue* printed in red ink, you'll be tempted to say "blue" when you should say "red." On the incongruent trials (the word *red* written in blue ink and the word *blue* written in red ink), subjects who were primed to feel powerless made more mistakes than did those who were primed to feel powerful and those in the control condition. In short, feeling powerless made it hard for people to block distracting information and to control their cognitive impulses.

In another study, subjects wrote about one of three things: a time when they had power over another person, a time when another person had power over them, or what they did the previous day. Then they played a version of what is called the Tower of Hanoi task on a computer, which requires strategically moving rings from post to post to get them all onto a target post. The measure of subjects' "planning" ability was how many extra moves (beyond the minimum number required) they made on trials that required counterintuitive strategies (in which one or more rings first had to be moved away from the target). Subjects primed to feel powerless required more extra moves in these trials than did those primed to feel powerful and those in the control condition. The study showed that powerlessness impairs planning, another critical executive function. The same authors also found that powerlessness induces something called goal neglect — the general phenomenon of failing to remain focused on a goal, which prevents you from executing the necessary task.

As these studies make clear, without access to our executive functions, we can't accurately present our abilities. Powerlessness blocks them, making it tough for us to show what we know.

Powerlessness Makes Us Self-Absorbed

So here we are, deprived of reason, focus, working memory, and lucidity, desperately attempting to navigate our way out of powerlessness. As if all this weren't bad enough, anxiety deals us another blow — it alienates us from others. Some research suggests that social anxiety interferes with our ability to see the world through others' eyes.

In a series of experiments led by social psychologist Andy Todd, participants had to identify the spatial location of an object — either from their own perspectives or from the perspectives of other people.[15] Subjects who had been primed to feel anxious were significantly worse at accurately identifying the location of the object when they were asked to do it from others' perspectives. In another experiment, participants viewed a photo of a person sitting at a table and looking at a book to the photographed person's left. Later, when asked to recall which side of the table the book was on, anxious participants were more likely to describe the book's location from their own perspective (e.g., "The book was on the right side of the table"), as opposed to the perspective of the person in the photo (e.g., "The book was on the left side of the table"). The more anxious participants were, the more acutely they showed this bias.

Put simply, the anxious subjects were unable to get out of their own heads and see things from another person's point of view. You can imagine how this momentary inability might affect your performance during high-pressure interactions that require you to hear and process what the other person is saying — like the interactions Reverend Jeffrey Brown was having with the young people in Boston.

The link between anxiety and self-absorption is bidirectional; they cause each other. In a review of more than two hundred studies, researchers concluded that the more self-focused we are, the more anxious — and also the more depressed and generally negative — we become.[16] Self-focus even makes us more sensitive to physical difficulties, such as stomach upset, nasal congestion, and muscle tension.[17]

On one occasion, I was speaking to a major-league baseball team, listening to players and coaches talk about the things that undermine their performance. One player mentioned the burden of something that's a huge part of the game — the public broadcasting of statistics. "Sometimes your batting average is no good," he said. He explained how it fluctuates, especially early in the season. When you're up to bat, he explained, you walk out and see the Jumbotron, which shows a huge picture of your face, your name, your batting average, and other stats. He described it as feeling like a heavy weight — feeling like everyone in the stands is looking at it and thinking about it. He said it's not just a bad feeling, it's also very distracting.

Perfectly understandable, but here's the thing. When you're a pro ballplayer and you're at bat, yes, a lot of people are looking at you. And some of them may be making snarky comments about your hitting ability. But a lot of people are also sipping their beers or taking selfies with their friends, and they're missing your at-bat altogether. And then they say — perhaps feeling embarrassed that they weren't paying attention — "Oh, I missed that. What just happened?" The reality is that people just aren't thinking about you as much as you think they are — *even when you actually are the center of attention.* And if they are, there's nothing you can do about it anyway. All you can do is hit the ball.

This is called the spotlight effect, and it's one of the most enduring and widespread egocentric human biases — to feel that people are paying more attention to us than they actually are... and usually in a bad way, not a good way. It's very difficult to turn that off. *What are they thinking of me? Does that person think I'm stupid? Do I have something in my teeth?* An exceptionally effective teacher once told me about the moment she overcame her anxiety about teaching: "In the middle of a class session, I noticed that I was no longer paying attention to what the students were thinking of *me*; I was just paying attention to what the students were *thinking.*" She was able to meet them where they were with the course material by removing herself from the analysis.

Dozens of experiments have demonstrated the spotlight effect. In one somewhat awkward study, a group of students was randomly assigned to wear brightly colored Barry Manilow T-shirts to a large introductory psychology class. They were then asked to estimate what percentage of their classmates noticed. The students greatly overestimated the number — they thought nearly half their classmates had noticed the shirts, when in reality fewer than a quarter of them had. In a follow-up study with less unusual T-shirts, the discrepancy between the estimated and actual percentage of students who'd noticed was even greater — participants thought that nearly half the class had noticed, whereas the actual number was less than 10 percent.[18]

We don't overestimate the amount of attention we're getting because we're egotistical or narcissistic. We do it because we're each at the center of our own universe, and we can't help but see the world from our own perspective. That leads us to think that others see it from our perspective, too. This is especially so when we're feeling awkward, having a bad hair day, or when we've said something dumb. In all such cases, most of us will overestimate the number of people who notice.

Powerlessness Prevents Presence

The harmful side effects of powerlessness don't stop there: the more anxious and self-focused we are during an interaction, the more time we spend *post-event processing* — ruminating about the interaction — even days later.[19] I've mentioned this unfortunate habit of endlessly replaying an interaction after the fact, but what we now know about the ways powerlessness and anxiety impair our brains puts a whole new spin on it: the thing we're ruminating about *isn't even real* — it's a seriously flawed memory of an interaction. We were so anxiously self-absorbed during the interaction that our memory of it is warped and full of holes. And yet still we obsess. We take that mangled memory and mangle it even further, ceaselessly running it through our rusty "What do they think of me?" filters. Unable to stop thinking about the situation after we've left it, we remain frozen in time.

In a nutshell, anxious self-focus makes it nearly impossible for us to be present — before, during, and even after a big challenge.

I realize it's not news that anxiety about how others see us stinks. But it's worth understanding how it saps us of our power.

The Benefits of Feeling Powerful

If feeling powerless inhibits us, depletes us, and generally throws us off our game, it's also true that feeling powerful does the opposite. But to understand how that works — how power might help us — you'll have to set aside any negative stereotypes you might hold about power, at least for now.

Power Can Protect Us

A growing body of research suggests that power is a buffer against negative emotions — it seems to thicken our skin against judgment, rejection, stress, and even physical pain.

In one study, researchers at the University of California, Berkeley, asked students who were in romantic relationships to fill out a survey each night for two weeks.[20] They were asked questions designed to measure how powerful they felt, questions such as "Who had more power in your relationship today?" and "Who made more of the decisions today?" Then, to measure their feelings of rejection, the students rated how hostile their partners had been toward them. They were also asked to report how strongly they experienced four negative feelings: anger, anxiety, sadness, and shame. On the days when rejection was high, feeling powerful reduced the negative emotions they felt, protecting them.

Even hypothetical power can work magic. In another study by the same researchers, subjects were assigned roles — either a high-power or a low-power company employee — and asked to imagine that they had not been invited to a regular happy hour. The colleague who decided not to invite them either had a higher rank, a similar rank, or a lower rank than they did at the firm. Subjects were then asked to rate their own emotions and self-esteem. The more powerful they were compared to the employee who rejected them, the less negative emotion they felt and the higher their self-esteem.

In a third study, students were first told that they would be paired with partners and asked to solve brainteasers. Then they were told that they would be assigned to play either the boss (a powerful role) or the employee (a powerless one). After their hidden (and fictional) partners learned a bit about them, they expressed either mild pleasure or displeasure at the prospect of working together. The less powerful participants (i.e., the "employees") felt worse and had lower self-esteem when their partners expressed displeasure versus pleasure. The more powerful participants seemed not to care.

In an experiment led by Berkeley professor Dana Carney, subjects were first asked to fill out a questionnaire about their leadership experience. They were then assigned either high-power or low-power roles. Though they believed the assignments were based on the questionnaire results, they were in fact random. The high-power and low-power people were asked to work in pairs to make a decision about bonuses awarded to other colleagues. Those in the high-power role were given much bigger offices, more control in meetings, and the final say in the decision about how much (if any) of a twenty-dollar "paycheck" would be paid to their low-power counterparts. Carney and her team used a stressor — physical pain — to measure the effects of feeling powerful on the stress response. They asked each subject to submerge his or her hand in a bucket of ice water (kept at around forty-eight degrees Fahrenheit), telling them they could remove their hands at any time, and measured how long each subject held out. Not only did people in the high-power roles keep their hands in the water nearly forty-five seconds longer than the powerless subjects did — that's nearly *twice* as long — they also showed fewer non-verbal signs of pain (grimacing, bracing, and restless motion)...because they were experiencing less pain.[21]

Power Can Connect Us

Feeling powerful can sometimes improve our ability to read and relate to other people.[22] In one experiment, subjects were subtly exposed to words either suggestive of having power (e.g., *royal, leadership, control*) or lacking it (e.g., *obey, serve, subordinate*). Then they watched videos of partners working on a task together and wrote down what they thought the partners were thinking and feeling throughout the interaction. When these notes were compared with what the interacting partners had written about their actual internal states, subjects primed to feel powerful were found to be more accurate.

In a companion experiment, subjects wrote about a time they had power over someone else, a time someone else had power over them, or what they did the previous day. Then they viewed twenty-four photos of faces expressing happiness, sadness, anger, or fear and selected which emotion was expressed. They also answered several questions related to their leadership styles. Subjects made to feel powerful judged emotional expression more accurately than did those made to feel powerless — unless they tended to wield power with a combination of lots of egoism and little empathy.

People who feel powerful are also more likely to forgive others, especially those they feel committed to.[23] In one experiment, subjects were asked to describe in writing a time they had power over someone else or vice versa. Then they imagined themselves in several scenarios in which a person hurt them — for instance, by sharing embarrassing stories about them. People primed to feel powerful said they'd be more forgiving of the transgressor compared to people primed to feel powerless. When we feel powerful, rather than adopting a vigilant stance toward others, we allow ourselves to be open — maybe even vulnerable. (Even powerful monkeys are less vigilant than monkeys without power.[24]) In a series of studies, people who felt powerful were more likely to see their interaction partners as friendly rather than threatening; people who felt powerless saw the opposite — inferring threat, not friendliness, from unfamiliar interaction partners. Feeling safe with their partners, powerful people in these studies were also more likely to express their true attitudes.[25]

In an early study on power and management, supervisors who felt powerless used more coercive power — threats of punishment or even being fired — when dealing with a "problem worker," whereas supervisors who felt powerful used more personal persuasion approaches, such as praise or admonishment.[26] In another study, managers who felt powerless were more ego-defensive, causing them to solicit less input. In fact, managers who felt powerless judged employees who voiced opinions more negatively.[27]

Power Can Liberate Our Thinking

Whereas a lack of power impairs our cognitive function, power seems to enhance it, improving our ability to make good decisions under complex conditions. Pamela Smith has conducted dozens of studies on the ways power and powerlessness affect our thinking.

According to Smith, compared to those who feel powerless, "the powerful process information more abstractly — integrating information to extract the gist, detecting patterns and relationships."[28]

Power makes us fearless, independent, and less susceptible to outside pressures and expectations, allowing us to be more creative. In one study, subjects were asked to imagine that they were applying for jobs at a marketing firm and had to come up with names for new products, including a pain reliever and a type of pasta.[29] They were given examples for each category — all the pasta names ended in *na, ni,* or *ti,* and all the pain pills ended in *ol* or *in.* The power-primed subjects invented more novel names rather than using the sample endings provided to them. When we feel powerful, we're less self-conscious about expressing our feelings and beliefs, and that frees us to think and do great things.

Power Can Synchronize Us

I wrote in chapter 1 about synchrony — the harmonizing of the various elements of the self. It turns out that feeling powerful synchronizes our thoughts, feelings, and behaviors, bringing us closer to presence. In one experiment, when people who felt powerful engaged in discussions with strangers, their nonverbal expressions closely matched their self-reported emotions. If they were feeling happy and telling a happy story, they were smiling. The expressions and self-reported feelings of powerless pairs were not so tightly linked.[30]

Powerlessness can also cause us to adapt our behavior to match the behavior or perceived expectations of others around us.[31] We become insincere — not necessarily in that we intend to deceive but in that we wish to protect ourselves. After all, it's better to blend in and please when you have no power.

Power Can Incite Action

> *I am no longer accepting the things I cannot change.*
> *I am changing the things I cannot accept.*
> — Angela Davis

A lab researcher leads you into a private room and asks you to sit in a chair and wait. After a few moments you notice a fan that's blowing directly in your face. It's annoying. What do you do? Move the fan? Turn it off? Or just try your best to ignore it?

Here's another quandary: you are part of a three-person debate squad about to go into the final round of a competition. Your team gets to choose whether to speak first or second. One of your teammates says you should go first — that way you will be able to frame the argument and set the tone. Your other teammate disagrees — if you go second, you'll be able to rebut your opponents' specific arguments. So now it's up to you to decide — does your team go first or second?

Both of these scenarios were used in experiments conducted by researchers trying to understand how power or its absence affects whether or not we act. In the fan study, all the subjects were first primed in the ways I described earlier to feel either powerful or powerless.[32] While 69 percent of the powerful participants redirected or turned off that annoying fan, only 42 percent of the powerless participants did. The rest just sat there and took it. After all, no one told them they could touch the fan. In the absence of power, they needed the permission of someone with authority to act. In the debate study, subjects who were primed to feel powerful were four times as likely to choose to go first in the debate competition compared with participants who weren't made to feel powerful.[33]

Endless studies back up the notion that feeling powerful makes people proactive. For example, one study showed that powerful subjects are also much more likely to haggle over the price of a new car and make the first offer in a job negotiation.[34] Why? Feeling powerful gives us the freedom to decide, to act, to *do*. Subjects in another study were first primed to feel powerful or powerless, then asked how long they would take to make a decision in various scenarios (selecting a roommate, buying a used car, visiting potential workplaces).[35] The powerless subjects said they'd need more time than the powerful ones. It's worth noting: acting more quickly isn't necessarily the best course of action; taking more time to think might have been prudent. But the general pattern is the same — power causes people to act. And in a companion study, subjects were asked to imagine how close to a deadline they would take action in circumstances such as applying for a fellowship or moving to a new apartment. The powerful subjects said they'd check these off their to-do lists sooner. In those cases, acting sooner is probably better. Finally, subjects were told to trace a figure without lifting their pencils or retracing any lines, a task that was actually impossible. The powerful subjects persisted longer and began more new attempts than the powerless ones.

The decisiveness of power is rooted in knowing that we will always have access to the resources we need. That sparks in us a greater *feeling of control*. I'm not talking about control as in being a controlling personality. The feeling that arises from personal power is not the *desire* to have control; it's the effortless feeling of *being* in control — lucid, calm, and not dependent on the behavior of others. This kind of power, as I hope to show you, becomes self-reinforcing. The thinking, communication, and action that proceeds from it can only enhance it.

In a similar way, powerlessness can lead to inaction that is directly self-defeating. People who feel socially powerless are, by definition, dependent on powerful others to lead the way. This causes the powerless to endorse the unfair systems that reinforce their state. In representative samples, economic powerlessness in the United States was correlated with greater perceived legitimacy of political agendas and policies that reinforce the subjects' power-lessness. As the authors of the study explain, these findings are "counterintuitive because it is clearly not in the interest of the powerless to endorse a system in which they are powerless. . . . The processes we identify are likely to perpetuate inequality insofar as the powerless justify rather than strive to change the hierarchical structures that disadvantage them."[36]

Power Can Make Our Actions More Effective

Power particularly affects performance when the pressure's on, providing a lift in high-stakes situations. Powerlessness does the opposite, deflating performance when the stakes are high.[37] This is, again, explained by the approach-inhibition theory of power: when we're feeling powerful, high-stakes situations activate "approach goals," inspiring us to go for it, whereas high-stakes sit-uations activate "inhibition goals" for powerless people, extin-guishing our desire to engage in what could be a risky or threatening situation.

Feeling powerful even changes our interpretation of the emo-tions that come up when we're under pressure: people who reported high levels of self-confidence — essentially, people who felt powerful — interpreted competitive anxiety as improving their performance, not inhibiting it. They also reported higher satisfac-tion with how they performed. Subjects who reported low levels of self-confidence, on the other hand, felt that competitive anxiety damaged their performance.[38]

A review of 114 studies looking at the relationship between work performance and self-efficacy — akin to personal power but limited to a specific task — revealed a clear albeit not particularly surprising correlation between the two: when people possess a strong belief that they will be able to perform the task at hand, they are more likely to perform it.[39]

Power Affects Our Physiology

So far, most of the power research we've examined has to do with its psychology — power and powerlessness as cognitive and emotional states. How they make us *think and feel*. That leads to a logical question: Is power all in our heads?

It would be surprising if that were the case, for the simple reason that our notion of power so often has physical, active connotations. Power isn't just a state of mind, it's a force of nature. Raw power. Firepower. Horsepower. Thermonuclear power. Power chords. Nobody has to explain that power is at least to some degree physical. We know it because we feel it. *We're* physical. Does this mean our power — even our internal, personal power — has a physical aspect, too? Recent research on hormones gives us fascinating clues.

But before I tell you what those clues are, I ask you to consider the following caveats. Not only is the relationship between hormones and behavior complex; the study of it is also quite new and rapidly evolving. The overview I provide here is not intended to explicate the many nuances and qualifications. Further, hormones exist alongside countless other variables that determine how we think, feel, and behave, like our relationships with our parents, how much sleep we got last night, the weather, what we ate for breakfast, how much coffee we consumed, the stability of our closest friendships, on so on. Why all the disclaimers? Because I've noticed something that happens when I say "hormones": ears perk up. People tend to disproportionately weight the importance of hormones studies, perhaps because hormones are more concrete than thoughts and feelings; they seem more "real." But the truth is that, at this point in time, behavioral scientists probably know more about how thoughts and feelings affect behavior than they do about how hormones relate to behavior. So please consider this as one piece of a bigger puzzle.

Back to the story about power and hormones...

Testosterone, a steroid hormone that is secreted by the testes in males and by the ovaries in females, aids in the development of muscle and bone mass, physical strength, reproductive tissue (in males), and even in the prevention of osteoporosis. But testosterone's effects aren't just physical; they're also behavioral.[40]

Referred to as the "dominance hormone" or the "assertiveness hormone," testosterone tracks with dominant behavior in humans, chimpanzees, baboons, lemurs, lambs, birds, and even fish and reflects changes in an individual's status and power.[41] High-status individuals — i.e., those who possess social power, the alphas — tend to have high levels of basal testosterone. In his studies of baboons, for example, Stanford professor Robert Sapolsky found that individuals with high testosterone were more likely than others to engage in competitive, "status-seeking" behaviors when opportunities arose to ascend the hierarchy and assume the top rank (e.g., when an established alpha is injured).[42] And this relationship between status and testosterone is reciprocal: not only is basal testosterone a good predictor of who will rise to the top, but rising to the top also increases an individual's circulating levels of testosterone. As status is gained, testosterone rises.

In humans, basal testosterone has been linked to socially dominant, assertive, and competitive behavior in both men and women. Testosterone levels, whether relatively stable or quite temporary, both result from and cause some of the behaviors that help us courageously approach and perform well in challenges.

But that's only half the story.

That high testosterone would correlate with power doesn't come as a surprise to most of us — it's kind of intuitive, given that we think of it as the dominance hormone. Less intuitive, and more interesting, is the role of a second hormone, cortisol, commonly referred to as the "stress hormone." Cortisol is secreted from the adrenal cortex in response to physical stressors, such as running to catch the train, and psychological stressors, such as fretting about taking an exam. Its primary function is to mobilize energy by increasing blood sugar and helping to metabolize fat, protein, and carbohydrates. It also helps to down-regulate other systems, including the digestive and immune systems. Cortisol spikes in the morning, encouraging you to wake up, then falls and levels off in the afternoon. And, like testosterone, it affects our psychology and behavior, increasing our sense of threat and the likelihood that we will avoid challenging situations.[43]

This idea — that low stress is a fundamental aspect of feeling and being powerful — runs contrary to some popular myths about leadership. It's lonely at the top, we've been told, and stressful, too. "Uneasy lies the head that wears the crown" and that sort of thing. We tend to imagine that our leaders in business and politics go through life burdened with the pressure and worry of having to wield so much power day in and day out. In response to this cliché, books and articles about how to deal with "leadership stress" abound.

Sure, some powerful people are undoubtedly stressed by their load of responsibilities, but the research doesn't support any broad trend. In fact, if anything, having real-world power seems to protect us from anxiety.

In 2012 I teamed up with Jennifer Lerner, Gary Sherman, and several other researchers at Harvard to investigate the relationship between power and stress. We recruited high-ranking leaders, including military officers, government officials, and business leaders, all of whom were participants in executive education programs. First we questioned them about how much anxiety they felt. Then we took saliva samples so we could measure their cortisol levels. Compared to members of the general population whose samples were taken under the same circumstances, the leaders had much lower cortisol and self-reported anxiety.

When we singled out the most powerful people among our group of leaders, we found that their cortisol and reported anxiety levels were even lower than those of their less mighty peers. It turned out that the most powerful leaders felt the greatest sense of control over their lives — another variable we measured — and that the sense of control seemed to make them calmer and less anxious than everybody else.[44] In fact, people who have a high sense of personal control — as opposed to people whose locus of control is external to them (i.e., it's centered on other people or on outside forces) — cope significantly better in crises (big, stressful challenges) because their executive functions are intact and they do not appraise the situation as particularly threatening, given that they feel personally in control.[45]

The strength of our study was that we didn't have to induce feelings of power in a laboratory setting — we were measuring people with actual worldly power. The limitation of the research is that because we can't randomly assign subjects to be real-life leaders and nonleaders, it's difficult to know whether power is a cure for anxiety or whether calm, confident people — the ones who possess ample personal power — just naturally ascend to leadership positions. But the connection is clear, and lab studies suggest that, as with testosterone, the relationship is bidirectional.

Two leading social neuroendocrinology researchers, professors Pranjal Mehta and Robert Josephs, have proposed that testosterone is related to power only when cortisol is low, which they refer to as the dual-hormone hypothesis.[46] Just as powerlessness saps our executive function and makes us anxious, so, too, does high cortisol. So when cortisol is high, high testosterone does not relate to powerful feelings and behaviors. This especially makes sense when you think of power as a characteristic that, as I've described in this chapter, causes us to feel not only risk tolerant and assertive but also calm, focused, controlled, and present. Risk tolerant and assertive mixed with anxious, scattered, and stressed is not a recipe for power. In fact, it's a recipe for a pretty unpleasant boss (most of us have worked for one of these people). Mehta, Josephs, and other researchers have found strong support for this dual-hormone relationship both inside and outside the lab.

In the leadership domain, this relationship is empirically supported. For example, a recent study of seventy-eight male executives also demonstrated that the high testosterone–low cortisol sweet spot is an excellent predictor of the number of people the executives had working for them.[47] And students in another study performed a leadership exercise during which they were rated on assertiveness, confidence, and overall leaderlike qualities. Again, high testosterone levels correlated with these traits, but only for people who also had low cortisol.[48]

Researchers have also measured levels of these hormones after athletes either won or lost a game (badminton, in one particular study), and they found the same effects in men and women: defeat leads to increased cortisol and lowered testosterone.[49] And among elite female athletes, players' testosterone levels have been shown to rise during competition, but only if their pregame cortisol levels were low.[50]

Emory University psychologists David Edwards and Kathleen Casto conducted an impressive six-study analysis of hormones and behavior among elite female college athletes.[51] Women who played collegiate soccer, softball, tennis, and volleyball were asked to evaluate their teammates on a scale of 1 to 5 on a questionnaire measuring qualities such as sportsmanship, leadership, and effort. The questionnaire included statements such as:

- She inspires her teammates to play at their highest level.
- She has an excellent sense, from moment to moment, of what the team needs to play at its highest level.
- By her words and/or actions, she has a consistently positive effect on team morale.
- She keeps a positive outlook, even when faced with adversity.
- She is able to be constructively critical of her teammates when necessary.
- She works effectively with her teammates to help create a sense of team unity.
- She is willing to make personal sacrifices when they serve the best interests of the team as a whole.
- She plays and competes with a passion for the game.
- She accurately represents her teammates and constructively communicates their concerns and frustrations.

- She is consistent, fair, and authentic in her interactions with teammates on and off the playing field.
- She is constructively motivated by defeat.

All the athletes also submitted saliva samples so that hormone levels could be measured. As it turns out, the women who had been ranked by their teammates as the most inspiring, communicative, hardworking, passionate, supportive, and optimistic also had the highest testosterone levels and the lowest cortisol levels in the group.

The researchers concluded that, "at least for individuals with low levels of cortisol, perhaps the higher an athlete's testosterone level, the greater her ability to reach the delicate balance between being gentle and being overbearing in matters of authority in interactions with teammates."

In fact, looking at testosterone and cortisol even gives us some insight into who is most likely to cheat. Harvard psychologist Jooa Julia Lee and her collaborators tested this prediction. Subjects were instructed to take and then to privately self-grade a math exam, with financial incentives increasing as the exam score increased. The situation was designed to make it easy and somewhat desirable for people to cheat. The people most likely to cheat were those who had both high testosterone *and* high cortisol. As study coauthor Robert Josephs explained, "Testosterone furnishes the courage to cheat, and elevated cortisol provides a reason to cheat."[52] In other words, while testosterone may cause people to be more risk tolerant, without the high cortisol and the accompanying fear of not having the control to meet the demands of the situation, testosterone does not predict cheating.

What's most interesting to me about this large body of research is not that high testosterone combined with low cortisol is related to power. It's that this hormone profile is related to responsible power, at least among humans. The testosterone boosts our assertiveness and likelihood of action, while the low cortisol safeguards us against the kinds of stressors most likely to throw us off course during our biggest challenges. It correlates with effective, team-focused leadership, an ability to calmly provide constructive feedback to others, and the courage and resilience to steadily push forward through challenges. Is it, in fact, confidence without arrogance?

Does Power Corrupt?

Which of the following is more likely to happen:

A. Your boss remembers your birthday.
B. You remember your boss's birthday.

I have an answer for that, though I'm not proud of it. On the day I started working on this chapter, which happened to be the week of my birthday, I arrived at my office to find a present waiting for me on my desk. It was from my assistant, Kailey, whose birthday I didn't know (but now do).

Power helps us fixate less on what other people think, which is liberating, but it can also cause us to think less about other people, period — and to think carelessly about them when we do. Susan Fiske has pointed out that those with social power can all too easily fall into the lazy habit of seeing and treating the less powerful (employees and subordinates, for example) not as individuals but as rough, stereotyped sketches of people. One reason for this, she says, is that attention runs up the hierarchy, not down. We pay attention to people who control our fate because we want to be able to predict how they'll act.[53] My assistant remembering my birthday might be a case in point (although she's also just a very thoughtful person).

The powerful, on the other hand, can afford to be inattentive to the less powerful — their fate doesn't depend on their subordinates (or, if it does, that subordinate has just become powerful). This is compounded by the fact that people in power often have more demands on their attention already and thus less of it to spare.[54] In one study, Fiske, along with Stephanie Goodwin and her colleagues, gave a group of undergraduates the power to evaluate high school students' summer job applications.[55] They found that the more say the undergrads had in the evaluations of the applications, the less attention they paid to each individual applicant's unique qualities and qualifications.

Here's the silver lining: when the researchers primed the undergrads to feel a sense of responsibility by having them reflect on several egalitarian values, the undergrads' attention to the unique qualities of each of the "subordinate" high schoolers they had power over increased substantially.

So does power corrupt? It certainly can, as many studies — not to mention history and experience — have shown. All too often, social power creates the kind of asymmetric interdependence that breeds inequity, injustice, and antisocial behaviors such as stereotyping. This is why I strongly favor the development of non-zero-sum personal power over the acquisition of zero-sum social power. But as the study above suggests, we can work to overcome our negative biases, using social power not only to do well for ourselves but also to do good for others. In fact, it turns out that many of the negative effects of social power diminish when people are motivated by their perception of themselves as fair and decent, their desire to be accurate, and their sense of accountabil-ity for others or responsibility to meet their organization's goals — when, for example, the boss feels accountability for her employees' development, well-being, and performance or when she feels responsible for her organization's success.[56]

And lack of personal power can be as dangerous as possession of social power. Claremont Graduate University professor of behavioral and organizational sciences Tarek Azzam and his col-leagues showed, in a series of studies, that the more powerless people believed they were, the more they felt anxiety about — and aggression toward — outsiders and immigrants. (This effect was even stronger for men who felt powerless.)[57]

Here's my hope: because personal power is infinite and does not require us to in any way control someone else, we don't have a sense of scarcity about it. We don't feel that we have to compete to keep it. It's ours, whatever happens. It can't be taken away by someone else. And that knowledge, that understanding, facilitates the desire to share it, to help others realize the same. And so I believe that personal power, unlike social power, becomes conta-gious. The more personally powerful we feel, the likelier it is that we'll want to help others feel the same.

Pulitzer Prize–winning biographer Robert Caro, who spent decades chronicling the life and machinations of Lyndon John-son, once told *The Guardian*, "We're taught Lord Acton's axiom: all power corrupts, absolute power corrupts absolutely. I believed that when I started these books, but I don't believe it's always true anymore. Power doesn't always corrupt. Power can cleanse. What I believe is always true about power is that power always reveals."[58]

Power reveals. That makes sense to me. As I've tried to con-vince you in this chapter, I think personal power brings us closer to our best selves, while the lack of it distorts and obscures our selves.

But if power reveals, then we can only know the truly powerful, because only they are bold enough to show who they are without subterfuge and without apology. They have the courage and the confidence to open themselves to the gaze of others.

In that way, the path to personal power is also the path to presence. It's how we, and others, discover and set free who we truly are.

6

Slouching, Steepling, and the Language of the Body

What you do speaks so loud that I cannot hear what you say.
— RALPH WALDO EMERSON

THE FIERCEST DISPLAY OF power at a New Zealand rugby match occurs before actual play begins.

Rugby is serious business in tiny New Zealand (population: 4.5 million). Their national men's rugby team — the All Blacks — is a tremendous source of pride. Playing since 1884, the All Blacks are, by virtually every measure, the greatest rugby team in the world.[1]

New Zealand is a unique country, with three official languages — English, Māori, and New Zealand Sign Language — and a population that includes people of European (74 percent) and Māori (15 percent) descent.[2] But what really distinguishes it, socioculturally, is the extent to which the cultures of the indigenous Māori and the European settlers have integrated.

I'm going to guess that most of you don't follow rugby. And if I'm right about that, then chances are most of you won't have seen the extraordinary thing that happens on the field before an All Blacks match. It starts as most pro sports games do — the spectators stand as the national anthem is sung. But then the team, comprising fifteen of the burliest, most herculean humans you can imagine — comic-book huge, almost — arrange themselves into a tight formation on the field, facing the opposing team, who typically stand in a single row, arms linked over each other's shoulders.

The crowd is waiting for this moment. The buzz of energy is, as some have described, "intoxicating." Many New Zealanders see this moment as far more meaningful than the singing of their national anthem.

Feet apart and firmly planted, knees slightly bent, the All Blacks wait. Their leader paces back and forth among his teammates like a tiger in a cage, then yells a command in Māori. At once, with controlled ferocity, his teammates call back to him while simultaneously moving into the first pose of what will unfold as a potent and provocative dance. Synchronized, they slowly but vigorously move through a series of very powerful postures, gestures, and facial expressions — eyes widened as far as possible, chests bulging, hands slapping thighs, feet stomping the ground. Their chant is loud and deep. With every movement, they seem to be both expanding and shooting roots down into the ground. Slowly, inexorably, they advance toward their opponents, finishing with eyes wild and tongues protruding.

This is called a haka, a traditional Māori dance, and the team has been performing it before matches since 1905. People commonly refer to it as a war dance, but a haka is much more than that. Although it was often used on the battlefield, it was (and still is) also performed when groups come together in peace. At funerals, it is a profound show of respect for the deceased. Typically, the All Blacks perform a haka called ka mate, which was created in 1820 by the Ngāti Toa tribal chieftain Te Rauparaha. On special occasions, the team performs the kapa o pango, created by Māori cultural consultant Derek Lardelli, who explained in a recent documentary that it is intended "to reflect the multicultural makeup of contemporary New Zealand — in particular the influence of Polynesian cultures."[3] The kapa o pango ends with the players drawing their hands across their necks, which some people interpret as an aggressive throat-slitting gesture. Lardelli explained that the intended meaning is not throat slitting but "drawing vital energy into the heart and lungs."[4] I encourage you to search for the All Blacks on the Web and watch them perform.[5]

Another striking moment of choreography is called a pukana. "The pukana is the act of defiance, which is exhibited by the protruding tongue," explained Hohepa Potini, an elder of the Ngāti Toa tribe. "So when you see the All Blacks' pukana at the end of the haka, that's them telling you: 'Bring it on.'"[6]

Watching the All Blacks perform a haka from a seat high in the stadium is intimidating. It's startlingly fierce, even in an online video. I can't imagine how it might feel to a player on an opposing team.

The first time I watched the All Blacks perform a haka, I thought, "This is the most extreme, fearsome display of dominant body language that I've ever seen among humans." A physical cease-and-desist letter. Over the top. Primitive, even.

If body language is about communication between people, then this message looked simple and direct: it was raw intimidation of one party by another. Or so it seemed at first.

Slouching, Steepling, and the Language of the Body

Power Expands Our Body Language

Power doesn't just expand our minds; it also expands our bodies. Expansive, open body language is closely tied to dominance across the animal kingdom, including humans, other primates, dogs, cats, snakes, fish, and birds, and many other species. When we feel powerful, we make ourselves bigger.

Whether temporary or stable, benevolent or sinister, status and power are expressed through evolved nonverbal displays — widespread limbs, enlargement of occupied space, erect posture. Think of Wonder Woman and Superman. Any John Wayne character. Kevin Spacey's Frank Underwood on *House of Cards*. An Alvin Ailey dancer expressing liberation and freedom. When we feel powerful, we stretch out. We lift our chins and pull our shoulders back. We puff up our chests. Spread our feet apart. Raise our arms.

Every four years we all get very excited about gymnastics. (Funny how a sport can seem so important to us during the Olympics only to be forgotten shortly after the closing ceremony.) I'm sure you've noticed that gymnasts go through a short choreographed display before they even begin their routines. They walk to the mat, raise their arms above their heads in a V, lift their chins, and open their chests. Why, of all the possible postures one could adopt, did the gymnastics powers that be choose this one?

To answer that, I want you to imagine you've just won a race. You cross the finish line, breaking through the ribbon: What do you do with your body? Or imagine watching as your favorite soccer team just scored the tie-breaking goal to win the World Cup: What do you do with your body? There's a very good chance you'd throw your arms in the air into a V, lift your chin, and open your chest. Why? Because that particular pose signals triumph, victory, and pride — psychological states of power. And by nonverbally displaying that triumph, we are communicating to others our status and power, however fleeting they might be.

Before I say anything else about humans, let's talk about other primates. I love nonhuman primates. Like many people, I find them beautiful, funny, fascinating. I see myself in them. I feel like I'm watching children play. But as a social psychologist studying power, I especially love observing primate behavior because nonhuman primates provide an unfiltered picture of how power shapes body language. Human behavior is controlled — by language, by impression management, by cultural norms, by stereotypes, by religion, by formal rules, and so on. All these things make human behavior noisy and hard to interpret. Am I watching someone do what she wants to do, or is she doing what she thinks other people want her to do? Nonhuman primates' social behavior is far less constrained. As renowned primatologist Frans de Waal explained:

> I am just grateful that I study social inequality in creatures who express their needs and wants blatantly, without cover-ups. Language is a fine human attribute, but it distracts almost as much as it informs. When watching political leaders on television, especially when they are under pressure or in debate, I sometimes mute the sound so as to focus better on the eye contact, body postures, gestures, and so on. I see the way they grow in size when they have dealt a verbal blow.[7]

The fact that dominant, powerful primates — alphas — enact expansive, open body language is clear to most untrained observers. When chimpanzees hold their breath until their chests bulge, they're signaling their rank in the hierarchy. Male chimpanzees, to show their status to a subordinate male, expand by walking upright and even holding pieces of wood to extend the perceived length of their limbs. The hair on their bodies also stands on end (a phenomenon known as piloerection). And male silverback gorillas do indeed beat their fists against their expanded chests to communicate strength and power when an unwelcome male is encroaching on their territory. Primates also demonstrate their power by occupying spaces that are central, high, and particularly valuable, making themselves visible and putting themselves physically above the others.[8]

Our more distant animal relatives are even less restricted by social pressures. When peacocks raise and spread their kaleidoscopic tail feathers, they're boldly displaying their dominance to potential mates; they don't hold back. When a king cobra wants to show someone who's boss, it has no second thoughts about rearing up the front part of its body, inflating its hood, and "growling." And impression management — in the human, metaperceptive, what-do-they-think-of-me sense — is certainly not a concern for a mama bear standing on her hind legs to scare off a predator eyeing her cubs.

Nonverbal behavior operates through many channels — facial expressions, eye movements and gaze, body orientation and posture, hand gestures, walking style, vocal cues such as pitch and volume, and others. Social psychologists Dana Carney and Judith Hall have carefully studied powerful and powerless body language. In one set of studies, they asked participants to imagine how powerful people were most likely to conduct themselves nonverbally.[9] Participants were given a long list of behaviors and were asked to select the ones characteristic of powerful people.

High-power individuals were expected to initiate handshakes, make more and longer eye contact, use broader gestures, have erect and open posture, lean forward and orient the body and head toward others, and be animated and self-assured in their physical expressions.

Even our hands and fingers can signal power. Hold your hands in front of your face with your palms facing each other and your fingers pointing upward toward the ceiling. Then curl the fingers of each hand toward those of the other until the tips meet in the middle, and spread your fingers as far apart as you comfortably can. If those instructions aren't clear, look for pictures of *The Simpsons* character Montgomery Burns. Even this gesture, which psychologists refer to as steepling or finger tenting, is a sign of confidence. It may be subtle, but it's still spatially expansive compared to how we typically hold our hands. In fact, former FBI agent and body language expert Joe Navarro explains, "Steepling communicates that we are one with our thoughts, we are not wavering, we are not vacillating. At that precise moment when we steeple, we are communicating universally that we are confident in our thoughts and beliefs, sure in our affirmation, trusting of ourselves."[10]

Power also affects how we perceive our own and others' stature. Feeling powerful even leads people to overestimate their own height. How is this possible? Most of us know how tall we are: Is power really going to cause us to misremember our own height? Of course not. I know I'm five feet five all the time, regardless of how confident or strong I'm feeling. But my judgment of my *relative* height is prone to subjectivity.

Psychologists Michelle Duguid and Jack Goncalo showed in a series of three studies that people — regardless of their actual height — tend to choose a tall avatar to "best represent themselves" in a virtual reality game. And in a pair of experiments led by Andy Yap, participants who were primed to feel powerful underestimated the size of a stranger in a photograph and another person with whom they had interacted during the study.[11] In short, power causes us to see ourselves as taller than we actually are and others as smaller than they actually are.

But are these behaviors learned or is something more fundamental going on? That is, is body language culturally learned or hardwired? Is it nurture or nature?

In 1872, Charles Darwin proposed that many expressions of emotion are biologically innate and evolutionarily adaptive, signaling important social information. He argued that expressions of emotion serve us by prompting an immediate action that benefits us, given our environmental circumstances. If we see an angry face coming at us, we flee. But to know that the face signifies anger, we first have to recognize that particular expression. In other words, Darwin was suggesting, certain expressions of emotion are universal — recognized in virtually all cultures.[12]

As I described in chapter 1, researchers have documented evidence of the universality of many facial expressions of emotion. For example, regardless of where we're from, when we feel disgust, we wrinkle our noses and raise our upper lips. When we feel surprised, we raise our brows, widen our eyes, and slightly open our mouths. (You can try it if you'd like.)

But the expression of emotional states does not end with simple emotions. More complex signaling of power and powerlessness, involving body postures and head movements, might also be universal.

No one knows more about this than Jessica Tracy, a professor of psychology at the University of British Columbia. Tracy has extensively studied the complex emotion of pride, which arises from feelings of power, strength, and victory, and her research shows that it, too, may be an evolved part of us — an idea also proposed by Darwin.

Pride takes over the whole body. As Tracy and her colleagues write, the prototypical proud expression includes "an expanded and upright posture, head tilted slightly upward (about 20 degrees), a small smile, and arms either akimbo with hands on the hips or raised above the head with hands in fists."[13] In a study she and Richard Robins reported in 2004, college undergraduates viewed images of people posing with expressions of pride, happiness, and surprise and had to describe the emotion they saw.[14] When they viewed the pride displays, two-thirds of the students used related adjectives (*proud, triumphant, self-confident*, and so on), while almost no one described happy or surprised poses as expressing pride. This indicates that we can easily distinguish pride from other expressed emotions.

Spontaneous expressions of pride also appear to be universal. Tracy and David Matsumoto analyzed photos of athletes from more than thirty countries taken after they won or lost judo matches in the 2004 Olympics and Paralympics.[15] Athletes from all over the world tended to show the same behaviors after winning (smiling, head tilted back, arms raised in V, chest out) and losing (shoulders slumped, chin down, and chest narrowed). This was true even in competitors from collectivistic cultures, where pride is less appreciated — even discouraged, in some cases. But perhaps the strongest evidence of the innateness of these expressions is the fact that even congenitally blind athletes — athletes who had never seen another person express pride or power or victory — did the same thing with their bodies when they won.[16]

Let's pause for a minute to think about how one might feel

after running one hundred meters faster than any human in history, as Jamaican sprinter Usain Bolt has done three times. The word *exhausted* certainly comes to mind. From one evolutionary perspective, continuing to expend energy by puffing your chest out and lifting your arms after you've already succeeded may seem like a waste of effort. Shouldn't we conserve whatever shreds of energy remain after having burned so much of it?

In fact, these victory expressions serve a different purpose. Tracy and her collaborators suggest they may have evolved to produce physiological changes, such as increasing testosterone, that would allow us to continue to dominate a situation and defend a victory. They then may have evolved a social function, as they became recognized as a signal of victory, thus communicating high status or power.[17] Indeed, people automatically interpret displays of pride as signs of status. In one study, when participants looked at pictures of people in expansive, powerful postures, they were more likely to accept that person's suggested answer to a trivia question, taking pride as a clue to competence.[18]

The signals communicated by these displays can be so strong that they neutralize or overcome other signs of a person's status. In a 2012 study, Tracy and her colleagues showed subjects an image of a man described as a team captain and one of a man described as a water boy.[19] When the captain slumped and looked ashamed, and the water boy stood tall and looked proud, people more quickly paired the water boy with high-status words and the captain with low-status words than they did when the postures were reversed. At least implicitly, posture was a stronger signal of status than information about roles on the team.

Walking and Talking with a Swagger

We've discussed powerful postures and gestures, but what about our bodies in motion? When we feel powerful, do we walk a certain way? To find out, my team collaborated with Nikolaus Troje, a biologist who directs the BioMotion Lab at Queen's University in Ontario. Troje and his colleagues are applying advanced computational analysis to three-dimensional motion data (captured with incredible accuracy through a technique called digital motion capture) to find the relationships between biological movement (the movement of a body) and various emotions, such as happiness, sadness, relaxation, and anxiety.[20]

In a study we completed with Troje, we asked one hundred online participants to rate a random selection of one hundred walking figures according to how powerless or powerful each

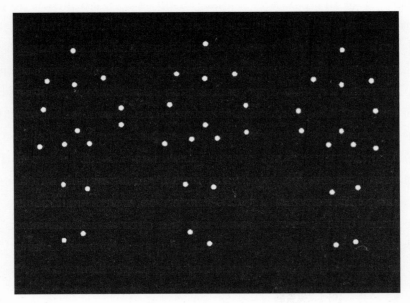

Powerful Walker

seemed. These walking figures were graphically, dynamically portrayed on a computer screen by fifteen moving dots representing the major joints of the body, resulting in a stunningly vivid image of the human body in motion. Using those ten thousand ratings (one hundred people rating one hundred walkers), we were able to analyze mathematically the kinematics of powerless and powerful movement as perceived by others and create a single computerized figure that could be manipulated on a continuum from one extreme of power to the other.

As you can see, powerful walking, relative to powerless walking, is expansive, with more arm movement and a longer stride. Although it's difficult to detect in these still images, powerful walking also involved more pronounced vertical head movement. Powerless walking is much more restricted, with very little arm movement, a virtually stationary head, and a shorter stride.[21] (You can look at some of Niko Troje's computerized demos on his website.[22])

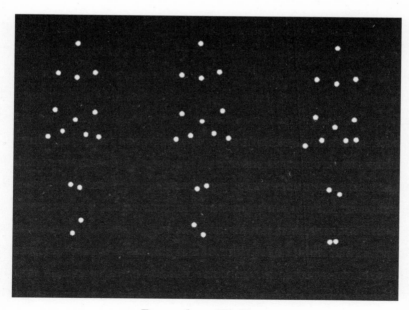

Powerless Walker

Even our voices communicate power — and not just through the words they speak. Just as our bodies expand and take up physical space when we feel powerful, our voices grow. Powerful people initiate speech more often, talk more overall, and make more eye contact while they're speaking than powerless people do. When we feel powerful, we speak more slowly and take more time. We don't rush. We're not afraid to pause. We feel entitled to the time we're using.

When people feel powerful or are assigned to high-power roles in experiments, they unconsciously lower their vocal frequency, or pitch, making their voices expand and sound "bigger." And when people speak at a low pitch, they are judged to be powerful by strangers.[23] How does this relate to expansiveness? Well, our voices are affected by anxiety and threat — both of which cause us to speak at a high pitch. When we are feeling strong and secure, the muscles in the larynx expand rather than tighten, and pitch automatically lowers.

Powerlessness Collapses Your Body

The flip side, of course, is that powerlessness doesn't just constrain our thoughts, feelings, and actions, it also shrinks our bodies. When we feel powerless or subordinate, we constrict our posture, tightening, wrapping, and making ourselves smaller (limbs touching torso, chest caved inward, shoulders slumped, head lowered, posture slouched). We also use restricted gestures and speech, by hesitating, rushing, using a small vocal range, a high pitch, and so on. Powerlessness even inhibits our facial expressions, evidenced through constricted facial muscles, such as lip presses.[24] Our study of walkers showed that powerless people are seen as moving with a stunted, collapsed gait — their stride is short, and they move their arms and heads significantly less than powerful people do. Even when they walk, they're trying to take up less space. They're trying to disappear.

One particularly telling gesture of powerlessness may not look dramatic at first glance: wrapping a hand around the neck. We do this when we feel especially uncomfortable, insecure, and unsafe, physically or psychologically, and we are clearly signaling fear and the sensation of being under threat. Why do we make this gesture? To protect ourselves from the jaws of a predator by literally covering the carotid artery. Next time you're around a lot of people, notice who does this and when. People do not do it when they feel powerful. Really. When you feel powerless, you start folding in on yourself, to protect, cover, and swaddle yourself, returning to the fetal position.

Other animals do the same thing. Low-ranking chimpanzees slouch, pull their knees in, and wrap their arms around their legs and torsos, adopting a fetal-like position, almost as if they're trying to become invisible. Submissive dogs pull their tails between their legs, lower their bodies, and flatten and pull their ears back, indicating absolute surrender. And low-status whooping cranes hold their bodies nearly horizontal to the ground, bending their necks and lowering their heads below the level of other birds in the area. If approached by a dominant crane, the submissive one will quickly move out of its way.

Elizabeth Baily Wolf, a doctoral student I've worked with at Harvard Business School for four years, was telling me one day about a soccer game she and her husband had been watching. She asked me, "Have you ever noticed what people in the stands do with their hands when they see their team make a mistake or miss a shot? They all do the same thing — they cover their faces." She was right. Watch spectators when their team makes a critical mistake and you'll see it: they immediately raise their hands and cover their faces or heads. In fact, watch the athletes themselves — many of them do the same thing when they make an error or miss a chance to score.

Wolf decided to conduct some experiments to study this phenomenon. She showed photos of people covering their faces and heads in a variety of ways to hundreds of participants, then asked them to describe the pictures in terms of certain traits. As expected, she found that people who had a hand on their faces were seen as less powerful and more distressed, embarrassed, and shocked than those with uncovered faces. Touching the face with both hands amplified these impressions.[25]

When we are feeling powerless, in virtually every way that we can, we make ourselves smaller. Rather than take up more space, we take up less — through our postures, our gestures, our walking, and even our voices. We shorten, slouch, collapse, and we restrict our body language. And when other people watch us doing those things, they can't help but see us as powerless and frightened.

Body Language and Gender

One of the questions I'm asked most often when I give talks about body language is "Don't men use much more expansive body language than women?" Yes. Absolutely they do. Men display generally more nonverbal dominance and expansiveness, talk more, and interrupt more than women do. Women show generally more submissive, contractive nonverbal behavior, talk less (yes, the stereotype that women are more talkative than men is just plain wrong[26]), interrupt less often, and are interrupted more often.[27]

When it comes to walking, gender differences are enormous. In our walking study, the relationship between gender and powerful movement was very strong: women's walking was far more restricted than men's walking on the dimensions we identified as relating to power — arm movement, head movement, and length of stride.[28]

Columbia Business School professor and expert on the psychology of power Adam Galinsky makes the compelling data-driven case that gender differences equate with power differences: behaviors typical of women are also typical of powerless people and vice versa. In virtually every society, women still have less formal social power than men — in other words, power and gender are almost always confounded, making it difficult to know which has a bigger influence on people's behavior. In fact, Galinsky has demonstrated that prototypical gender behavioral differences can be elicited by manipulating how powerful a person feels, regardless of his or her gender.[29]

That's not to say that some biologically based gender differences don't exist; of course some do. But those differences are far smaller than people tend to perceive them to be — it's not that "women do this and men do that." And these differences are greatly reinforced through stereotyping and the cognitive biases that lead us to look for information that confirms those stereotypes. In short, many of the differences that we observe between how women and men behave — including body language — are actually grounded in power differences, not biological differences.

To further complicate things, culture moderates these differences, thereby widening or narrowing the gender-based power gap. A woman named Sadaaf, born and raised in Bangladesh but now living in Dallas, Texas, wrote to me not long after my TED talk was posted. "Women tend to make themselves smaller compared to men. I grew up in Bangladesh, and culturally we are not taught to feel powerful. Men are the dominant sex, and it is a struggle for women to feel and be powerful in [the] same room. It certainly reflects in the body language." She went on to explain: "After seeing your talk I always remind myself to take a little bit more space than I [am] used to. I am not doing anything extreme but just enough to feel like I own my bubble! I will not become smaller! I will use all this space. It makes me feel a little bit more in charge."

I also received a deeply touching e-mail from a young Vietnamese woman, Uyen, reflecting on her experiences as a newcomer to the United States. She was stunned by the differences in women's body language between the United States and Vietnam and confused about how to square these differences with what she'd been taught as a child by her female elders (e.g., "Don't maintain eye contact while talking with Dad," "Barely shake hands with Dad's friends when they visit us," "Cross your legs while talking with your colleagues," and even "Women are unimportant — we should make ourselves small and hide our significance in front of others"). At the time she wrote me, she said, she was "sitting in a coffee shop in Boston, watching women coming in and out, and noticing their body language. American women confidently maintain eye contact while ordering cups of coffee with baristas; they open their arms while talking with friends and colleagues." How could she respect what she was taught by her well-meaning elders in one culture while growing her sense of power and pride in another?

But although these gender prescriptions might be exaggerated in some countries, the United States is certainly not in the clear, as my colleagues and I discovered in an experiment involving American children.

Parents of young children — actually, anyone who's observed young children — might have noticed that both boys and girls freely use expansive postures and movements. Unconstrained by cultural norms, little girls seem to be just as likely as little boys to throw their arms in the air, stand with their shoulders back, and plant their feet apart. But at some point, this appears to change: boys continue to expand, and girls begin to collapse. When my son entered middle school, I watched his female friends change the way they carried themselves. They began to draw their bodies inward, hunching their shoulders, wrapping their arms around their torsos, twisting up their legs and ankles, lowering their chins. There could be any number of reasons why this happens, but surely one of them is that girls, around that age, become more attuned to cultural stereotypes prescribing — accurately or not — what is attractive to the opposite sex. And this may be why your once effervescent child begins to wilt when she enters middle school.

My colleagues and I began studying the role of gender in children's body language by accident. Annie Wertz — developmental psychologist at the Max Planck Institute in Berlin (also my childhood next-door neighbor, "babysittee" for ten years, and daughter of my third-grade teacher, Elsa) — Kelly Hoffman, Jack Schultz, Nico Thornley, and I were launching a social development study to identify the age at which kids start to associate expansive postures with power and contractive postures with powerlessness. We considered several ways of presenting the poses to the kids: we could stand in various poses ourselves; we could show them pictures of other people in various postures; we could use cartoon characters or stick figures adopting various postures...lots of possibilities. It was important to use gender-neutral stimuli to make the experiment as clean as possible, and in a brainstorming session we came up with the idea of using a wooden artist's mannequin, or doll, which is easy to manipulate. So we bought one and configured it into a bunch of high-power postures and low-power postures, then took photos of them. We thought we should probably pilot-test our photos of the dolls with a "convenience" sample (i.e., our friends' kids) to get their initial reactions before launching the actual study, especially since social development studies involving young kids are very time- and labor-intensive; we wanted to be sure we were using the right methods. When we did that, we accidentally found something troubling: the kids seemed to think the powerful dolls were boys and the powerless dolls were girls. So we slightly changed course, and instead of examining the age at which kids might associate expansive postures with power, we decided we'd examine the age at which they might start to associate expansive postures with gender.

We then collected kids' impressions by having them look at sixteen pairs of images, each consisting of one image of a doll in a high-power pose and one image of a doll in a low-power pose. After they had viewed each pair, we'd ask the kids to tell us which doll was the girl and which was the boy. A score of 9 or higher would indicate a male-powerful bias; a score of 8 or below would indicate a female-powerful bias. A score of 16 would mean that a child saw every powerful doll as a boy and every powerless doll as a girl. A score of 0 would mean that a child saw every powerful doll as a girl and every powerless doll as a boy.

Around sixty kids, recruited at a children's museum, participated in the study: half were four-year-olds and half were six-year-olds. Based on research on timing of the development of gender identities and adoption of cultural stereotypes, we hypothesized that the children would label dolls in the high-power poses as male and dolls in the low-power poses as female and that the effect would be stronger in the six-year-olds. We wanted to know what percentage of the children showed a male-power bias. While 73 percent of the four-year-olds showed a male-power bias, 85 percent of the six-year-olds did. The results are even more startling when you consider the percentage of "perfect" male-power scores — scores of 16. While only 13 percent of the four-year-olds scored 16, 44 percent of the six-year-olds did. In other words, while both groups showed a strong male-power gender bias, compared to the four-year-olds, the six-year-olds were about three times as likely to see *every* powerful doll as male and *every* powerless doll as female. And there were no differences between the scores of girls and boys — they were equally biased.

What do we do about this, you might wonder?

I am issuing a challenge to all of us, and it's one that I do not take lightly: *Let's change it.* When you see your daughters, sisters, and female friends begin to collapse in on themselves, intervene. Show them examples of girls and women in triumphant postures, moving with a sense of power, speaking with authentic pride. Change the images and stereotypes that kids are exposed to. We don't need to tell women to be like men. But we do need to encourage girls not to be afraid to express their personal power. Let's stop thinking about powerful postures as masculine and powerless postures as feminine. I'm not advocating that you sit with your knees wide apart or your feet up on the desk while in a meeting or that you engage in alpha body language in your interactions — whether you are a man or a woman. I'm telling you that you *deserve* to adopt open, comfortable postures and to take up your fair share of space regardless of your gender.

Should We Just Dominate Everybody with Our Body Language?

In 2014, someone from Washington State sent me a link to a public service announcement explaining what to do if you encounter a cougar in the wild. (Let me point out that, as noted in the PSA, the chance of this happening is extremely small, and Washington State's only known cougar-caused human fatality happened in 1924.) In the video, the narrator, ecologist Chris Morgan, explains, "Knowing a few things about cougars will keep you, your family, and cougars safe." One of those safety precautions, he advises, is: "If you *do* have an encounter, don't run; be big!" This is accompanied by a clip of a man standing in the woods and pulling the back of his jacket up above his head to make himself appear taller.

I described this PSA when I was giving a talk last year. A man in his fifties came up to me afterward and said, "I know this sounds crazy, but when I was a little kid, my dad and I had a cougar encounter while we were fishing in Oregon — and that's exactly what we did. In fact, my dad said, 'Get up on my shoulders and pull the back of your shirt up above your head so we look bigger than the cougar.' Of course I listened to him. And the cougar just ran off! Now I get it."

Recall the chimps who hold sticks to make their limbs appear longer? Same idea.

Powerful body language signals others to either approach or avoid. In this case, of course, we want to signal the cougar to avoid us — to let her know that we are big, dominant, strong, and dangerous.

But here's the thing: most of us will never have to scare off a cougar. Or any other wildcat. Or large predator. While these postures, which I often refer to as cowboy poses, may have been evolutionarily adaptive when we were trying to avoid being eaten by a saber-toothed tiger, they are not particularly useful in business meetings, classrooms, or family discussions. In fact, they often backfire when we intentionally use them for effect.

When I speak to audiences — from college students to physicians to executives to librarians — one of their most common questions is, "What should I do if I work with a person who is always using dominant alpha body language?" These questions show that most of us are turned off by attempts to dominate through body language. Now, that might seem to contradict all we've learned about the importance of posture to power. But there are several reasons that trying to use high-power nonverbal expressions to get our way is a bad idea.

Intimacy, Not Intimidation

While status and power are not synonymous, they are closely related. Research shows that we pay extra attention to high-status, dominant individuals, just as nonhuman primates do. And that makes sense, because dominant members of a group generally have the capacity to allocate resources, influence group decisions, set norms for appropriate behavior, incite conflict, and resolve disputes.

But chimpanzees and gorillas *avert* their gazes from individuals who are overtly *displaying* dominance (i.e., using expansive body language). Displaying dominance differs from occupying a dominant, high-status role in the hierarchy; one can do the latter without overtly displaying it. So an overt display of dominance, particularly by a high-status member of the group, means something. Gaze aversion is a sign of submission. Do humans show the same gaze deference as their primate counterparts?

In a pair of experiments, Elise Holland, Elizabeth Baily Wolf, Christine Looser, and I posed this question.[30] We asked people to view a series of photos of men and women: sometimes the people in the photos were adopting dominant, powerful postures — e.g., standing with their hands on their hips and their feet apart; sitting with their knees apart and their fingers interlaced behind their heads, elbows pointed out — and sometimes they were adopting submissive, powerless postures, e.g., standing with their ankles crossed and their arms wrapped around themselves; sitting with slouched shoulders, lowered chins, and hands folded.

Using a video-based method called eye-tracking, we were able to measure the exact gaze patterns of the subjects as they were viewing the photos. While the participants sat in a chair and looked at the images depicted on the computer screen, a camera focused on and recorded the movements of their eyes, capturing exactly what they were looking at, when, and for how long. Because people find it very difficult to intentionally control their gaze patterns when they first glance at something, eye-tracking acts as a bit of a mind reader — by showing us what you're looking at, it tells us something about what you're thinking.

The difference between gaze patterns when the subjects were looking at dominant versus submissive poses was stark: participants viewing the dominant poses quickly averted their gazes from the faces, looking down at the legs and feet or away from the person in the image altogether. When looking at people in submissive poses, subjects' gazes followed more normal social patterns — they looked at people's faces. And these gaze patterns mimic the way we would interact with people in the real world — we don't want to engage with people who are conspicuously displaying dominance. We sense that their behavior is asynchronous, and they seem too dangerous.

Jessica Tracy found another reason we humans are turned off by excessive eye contact: we take it as a blatant, arrogant attempt to dominate us, and we resent it. She wrote, "When people gaze upwards, rather than directly at those they're engaging with while showing the pride expression, their expression is perceived as more authentic, less hubristic. This may be because of the sense of dominance conveyed by direct eye gaze."[31] That's another reason to tone down those piercing eyeball-to-eyeball staring contests in business meetings.

As I've said above, in most social situations, we tend to unconsciously mimic each other's body language, which serves to make interactions smoother. Sometimes, though, instead of mimicking our companions' body language, we complement it. This phenomenon is particularly common when there is a power imbalance between the people involved. The higher-power person is likely to use exaggerated power postures, which leads the lower-power person to use exaggerated powerless ones.[32]

In these situations, getting bigger just makes others smaller (and vice versa), which only makes it harder to establish a rapport. Remember, we want power *to*, not power *over*. We want to look confident and relaxed, not as though we're trying our best to dominate. The goal is intimacy, not intimidation. Commanding a room as though you were a silverback leaves little space, physically or emotionally, for anyone else.

To illustrate how public posturing might go wrong, the website Vooza made a satirical video set in a corporate conference room during a meeting. A man enters and begins coaching one of his colleagues to seem more confident and powerful by adopting ridiculous poses such as "the confident gorilla" and "the double mountain man." As these displays become more aggressive and exaggerated, the meeting participants' eye rolling and disgust only deepens, until finally "the angry moose" gets a face full of mace. It's funny because it's familiar: we all know that jerk. We don't want to be him.

And perhaps you've heard of "manspreading." It's an issue in cities where subway cars are painfully crowded. The term describes the habit of some male riders to sit with their legs sprawled inelegantly wide, taking up two or even three seats while other people are forced to stand. And glare. If you ride a New York City subway, you're likely to see posters with slogans that read DUDE . . . STOP THE SPREAD, PLEASE.

We're often tempted to take charge of a situation by using ultraerect postures or extra-firm handshakes. This is particularly common in job interviews. And research shows that the benefits are . . . well, almost nonexistent. For example, in one study, job candidates trying to make a strong impression by using frequent eye contact did not do well in interviews. And the longer and more structured the interview was, and the better trained the interviewer was, the more often nonverbal impression management tactics led to bad outcomes. Remember our discussion of synchrony in chapter 1? This, too, is a factor. Perhaps most important, interviewers viewed candidates making obvious use of body language as inauthentic and manipulative. Suffice it to say, they didn't get hired.[33]

You Might Be Violating Cultural Norms

Body-language norms vary widely among cultures, and understanding these idiosyncrasies can make or break cross-cultural interactions. They differ on many dimensions: How much eye contact? Do you shake hands? How firmly? Who reaches first? Do you bow? How long? Who bows first? Do you sit or stand?

Where do you sit? How do you make a toast? How much space do you leave between you and someone else?

In a study by University of Waterloo organizational behavior professor Wendi Adair, Canadian negotiators used far more relaxed body language and more negative facial expressions than their Chinese counterparts. But the Chinese negotiators took up more space at the table than did the Canadians. These differences affected both concrete negotiation outcomes and the participants' sense of satisfaction with the process.[34]

Adair also studies the ways people of different cultures try to adapt to each other in business settings. She found that when Western negotiators try to use space as their Eastern counterparts do, they might be seen as displaying inappropriate dominance. Cultural misunderstandings about body language can lead people to walk away from potentially lucrative deals.

Cowboy poses might go over well in Texas, but you'd be prudent to avoid using them in Japan. Draping your arm on the shoulder of a new acquaintance in Brazil might be just fine, but you'd likely get a different reaction in Finland. Not taking the time to understand these differences can result in business deals and job offers falling apart, and worse.

All of which brings us back to rugby, the All Blacks, and the haka.

Haka is "about the triumph of life after death," Hohepa Potini, the Ngāti Toa elder, explained.[35] "New Zealand is a small country, and so when we go out and face these countries that are three, four times larger than ourselves, we strive to survive and uphold our own selves — our *mana*, our integrity. [The All Blacks] do it with immense pride. And that's what this haka gives them. . . . It's our cultural heritage. Issuing a challenge. Celebrating in victory."

And the All Blacks players themselves talk about haka with

great reverence, as something they only dreamed of doing. "We are really proud of our heritage, and when we do the haka together, that's a chance for us to look along the line and see our teammates and really connect with the man next to us," said All Blacks player Keven Mealamu. "A lot of kids growing up as young boys in New Zealand always practiced the haka and wished one day they [would] get an opportunity to do it," added teammate Aaron Cruden, who said the haka was about "spiritually gaining strength from the guys beside us, from the ground that we stand on."

But what does the haka have to do with us?

Well, it's clear that thoughts and feelings shape body language and that each person's body language speaks to others. Using a purely physical vocabulary, our inner lives communicate, person to person, back and forth. We're holding entire conversations, exchanging important information, without ever saying a word.

But there's also something else going on, something that doesn't really register in such an obvious way: our body language is also speaking to *us* — to our own inner selves. And it's not simply telling us what we're feeling — it's even more complicated than that. Maybe the power of the haka is not simply its effect on the opposing team members. Maybe the power of the haka also lies in what it does to the All Blacks players themselves. (Portentous drumroll, please.)

7

Surfing, Smiling, and Singing Ourselves to Happiness

I had to decide to stay upright on my surfboard. I didn't know it would help me stay upright in my life, too.
— EVE FAIRBANKS

IF YOU HAPPEN TO marry an Australian, as I did, you are likely to become familiar with the demoralizing process of learning to surf. I've put in some time standing shakily on the board (and toppling off it), but it wasn't until I read journalist Eve Fairbanks on the subject that I realized how deeply connected to presence this process is.

Fairbanks believes that learning to surf taught her something about how to live on dry land.[1] As she wrote in the *Washington Post*, "Surfing distills into a pure physical moment the usually drawn-out, intellectual, complex challenge of simultaneously accepting what life throws at you and making the best of it."

Her analysis of learning to surf, a process that requires us to control our physical postures in order to change our psychology, perfectly captures the body-mind connection — how and why it works and why we, unfortunately, tend to overlook it.

Our first mistake, she said, is to focus too much on the specific skills we think are required to become a good surfer — or to be seen as good at our jobs or attractive to potential partners. Fairbanks wrote, "Amateurs imagine adventure sports are all about skills: We have to acquire strength and muscle memory before we can accomplish a sporting feat." With this mind-set, Fairbanks at first fixated on how she measured up, whether or not she had skill, and where she was on the learning curve — all of which made her insecure. "At first," she said, "when I fell, I felt a desperate desire for my teacher to tell me my mistakes were normal, that I didn't measure up poorly against the others he'd taught. It was so similar to my yearning, often, to be reassured that my mistakes don't reflect badly on my character."

But at a certain point she changed her approach. "After a mixed record of successes and failures, my teacher told me that at some point I just had to 'decide to stay on the board,'" she recalled. "It was astonishing to experience how great a difference simply making that decision and being tenacious about it made. Where I'd been falling most of the time, I began to catch every wave. Pleasure built upon pleasure, the certainty of my ability amplifying with each new trial."

Her experience suggests that we might have the "recipe for success" backwards. "Advisers often tell us we have to be confident about our decisions. That decisions come at the end of a certainty-acquisition process and simply ratify an inner truth. But in fact, it goes the other way: Decisions create confidence. That's what I learned on my surfboard."

The lesson stuck, and she soon found that it applied off the board as well. "Faced with on-land choices — the kind of choices I sometimes balk at — I felt my body on the board, choosing and succeeding to stay upright. It made it much easier to believe I could stay on the figurative board of a plan."

By staying on that board, Fairbanks's body showed her what she was capable of in a way that thinking never could. "The problem," she said, "is that what lies inside our minds is invisible. We can only imagine it. But we experience our bodies sensually. It's so powerful to get a sense of our character as our bodies express it, as all of our senses perceive it."

A sense of our character as our bodies express it . . .

"I'm Happy Because I Sing"

I am endlessly puzzled by the myth that the body, brain, and mind are separate and autonomous entities — and by the notion that seeing them as connected is a "fringe" idea. Is the brain not located *inside* the body? And if that isn't evidence enough, the body moves, speaks, responds, breathes, *lives* because of the brain. The body and brain are part of a single integrated, complicated, beautiful system. As Oakley Ray, revered former psychologist at Vanderbilt University, said, "There is no real division between mind and body because of networks of communication that exist between the brain and neurological, endocrine and immune systems."[2]

And can one have a mind without a brain? That the body, brain, and mind are connected should be among the least controversial ideas in all of science. Yet statements about this connection often elicit skeptical reactions. When I made a comment about the body-mind connection, a stranger snarkily replied, "Have you been smoking a pack of Chopras?" (Referring, of course, to the teachings of mindfulness guru Deepak Chopra.)

The Harvard University Department of Psychology resides in William James Hall. Its namesake, William James (1842–1910), must have been quite a guy. Many great psychologists have populated the halls of Harvard, but James's legacy outshines them all. He was the first educator to offer a college-level psychology course in the United States, he remains one of the most famous American philosophers ever, and he is known as the father of American psychology.

Although countless Jamesian ideas have helped shape what today's psychologists study, the one that struck the deepest nerve with me comes through in his famous assertion "I don't sing because I'm happy; I'm happy because I sing."

This provocative idea asserts that bodily experiences cause emotions, not the other way around. According to James, we experience or perform a physical sensation or action with our bodies, and that causes us to feel a certain way. "A purely disembodied emotion is a nonentity,"[3] he wrote in 1884. James, it should be clear, was not "smoking Chopras"; Deepak Chopra wouldn't be born for another sixty-three years.

Believing that our emotions are interpretations of our bodily, visceral experiences, James theorized that we can fake an emotion until we actualize it — that we can sing ourselves to happiness or cry ourselves to despair. James, a great intellectual — a term that is these days too often confused with "cynic" — was also full of hope, encouraging people to "begin to be now what you will be hereafter."

Perhaps James's theory doesn't strike you as particularly controversial, but keep in mind that humans — typically stuck in our heads — do tend to believe that emotions happen first, before physical sensations, and that what happens in our minds is the *cause* of what our bodies do and feel, not, as James proposed, the *outcome*.[4] He wrote: "Common sense says, we lose our fortune, are sorry and weep; we meet a bear, are frightened and run; we are insulted by a rival, are angry and strike. The hypothesis here to be defended says that this order of sequence is incorrect...

and the more rational statement is that we feel sorry because we cry, angry because we strike, afraid because we tremble."[5]

James even suggested — again, in 1890 — that one way to test his theory would be to examine the emotions of people with no bodily sensations. It took more than a hundred years for a group of researchers, led by Hugo Critchley, to follow his advice and measure the emotional experiences of patients with pure autonomic failure (PAF), which leads to degeneration of the feedback mechanics of the sympathetic and parasympathetic nervous systems — meaning that people with PAF have significantly decreased bodily sensations.

Compared to the rest of us, the study found, people with PAF reported muted emotional experiences, less fear-related neural activity, and were less adept at understanding how other people's feelings were affected by a situation. In other words, an impaired connection with the body leads to a muffled connection with one's own emotions — and a somewhat diminished ability to read the emotional responses of other people.[6]

About Face

If you were going to conduct an experiment to directly test James's hypothesis that bodily expressions cause emotions, where would you begin? The face seems like a good place to start, but which facial expression? Which emotion? To create a proper test of how the body influences the mind, you'd have to get someone to make a facial expression without associating it with the emotion it connotes. A tricky thing to manage.

In 1974, the psychologist James Laird published the results of a study in which he'd set out to measure whether physically expressive behavior can create emotional experience — or, in English, whether frowning makes us angry and smiling makes us glad.[7]

Laird knew that telling his subjects the purpose of the experiment might bias their answers, so he constructed a clever ruse to throw them off. First he told the participants (undergraduate men) that the experiment's aim was only to study "the activity of facial muscles under various conditions." Then he attached electrodes to various points on their faces and connected them to fancy-looking machinery that in fact did nothing.

In order to arrange an "angry" expression, he would lightly touch the electrodes between their eyebrows and say, "Now I'd like you to contract these muscles." He'd also touch the electrodes at the corners of the jaw and ask the subjects to contract those, perhaps by clenching their teeth. For a "happy" expression, he asked subjects to contract the muscles at the corners of the mouth.

As subjects held these poses, they were asked to rate their emotions. Laird told them he needed these ratings in order to rule out any error, because sometimes emotions can create unwanted changes in facial muscle activity. Another falsehood to throw them off.

Even after excluding all the subjects who suspected what was up, Laird found that subjects felt angry when holding an angry expression and happy when holding a happy one. One participant even told him: "When my jaw was clenched and my brows down, I tried not to be angry, but it just fit the position. I'm not in an angry mood, but I found my thoughts wandering to things that made me angry, which is sort of silly, I guess. I knew I was in an experiment and knew I had no reason to feel that way, but I just lost control."

In a famous 1988 paper, Fritz Strack, Leonard Martin, and Sabine Stepper went even further, describing the results of a study that tested what had by then come to be known as the facial feed-back hypothesis.[8] Without explaining why, they instructed participants to hold a pen in their mouths in a way that engaged the muscles typically associated with smiling. Other randomly selected participants were told to hold a pen in their mouths in a way that inhibited the smile muscles. All participants were then given cartoons to read. People in the smile condition found the cartoons much funnier than the people who were unable to smile. That finding has been replicated in Japan and Ghana[9] and extended through the use of different methods and the analysis of different outcomes. For example, in other experiments, people whose muscles were made to smile showed less racial bias.[10]

As researchers discovered in the decades that followed, facial feedback is not limited to smiling and good moods: it also drives negative emotions. In a study led by a team in Japan, when experimenters dripped water onto subjects' cheeks near the tear ducts, these subjects felt much sadder than those who had been randomly assigned to the no-crying condition.[11] In other studies, researchers forced participants to furrow their brows — either by applying stretched adhesive bandages to their faces or by simply asking them to "push their eyebrows together" — inducing increases in self-reported feelings of sadness, anger, and disgust.[12]

In the same way that enacting certain expressions prompts corresponding emotions, *hindering* those expressions can *block* emotions, a finding that has been put to work in the treatment of depression by using, of all things, Botox. When we frown, certain muscles in the forehead — what Darwin called our grief muscles — are activated. Botox (botulinum toxin A) temporarily paralyzes these muscles, thereby reducing wrinkles in the forehead and between the eyebrows. This temporary paralysis also decreases the feedback from the injected muscles to the brain.

Initial evidence that Botox injections might affect emotions came from a 2009 study that compared depression scores of women who'd had forehead injections of Botox to those of women who'd had other cosmetic treatments, all in the previous seven days to three months.[13] The botulinum toxin A recipients scored much lower than the other group on a measure of irritability, depression, and anxiety. (Scores from before the treatments weren't available.) This despite no significant difference between the two groups in their self-rated attractiveness. The finding is compelling but a bit difficult to interpret, given that the researchers had not randomly assigned the women to a treatment condition and that they hadn't collected a pretreatment assessment of the women's feelings of irritability, depression, and anxiety.

Another group of researchers conducted a randomized controlled trial in men and women with treatment-resistant depression.[14] Half the subjects were injected in the forehead with Botox and half with a placebo. Six weeks later, the Botox subjects scored around 50 percent lower on a measure of depression than they had at the outset. The control subjects' scores dropped only around 10 percent.

Does this mean that Botox cures depression? Before you run out to banish those blues along with your wrinkles, consider another study, conducted by social psychologists David Neal and Tanya Chartrand.[15] They compared female subjects who had received Botox for forehead wrinkles and crow's feet to women who'd gotten dermal filler injections, which don't disrupt communication between the muscles and the brain. Between one and two weeks after the procedure, Neal and Chartrand had the subjects complete a computer task in which they viewed, one at a time, thirty-six black-and-white photographs of people's eyes and the immediate surrounding area of their faces (roughly the area that would be covered by an eye mask when you sleep). What made these photographs noteworthy was that each one expressed a subtly different emotion (e.g., the subjects appeared irritated, full of desire, flustered, pensive, and so on). The women's task was to identify the correct emotion for each picture by selecting from a list of four possible answers. Women who'd gotten Botox had a harder time: on average, they were around 7 percent less accurate than the other women at reading the subtle emotional cues hidden in people's eyes.

Why does this disconnect occur? It happens because one of the primary ways we decode others' emotions is by automatically mimicking their facial expressions. In everyday life, this mimicry is so subtle and quick (it takes about one-third of a second[16]) that we don't even know it's happening. Nonetheless, through the magic of facial feedback, this mimicry allows us to feel and understand other people's emotions. But botulinum toxin A, by disabling our facial muscles, thwarts this process. David Neal explained, "Mimicry gives us a window into other people's inner world. By disrupting mimicry, Botox makes that window just a little darker."[17]

And that's not the only reason to embrace your wrinkles. Keep in mind that Botox sometimes targets muscles and wrinkles that relate to both negative *and* positive emotional expressions — not just frowning but smiling, too, which involves the contraction of the same muscles around the eyes that cause crow's feet. It's hard to feel bad when you can't frown. But it's also hard to feel happy when you can't smile.

In short, by paralyzing or relaxing the muscles that allow us to express real emotions, we are dimming both our own emotional experiences and our ability to recognize those of other people. We become just like those PAF patients — less able to connect. Neal said, "It's somewhat ironic — people use Botox to function better in social situations. You may look better but you could suffer because you can't read other people's emotions as well."[18] There's a lesson here: be kind to your crow's feet, and they will be kind to you — and they will make it easier for you to be kind to others.

In the time since William James proposed his controversial body-mind theory of emotions, we've amassed a mountain of experimental research testing it. In a recent review of that literature, psychologists James Laird, who conducted the original facial feedback experiment, and Katherine Lacasse concluded: "In literally hundreds of experiments, when facial expressions, expressive behaviors, or visceral responses are induced, the corresponding feelings occur. In each of the types of behavioral manipulation, a variety of feelings have been induced or strengthened.... Preventing expressions has reduced many of these same feelings.... Overall, the reasonable conclusion, we believe, is that James was in fact correct: Feelings are the consequences... of emotional behavior and bodily response."[19]

So far we've been talking about the impact of small changes to the muscles that control our faces. But what if we move down to the muscles and bones that direct our below-the-neck expressions? Our shoulders, arms, hands, torsos, legs, and feet? They express, too. Is there such a thing as bodily feedback? Can our bodies teach us to feel powerful, confident, calm, and synchronized? Can they lead us to presence?

Presence Through the Body

He walked along the River Lee, his hands clasped behind his back. A new walk for him. Large and public. The attitude of a thinking man. He enjoyed the pose, found it conducive to the idea of himself.

— Colum McCann, *TransAtlantic*, describing
Frederick Douglass

The "idea of oneself" is an intriguing concept. The self can, presumably, be anything you want it to be. It can even be new, but that doesn't make it insincere or inauthentic. It suggests that you can think of yourself in a certain way and then take steps to bring that self into existence. In the example above, from a 2013 novel by Colum McCann, it means steps in the literal sense: Frederick Douglass, the nineteenth-century African American civil rights activist, walked a new walk, struck a fresh pose, and enjoyed it — he found it conducive to the idea of the person he thought himself to be.

Our bodies, McCann suggests, don't just carry us where we want to go: they can help carry us to who we want to be. And, as we're about to discover, the evidence seems to agree: where our bodies lead, our minds and emotions will follow.

To understand this phenomenon, it will help to look at what happens when the body betrays us, locking us into a defensive, fearful, hypervigilant state rather than leading us to greater personal power. I'm talking about post-traumatic stress.

Imagine all the components of powerlessness — anxiety, stress, fear, threat, self-doubt, negative mood, defensiveness, diminished executive function, memory problems, distracting thoughts, avoidance — and then multiply them. By a lot. That gives you a rough idea of how someone with post-traumatic stress, or PTS,[20] experiences life. Traumatic experiences can rob us blind of personal power.

Trauma, like powerlessness, causes profound disharmony between body and mind. Psychiatrist and longtime PTS expert Bessel van der Kolk observed that trauma "results in a breakdown of attuned physical synchrony." He wrote, "When you enter the waiting room of the PTS clinic, you can immediately tell the patients from the staff by their frozen faces and collapsed but simultaneously agitated bodies."[21] PTS breaks us apart, creating deep psychological fissures and conflicts as we struggle to engage in day-to-day life — to be present with our children, parents, friends, and our colleagues — while vigilantly protecting ourselves from perceived threats and trying to ward off the memories that haunt us. We are divided.

Traditional psychotherapy treatments for PTS assume that trauma lives in the mind, and they target it there. Cognitive behavioral therapy (CBT), based on the idea that thought guides behavior, seeks to rewire the PTS sufferer's thought patterns. Exposure therapy seeks to desensitize the sufferer to the trauma that haunts her by forcing her to recall it, reengage with it, and reexperience it.

But some, like van der Kolk, have questioned these approaches. "Trauma has nothing whatsoever to do with cognition," he told the *New York Times*. "It has to do with your body being reset to interpret the world as a dangerous place."[22] The idea that trauma lives in the body — and must therefore be sought and healed there — resonates intuitively. As Jeneen Interlandi wrote in the *Times:*

> In so many cases, it was patients' bodies that had been grossly violated, and it was their bodies that had failed them — legs had not run quickly enough, arms had not pushed powerfully enough, voices had not screamed loudly enough to evade disaster. And it was their bodies that now crumpled under the slightest of stresses — that dove for cover with every car alarm or saw every stranger as an assailant in waiting. How could their minds possibly

be healed if they found the bodies that encased those minds so intolerable?

Or, as the artist Frank Gelett Burgess put it, "Our bodies are apt to be our autobiographies."

Many people suffering from PTS, along with their families and friends, have asked me if body-mind interventions are being used to alleviate symptoms of this stubborn disorder. At least two-thirds of the e-mails I've received on this subject have come from military veterans or their families. The question has plagued me: If trauma is ultimately about extreme powerlessness and characterized by body-mind disconnects, can certain physical interventions help reduce feelings of threat while restoring a sense of pride? Perhaps the body could lead the mind out of states of post-traumatic stress.

As it turns out, a number of scientists have developed a strong body of research on this topic.

Much PTS research has focused on veterans. Experts conservatively estimate that one in five veterans suffers from PTS, and that number grows significantly among those who have experienced combat. PTS in veterans has proved particularly hard to treat with medication and traditional psychotherapeutic approaches, such as CBT and exposure therapy. In addition, dropout rates for PTS treatment programs are staggeringly high, especially among veterans, for a number of reasons, including concerns about stigma, competing life demands, and the understandable fear of revisiting the traumatic experience that caused the PTS in the first place. Meanwhile, the disorder is shattering the lives of countless veterans and their families.

In 2012, Stanford University scholar Emma Seppälä set out to investigate the effectiveness of body-mind treatments to help veterans with PTS.[23] Twenty-one American veterans from the wars in Iraq and Afghanistan participated in her study. Eleven of them were randomly assigned to a yoga treatment group; the other ten were placed on a waiting list. Every day for seven days, the eleven veterans in the treatment group were instructed for three hours in sudarshan kriya yoga, a breathing-based technique that other studies have found to be effective in reducing anxiety, depression, impulsive behavior, and even tobacco use while increasing optimism, well-being, and emotion regulation.[24]

Before going on, I have to come clean. I'm not a yoga person. Until I really dug into the scientific literature on it, I was a skeptic. It wasn't that I thought yoga was *bad* for people; it's that I just couldn't get on board with the idea that it was as *good* as its practitioners claimed. Sort of like a teenager, I tend to react against any trends that seem suddenly to be everywhere. In addition to all that, practically every day someone would ask me, given my background in ballet and my research interests, "You must do a lot of yoga, right?" Which made me resist it even more.

But I am a scientist, and so now I have to eat my resistance, because the evidence that yoga yields positive psychological and physiological results is nearly impossible to refute. Since yoga-based interventions have moved into the medical mainstream, there have been hundreds — maybe thousands — of empirical studies describing its many health benefits, from reducing blood pressure and cholesterol to easing chronic physical, emotional, and social pain.[25] Is every result valid? Was every study well done? Probably not; that's the nature of the scientific beast. But I no longer see yoga as an overhyped trend. When done properly, it can be extraordinarily effective.

Now, to try to explain, in just a few pages, every aspect of how yoga affects the body and the mind would be absurd. We're talking about an ancient practice, three thousand or so years old, that simultaneously engages physical movement, breath control, and meditative mindfulness, all interacting and flowing together. If you want to learn more about the potential health benefits of yoga, I recommend *Yoga for Pain Relief* by Stanford psychologist Kelly McGonigal. Here we're making what amounts to a short foray into yoga, going just far enough to examine how and why it might reduce anxiety and fear in PTS sufferers — and in the rest of us, too — while increasing strength and confidence.

I wanted to know more about Emma Seppälä's work with veterans, so I asked if she'd be willing to talk with me about her research. She enthusiastically agreed. Seppälä's yoga intervention for veterans, she explained, started with participants just "sitting comfortably — and taking deep breaths," which naturally expands the chest. The group practiced what in yoga is called victory breath, "what we do when we're in a deep state of rest," which — in an elegantly simple example of the body's ability to change the mind — triggers the calming reflex.

"Breath is such a wonderful way to reduce your physiological activation," said Seppälä. "Understanding that you can control your breathing is a first step in understanding how you can control your anxiety — that you have the tools to do it yourself. When your mind is racing, when something unexpected happens in a social situation, when you don't know what to do, you know you can calm yourself by controlling your breathing."

To assess the effectiveness of yoga on veterans in their study, Seppälä and her collaborators at Stanford took before-and-after measures of eyeblink responses to loud noises (i.e., the startle response, generally exaggerated in PTS sufferers), respiration rates (generally higher among people with PTS), and self-reported measures of anxiety (i.e., the frequency of traumatic memories and nightmares). Given the well-documented resistance of PTS to treatment, Seppälä was surprised by the results: a month after completing the intervention, veterans who took part in the week-long yoga program showed reductions on all measures of PTS. And she was stunned when, a full year later, the veterans' symptoms of PTS and anxiety were still dramatically reduced.

Seppälä described the study as "the most rewarding thing I'd ever done in my life." One participant wrote to her, "I remember everything that happened [about the traumatic experience], but it no longer has a hold on me." Another said simply, "Thanks for giving me my life back."

"Some of these people lived bunkered up in their basements and never left," she said. "Now they're going to work, dating, socializing, getting out. I see them smiling again. One of them told me that he'd gone on vacation with his dad and couldn't believe how happy he felt. But the most important thing to him was when his dad said, 'I have my son back.' And now he's gone on to become a spokesperson for the program."

You Already Have the Tools You Need to Become Present

In 1997, while working with the Truth and Reconciliation Commission in South Africa, Bessel van der Kolk attended a meeting of a group for rape survivors in Johannesburg and recognized, even in a setting utterly foreign to him, the universal body language of trauma. "The women sat slumped over — sad and frozen —[as they did in] so many rape therapy groups I had seen in Boston," he recalled in his book *The Body Keeps the Score*. "I felt a familiar sense of helplessness, and, surrounded by collapsed people, I felt myself mentally collapse as well."[26]

What happened after that sounds like an enactment of William James's words: "I don't sing because I am happy; I'm happy because I sing."

> One of the women started to hum, while gently swaying back and forth. Slowly a rhythm emerged; bit by bit other women joined in. Soon the whole group was singing, moving, and getting up to dance. It was an astounding transformation: people coming back to life, faces becoming attuned, vitality returning to bodies. I made a vow to apply what I was seeing there and to study how rhythm, chanting, and movement can help to heal trauma.[27]

Van der Kolk kept his promise, and he has been studying body-mind methods of overcoming PTS for decades, conducting research, treating patients, and offering workshops. His recent studies focus on women whose PTS is caused by domestic abuse, a group that, like veterans, has proved difficult to treat successfully.

In one study, van der Kolk recruited sixty-four women with chronic treatment-resistant PTS for a therapeutic program. Half were randomly assigned to a yoga group, and the rest were placed in a supportive women's health education group, a traditional talk-therapy approach. Each group met for a weekly one-hour class for ten weeks.

The women were evaluated pretreatment, midtreatment, and post-treatment on widely used clinician-administered assessments of PTS. At pretreatment, the groups did not differ from each other. At the midtreatment point, both groups showed a significant improvement, although the results were much better for those in the yoga group: 52 percent of those patients no longer met the criteria for PTS, compared to 21 percent in the other group. However, the post-treatment evaluations revealed that, unlike the patients in the yoga group, the women who received traditional treatment later relapsed, showing the same PTS symptoms they'd had pretreatment. For those in the yoga group, the effects stuck.[28]

The psychological and physiological benefits of yoga certainly aren't limited to people with PTS. And although the benefits of participating in long-term therapeutic programs are obvious, scientists have found that people experience beneficial effects even after a single fifteen-minute chair-based yoga session. In one study, participants held a series of gentle postures (e.g., arms extended above the head followed by a back bend and side bend) for approximately thirty to sixty seconds each; they then repeated the cycle. The participants showed significant decreases in self-reported stress as well as decreased breathing rates and increased heart-rate variability (HRV). Low HRV, which indicates lack of fluctuation in the heart rate in response to breathing, is linked to anxiety and emotional strain; high HRV indicates that breathing and heart rate are in sync. In other words, increased HRV, like a slow breathing rate, is generally good, an indication of basic well-being.[29]

We can probably all agree that what we're doing with our bodies when we do yoga has some seriously positive effects. But the really exciting thing is that those of us who don't plan on doing yoga anytime soon can achieve many similar outcomes, because the body-mind effects that yoga activates are available to all of us in our everyday lives. The tools we need to become present are built into our biology. One of them is an action so basic that we usually forget we're doing it: breathing.

Numerous psychophysiological mechanisms have been implicated in body-based interventions such as yoga, but most interventions end up zeroing in on two of them: the sympathetic nervous system (SNS), which stimulates our stress response, also known as our fight-or-flight response, and the parasympathetic nervous system (PNS), which stimulates our relaxation response, also known as our rest-and-digest response (it sets in, for example, after eating, during sleep, or when we're sexually aroused). These two complementary systems regulate arousal throughout the body. In basic terms, the SNS is the accelerator, and the PNS is the brake.

The key agent of the PNS is the vagus nerve, a cranial nerve that carries sensory information between the brain stem and many of our vital organs, including the heart and lungs. When the vagus nerve is doing its job (i.e., when we have high vagal tone), it signals the heart to slow down and the lungs to breathe more deeply, promoting a state of calm. (Endurance runners, swimmers, and cyclists tend to have high vagal tone.) In situations when your body has an acute stress reaction and the sympathetic nervous system takes over and triggers the fight-or-flight response, the vagus nerve is inhibited.

We don't need our vagus nerves to be on active duty all the time. Some situations that demand alertness and adrenaline — such as a tough mental challenge or a physical threat — naturally reduce vagal tone and elicit a stress response. But often our stress response kicks in unnecessarily, and that can take a negative toll. At rest, high vagal tone is associated with positive physical and mental health, while excessive and sustained vagal withdrawal has been associated with high self-reported levels of stress, anxiety, and depression.[30]

Here's the good news: we actually have some control over our sympathetic and parasympathetic nervous systems. Recall that the vagus nerve carries information between the brain stem and the organs; the traffic goes both ways. As van der Kolk explains, "Some 80 percent of the fibers of the vagus nerve (which connects the brain with many internal organs) are afferent; that is, they run from the body into the brain. This means that we can directly train our arousal system by the way we breathe, chant, and move, a principle that has been utilized since time immemorial in places like China and India."[31]

Take a second right now to focus on your breath: inhale quickly, then slowly exhale. One more time: inhale for two seconds, then draw out your exhale for around five seconds. Notice anything? Slow exhalation triggers your parasympathetic nervous system, decreases your blood pressure, and increases your HRV. Hundreds of studies have measured the effects of relaxation-focused breathing, with similar results. Psychological outcomes include reduced anxiety and depression and improved optimism, emotional control, and pain management. Behavioral outcomes include reduced aggression and impulsive behavior as well as improved addiction management and work and school performance.[32]

That's one of the reasons yoga can change the way you feel — it naturally prompts you to breathe slowly and rhythmically, as do practices such as chanting, tai chi, qigong, and meditation. But you don't need to do any of those; you can reap the benefits of breath control almost anywhere at any time. With a few deep, slow breaths, you've just changed your body and your mind. Considering that it's something we all do countless times a day, without any conscious effort whatsoever, breathing is pretty amazing — in ways we're just starting to understand.

Neuroscientist Pierre Philippot and his colleagues conducted a clever experiment in which they asked a group of subjects to alter their breathing to make themselves feel emotions such as joy, anger, and fear (one emotion at a time), then report exactly how they did it.[33] That sounds pretty weird, right? How do you create an emotion by changing how you breathe? Don't worry about it, the participants were told — just try it.

When they were done, they were asked to describe their breathing methods to a second group of subjects without mentioning anything about how the breathing was supposed to summon forth emotional responses. The second group then was asked to breathe as they were taught, after which they were asked what emotions they were feeling.

Can you guess the outcome? When the second group unknowingly followed the instructions for "joy" breathing, they felt joy. It also worked for anger and for fear.

So just by breathing faster or slower, more deeply or more nasally, or with tremors or sighs, people could change their emotions and their states of mind. The researchers noted that the effects of breathing like another person were at least as strong as those reported in facial-feedback studies.

By the way, if you want to feel a little burst of joy right now, here are the breathing instructions the second group of subjects received: "Breathe and exhale slowly and deeply through the nose; your breathing is very regular and your rib cage relaxed." Feel better?

We can indirectly measure the relaxation response of breathing by looking at physiological markers such as increased HRV and decreased heart rate, blood pressure, and levels of stress hormones such as cortisol. These have all been associated with emotional relaxation. They also tend to improve physical health. Reduced stress hormones, for example, predict a lower risk of heart disease, infection, and cancer.[34]

Posing Our Way to Presence

The verdict is in, and the science resoundingly says, "William James was right." Our bodies speak to us. They tell us how and what to feel and even think. They change what goes on inside our endocrine systems, our autonomic nervous systems, our brains, and our minds without our being conscious of a thing. How you carry yourself — your facial expressions, your postures, your breathing — all clearly affect the way you think, feel, and behave.

Eve Fairbanks, who learned to make decisions in the boardroom by standing up on her surfboard, may not have been thinking of yoga or William James as she did so, but she knew she was on to something. "How many other kinds of actions," she wondered, "might transform our ways of thinking?"[35]

This chapter has been an attempt to answer that question. We've discovered how holding a pen in your teeth makes the world seem funnier, how Botox injections can dull our emotional palettes, how paced breathing can instantly relax us.

What about going bigger, beyond facial expressions and breathing? Can we use our whole bodies — through posture, gesture, and movement (even imaginary movement) — to enhance our personal power in an adaptive way when we need it most? Can we pose our way to presence?

Well, why not?

8

The Body Shapes the Mind
(So Starfish Up!)

*Stand up straight and realize who you are, that you tower
over your circumstances.*

— MAYA ANGELOU

WHEN I WAS A little girl, I lived in a tiny stone house in the middle of a state park in eastern Washington State, perched on a cliff
more than a hundred feet above the mammoth half-mile-wide
Columbia River.[1]

In a town with a population that barely broke three hundred,
there weren't many kids to play with, so I spent a lot of time outside, trying to make friends with all the critters. I spent hours in
the gardens alongside the house, digging around, carefully turning rocks over to find the insects that lived beneath them. I always
had a soft spot for underappreciated creatures, and at the time, my
favorites were the insects that look like tiny armadillos — pill bugs.
I'm not sure where the name came from — maybe because when
you touch them they instantly roll up into a perfect little ball,
smaller than an aspirin. At least that's what I always believed.

When I found one, I'd gingerly pick him up and place him in the open palm of my hand, which I held perfectly still, hoping maybe he'd trust me enough to unfurl. But he rarely did. I felt guilty. I knew the little guy was terrified — giant, powerful me trying to commune with tiny, powerless him. Of course he made himself as small and protected as possible. All I wanted was for him to scurry around in the comfort of my hand, somehow knowing that he could trust me, an impossible thing to communicate no matter how gently I moved.

The next time I really paid attention to body language was after my car accident. Because I wasn't driving when we crashed, being a passenger — something I'd never thought twice about — had become viscerally scary. It's still unnerving today, but in the beginning it was terrifying. I felt utterly powerless to protect my own physical safety. When I sat in the passenger seat, I pulled my knees to my chest, wrapped my arms tightly around them, and burrowed my chin in between. I imagined myself as a little pill bug. It didn't matter if I was in the hands of a trustworthy driver. My body curled into a ball, as tiny as I could make it. And I shut down mentally, unable to engage in conversation, instead vigilant to every conceivable traffic hazard, my mind snaking through the worry gears. Friends and family sometimes felt hurt or annoyed at my behavior — why didn't I trust their driving? But I couldn't help it. It was instinctive. They held all the power; I held none. So I'd better prepare for the worst.

The tighter I held my knees to my chest, the tinier and less perceptible I became. And the faster my heart and mind raced.

But what would have happened if I'd pretended to be brave? If I'd tried to trick myself into feeling comfortable in the passenger seat? If I'd forced my body to oppose all the psychological forces working to collapse it? By not protecting myself, would I have felt a little safer? A little less powerless? A little more present?

Fifteen years later I still hadn't figured it out.

Then the insight came from an unlikely combination of two experiences that, serendipitously, occurred at around the same time.

First, I was worrying about the students I taught who weren't participating in the classroom. The stakes and standards for participation are high for every student at Harvard Business School: participation counts for half a student's final grade, and it isn't just about getting "airtime" — students are expected to contribute astute, thoughtful comments that provoke discussion, a tall order for anyone. And, as I mentioned earlier, some students find class participation terrifying. For many, it's their biggest challenge — the most daunting social-evaluative threat.

These nonparticipators confounded me. They seemed almost aloof in class. If I hadn't been interacting with them outside that room, I'd have assumed they were uninterested, disengaged, maybe even unprepared. But I knew that wasn't the case. I met and talked with these same young people during office hours, and I read their work. Without a doubt, they were as bright as the students who spoke up in class regularly. But I couldn't give them a respectable grade unless they found a way to engage. To be present.

Studying this problem, I began to notice details that hadn't struck me before, and the more I looked, the more I saw. In the moments before class began, while the participators were moving around, gesticulating, gravitating toward the center of the room, the nonparticipators went directly to their assigned seats and hunched over their books or phones.

When the participators raised their hands, they did so with conviction, sticking their arms straight up — not aggressively, but in a way that announced *I believe I have something meaningful to say. I have something to contribute.* If the nonparticipators raised their hands at all, they raised them apologetically — elbows bent and cradled in the opposite hand, arms wavering up and down, clearly ambivalent about calling attention to themselves.

The participators sat upright during class, shoulders back. Nonparticipators knotted themselves up with their own limbs, touching their necks, fidgeting with their hair, clothing, or jewelry, crossing their legs and wrapping their ankles (a position I call twisty legs). Their bodies communicated a wish to shrink, to hide in a magical invisibility cloak. During class they didn't move much or turn their heads to make eye contact with other students, even when responding to someone else's comment. *They looked ashamed.*

Reading these students' writings told me they were curious, passionate, and fully engaged in their intellectual lives. Reading their body language told a different story about their emotional lives: in the classroom, they felt powerless to believe their own thoughts. They couldn't bring themselves to trust that their classmates would treat them with respect. When they spoke they felt they were lying, in a way: they didn't believe their own stories.

They were there in the room, but they were also absent.

The second thing that happened was wholly unrelated. The chair of my department, an economist named Brian Hall, had become interested in the writings of Joe Navarro (the former FBI agent and body-language expert I told you about earlier). Brian invited Joe to spend a day at Harvard to brainstorm about ways in which his work might be applied in the MBA classroom, and Brian asked me to join the conversation and give a short presentation — which I did, along with social psychologist Dana Carney, then a professor at Columbia Business School.

Joe's an unusual practitioner. He understands that he's in the best position to advise and teach when he can pair his vast professional experience with the scientific evidence that supports it. He cares deeply about keeping up with the latest research. I was coming from the opposite corner, eager for real-life examples to inform my studies.

But Joe made me nervous. His own body language signaled dominance, and I was worried about how he'd read mine. I was only in the beginning of my second year as a junior faculty member, and there I was presenting to a former FBI agent, the chair of my department, my collaborator the nonverbal behavior expert Dana Carney, whom I dearly respected, and another esteemed senior colleague, Andy Wasynczuk, who, before coming to HBS, had been the chief operating officer of the New England Patriots (yes, the NFL team).

I desperately wanted to make a good impression and present well in this situation. Instead I was hung up worrying about what other people thought of me and trying to adapt to what I believed they expected. Being caught in my nervousness by an expert on body language was my worst nightmare, and, ironically, as a result of that fixation, I was struggling to be present. Sure enough, because we were discussing body language, Joe pointed out a few things I was doing during my talk to signal powerlessness and insecurity. I was touching my neck, playing with my hair, wrapping my arms around my torso — rookie mistakes very similar to the things I was observing in my classroom. Under stress, I was acting like a nonparticipator, even though what I wanted most in the world was to participate fully in the work under discussion.

Joe told us a story about a memorable interrogation. The suspect, as Joe explained it, was exhibiting dominant body language.

Joe interpreted the man's peacocking not as a message to the interrogator, however, but as a signal to himself — a way to puff up his nerve in a tough situation. I asked Joe if anyone had scientifically tested the hypothesis that one can make oneself feel more powerful by "faking" dominant body language. His response: "Not yet, but you're going to do it."

That's when it all came together. Fear was limiting me, and it was limiting my students, but maybe it didn't have to. We were going to do this research, damn it — we were going to study how the body talks to the mind.

This science isn't just about how people perceive us through our body language, and the story isn't only about whether or not college students speak up in class. The way we carry ourselves from moment to moment blazes the trail our lives take. When we embody shame and powerlessness, we submit to the status quo, whatever that may be. We acquiesce to emotions, actions, and outcomes that we resent. We don't share who we really are. And all this has real-life consequences.

The way you carry yourself is a source of personal power — the kind of power that is the key to presence. It's the key that allows you to unlock yourself — your abilities, your creativity, your courage, and even your generosity. It doesn't give you skills or talents you don't have; it helps you to share the ones you do have. It doesn't make you smarter or better informed; it makes you more resilient and open. It doesn't change who you are; it allows you to *be* who you are.

Expanding your body expands your mind, which allows you to be present. And the results of that presence can be far-reaching.

Taking control of your body language is not just about posing in a powerful way. It's also about the fact that we pose in a powerless way much more often than we think — and we need to change that.

Our Experiments in Power Posing

As scientists, the first thing we needed was a clear hypothesis.

This was our thinking: if nonverbal expressions of power are so hardwired that we instinctively throw our arms up in a V when we win a race — regardless of cultural background, gender, or whether we've seen anyone else do it — and if William James was right that our emotions are as much a result as they are a cause of our physical expressions, then what would happen if we adopt expansive postures even when we are feeling powerless? Since we naturally expand our bodies when we feel powerful, do we also naturally feel powerful when we expand our bodies?

If our experiment demonstrated that the answer is yes, it could provide the tool I'd been searching for to help students (and others) become present when they most needed to be, the tool that would help them bring their boldest selves to their biggest challenges.

Eager to test our hypothesis that expansive postures can cause people to feel more powerful, we decided to begin by looking at two key factors: feelings of power and confidence and willingness to take risks.

But before my collaborators Dana Carney and Andy Yap and I could begin our first experiment, we had to take care of some critical groundwork — identifying and testing appropriate poses. From a thorough review of the body-language literature, we selected five high-power poses (see figures 1–5) and five low-power poses (see figures 6–10). The high-power poses were both expansive (meaning that the body took up a significant amount of space) and open (meaning that the limbs were held far away from the body), and the low-power poses were constricted and clenched, as I was when riding in a car after my accident.

Powerful Poses

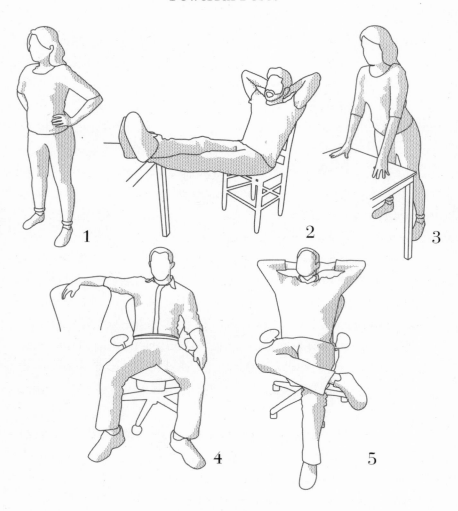

1

2

3

4

5

Powerless Poses

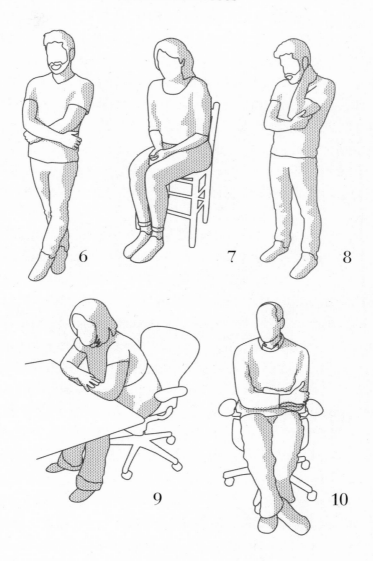

6

7

8

9

10

To be 100 percent certain that "regular" people (i.e., non-psychologists) would associate these positions with power, we conducted a preliminary study in which we asked participants to rate each of the poses from 1 (very low power) to 7 (very high power). As we'd hoped, they rated the expansive, open postures as whoppingly higher on the power scale (an average of 5.4) than the contractive, closed postures (an average of 2.4). We also needed to be sure that the poses didn't differ in degree of comfort, since holding your body in an uncomfortable way could definitely dampen your mood. So we recruited another group of subjects and had them hold the positions and then rate them for comfort, pain, and difficulty. The poses were rated the same on all counts.

With the preliminary work done, we launched our initial experiment, keeping it as simple as possible.[2] First we recruited a group of subjects. None of them was told anything about the purpose of the study. After arriving at the lab, each of them was taken to a small room containing a table, chair, and computer. Before the experimenter left, he explained that the computer screen would display photos of people in five different postures, and he instructed the subjects to view and mimic each posture for as long as it appeared on the screen — sixty seconds. Subjects did not know that they had been randomly assigned to view and mimic *either* high-power poses or low-power poses, the critical manipulation.

Each subject was paid the standard fee for taking part in research, but then, after the posing was finished, the experimenter gave participants a bonus of two additional dollars and explained that they could either keep the little windfall of extra money or risk it, double or nothing. They could roll a die and either win four dollars or lose the two dollars. (The odds were one in six, but no matter what happened they were reassured that they would be paid the full fee they were promised for their participation.)

Could standing in an expansive posture for a few minutes actually influence people's behavior in this situation? At this point, you should not be surprised to learn that it did: power posers were significantly more likely to roll the die. One-third of them, 33 percent, took the risk, compared with just 8 percent of the subjects who held powerless poses.

Finally, subjects were asked to rate how "powerful" and "in charge" they felt on a simple four-point scale. High-power posers felt significantly more powerful and in charge than did the low-power posers.

These results from our first experiment strongly suggested that the body shapes the mind. The nature of the poses influenced how powerful or powerless people felt and how willing they were to take risks.

But it occurred to us that the effect might have been caused by merely seeing the power poses on the computer screen. Perhaps just looking at a powerful posture — rather than mimicking it — primed the concept of power, making our subjects behave the way they did. That would have indicated a mind-mind effect, which wasn't what our research was after. We wanted to isolate and measure how the body influenced the mind.

So out of caution, we changed several details of the experiment. The second time we conducted it, the subjects didn't view pictures. Instead the experimenter verbally described the poses, then made sure the subjects correctly adopted each one for a full minute. We decreased the number of poses from five to two, resulting in a total posing time of only two minutes. We carefully concealed any possible references to power by employing a cover story: we hooked up subjects to three sham electrocardiography (ECG) leads and told them that the study was about how the positioning of the electrodes could affect heart rate. And because the chance of winning the die roll in the preliminary experiment was low, just one in six, in this second experiment we changed the odds to fifty-fifty, making the "risk" more rational.

A final, important change: this time we didn't measure only the subjects' self-reported feelings and willingness to take risks; we also measured hormonal changes. Recall from chapter 5 that testosterone (the assertiveness hormone) and cortisol (the stress hormone) fluctuate in response to changes in an individual's feelings of power and status. As power increases, testosterone rises and cortisol drops. This hormone profile is associated with high assertiveness and low anxiety, the ideal combination for facilitating presence in challenging moments.

If the power poses were truly causing subjects to feel more powerful — if they were actually altering people's internal physiological preparedness so that they would *be* more (or less) powerful — then those postures could also cause a measurable change in hormone levels. It was time to find out if they would. We hypothesized that adopting expansive postures would cause testosterone to rise and cortisol to fall, whereas adopting contractive postures would cause testosterone to fall and cortisol to rise.

A small study published in 2004 in the journal *Human Physiology* provided evidence that directly supported our predictions. The authors measured the physical effects of holding a very expansive hatha yoga pose known as the cobra for approximately three minutes.[3] You can try it: lie flat on the floor on your stomach, legs straight behind you, feet pointed, hands on the floor, and palms down right under your shoulders so that your elbows are bent and tight against your torso. Then straighten your arms so that your upper body — shoulders, chest, and belly — is arching up off the floor, and raise your head, gaze slightly lifted, the way a cobra rears back. (You can go online and find images to guide you.) This is a slight back bend, and it's not the most comfortable pose if you're not used to doing it.

The researchers were interested in one thing: the effect of the cobra on circulating hormone levels, including the ones that interested us — testosterone and cortisol.[4] So they collected blood samples immediately before the participants went into the pose and again a short time after they'd stopped holding it.

Here's what they found: every participant in the study showed an increase in blood serum levels of testosterone and a decrease in blood serum levels of cortisol. On average, testosterone rose by 16 percent and cortisol dropped by 11 percent, changes that were statistically significant for both hormones.

These intriguing findings showed that holding a single expansive pose can make significant, measurable differences in the hormones related to confidence and anxiety.[5] But could power posing — adopting simple non-yoga-based power poses — yield the same results as yoga, whose health benefits, as we've seen, have been well established? And could "powerless posing" do the opposite?

To measure hormone changes in our experiment, my colleagues and I collected saliva samples from subjects before and then fifteen to twenty minutes after the power pose manipulation.[6]

What did we find? In our sample of women and men, the high-power posers showed a 19 percent increase in testosterone and a 25 percent decrease in cortisol. Low-power posers showed the opposite pattern — a 10 percent decrease in testosterone and a 17 percent increase in cortisol, the exact pattern we'd predicted.

In addition, as in the first experiment, the degree to which posing affected the subjects' stated feelings of power or powerlessness was startlingly similar. The same was true for risk tolerance, and when the odds of winning improved to fifty-fifty, although every-one's willingness to risk two dollars naturally rose, the *difference* between the high-power and low-power posers remained virtually identical: 86 percent of high-power posers versus 60 percent of low-power posers (a difference of 26 percentage points). Compare this to the 33 percent versus 8 percent of participants (a difference of 25 percentage points) who were willing to take the risk when the odds were only one in six. In other words, the odds of taking the risk rose for everyone in correspondence with the odds of win-ning, but the absolute difference between high-power and low-power posers remained the same.

Our first studies provided strong evidence that adopting expansive, open postures — bodily displays of power — caused not just psychological and behavioral changes but also alterations in our subjects' physiological states. All of which perfectly paralleled the known effects of power.

We weren't the first psychologists to explore the effects of adopt-ing open versus closed posture. Although he had not linked pos-ture to power or presence, the psychologist John Riskind showed, in a series of experiments done in the 1980s, that holding an upright position rather than a slumped one can yield many bene-fits. Our feelings of confidence and self-control are enhanced while our feelings of stress diminish, we become more persistent problem solvers, and it even helps us react more constructively to performance feedback.[7] In the early 1990s, Sabine Stepper and Fritz Strack (the smiling-with-a-pen-in-your-mouth researchers) found that learning we'd succeeded on a task led to greater feel-ings of pride when we received the news while sitting in an upright posture versus a slumped posture.[8]

And in the time since our first experiments with power posing were published in 2010, there has been a substantial amount of inquiry into this and closely related body-mind phenomena, which together illuminate the many benefits of adopting expansive, bold poses and upright, "good" posture.

The Riskind work, as does much of the research conducted since then, uncovers something astonishing. It's not only bold power poses that have an effect: even very subtle types of expansion — such as simple, good, "sit-up-straight" posture — can also do the same sorts of things. Taking it even further, we'll see that expansive movement — and even vocal expansiveness, such as speaking slowly — can affect the way we think, feel, and behave.

Carrying yourself in a powerful way directs your feelings, thoughts, behaviors, and body to feel powerful and be present (and even perform better) in situations ranging from the mundane to the most challenging.

Let me explain.

Feeling

The results of the experiments my colleagues and I conducted to study the effect of power posing on hormones are sticky, as we say in psychology[9] — they fascinate people. *I* find them fascinating. But they are only one part of a much bigger picture. Perhaps the most important and robust finding is that, as we showed in our experiments, by adopting expansive, open postures, we make ourselves *feel* better and more effective in several ways. We feel more powerful, confident, and assertive, less stressed and anxious, and happier and more optimistic.

In our studies, my colleagues and I have often asked people to report their feelings after power posing by means of a variety of personal-power-related questions. Other researchers have used similar measures, and the effects on conscious feelings of power have been demonstrated many times.[10]

But the benefits of power posing are also apparent at a less conscious level. For example, psychologist Li Huang and her team compared the effects of power poses to the effects of traditional power manipulations — the kinds described in chapter 5 — such as role assignments (manager versus subordinate).[11] Each subject was assigned to a high-power or low-power posture condition and then to a high-power or low-power role condition. To surreptitiously change subjects' posture, Huang told them she was doing a marketing study on ergonomic chairs. In the expansive (i.e., high-power) posture condition (again, randomly assigned), subjects placed one arm on the armrest and draped the other on the back of a nearby chair. Huang also told them to cross their legs so the ankle of one rested on the thigh of the other, causing the knee to fall outward. The resulting posture resembled the one presented in figure 5 in our experiments. In the contractive (i.e., low-power) posture condition, participants sat on their hands, held their legs together, and drooped their shoulders. This posture resembled our figure 7 posture. Then the researchers assigned people to the role of manager (i.e., high-power) or subordinate (i.e., low-power). Managers were told they would direct, evaluate, and reward the subordinates in a shared puzzle-solving task; subordinates were told they would be directed, evaluated, and rewarded by managers in the task. (Note that the task never happened; simply assigning people to their respective roles is sufficient to manipulate power.)

After they completed their role manipulations, subjects' unconscious sense of power — the extent to which the concept of power became cognitively "activated" or "accessible" — was measured by having them complete a series of word fragments, each of which could be completed as a word related or unrelated to power, such as "l_ad" (the word *lead* is related to power; the word *load* is not). The subjects were told to complete the fragments with "the first word that comes to mind."

Although both adopting a powerful posture and adopting a powerful role increased conscious feelings of power, Huang found that only posture — but not role — affected unconscious feelings of power. Expansive postures caused people to complete more of the fragments as power-related words, thus reflecting the unconscious activation of powerful feelings. As Huang notes, "Our experiments [show] that posture actually has a stronger effect than role power on the behavioral and psychological manifestations of power [and] ... further bolster the notion that power is embodied, or grounded in bodily states. To think and act like a powerful person, people do not need to possess role power or recall being in a powerful role." In short, a simple bodily posture, held for just a couple of minutes, produces bigger feedback effects than being assigned to a powerful role.... That's quite exciting.

Do the effects of power posing hold up across cultural lines? To find out, psychologist Lora Park and her colleagues conducted a cross-cultural study comparing samples of American and East Asian participants. In many East Asian cultures, conspicuously dominant body language is generally frowned upon in public settings, suggesting that power posing might not work for people from those cultures. On the other hand, given the universal association between expansive posture and dominance — around the world and even across the animal kingdom — we should expect power posing (especially when done in private) to work most everywhere.

And indeed, Park found that her American and East Asian subjects felt the confidence-boosting benefits of power posing after adopting the expansive hands-spread-on-the-desk pose that I and my colleagues have used in our own studies and the expansive upright seated pose that Huang used in her studies.

But given cultural differences in the types of nonverbal displays that are considered appropriate, we should also expect some nuances — some poses might work better than others for certain people. Park found that among her East Asian sample, one specific posture — the one in which people prop their feet on their desks and put their hands behind their heads with their arms akimbo — did not make people feel more powerful or action-oriented.

Why not?

It might be because East Asians tend to express their physical expansiveness on a vertical axis whereas Westerners express it on a horizontal axis. East Asians' power postures are reflected, for example, in their decisions about whether to sit or stand, how low to bow, how high to raise a glass during a toast, and so on. Cultural psychologist Seinenu Thein found that in some parts of Myanmar, children are expected to keep their heads below those of their elders. A child in Myanmar remains seated on the floor until his parents have gotten out of bed in the morning. When a monk enters the house and sits in a chair, children and adults are expected to sit on the floor. One's place in the social hierarchy seems to determine one's degree of verticality: low vertical expansion reflects low status.[12]

While Westerners are at ease with horizontally expansive postures, such as putting their feet up on a table or gesturing widely with their arms out to their sides, in East Asian cultures horizontally expansive public displays are often considered socially inappropriate or rude. A simple Google image search for "American CEOs" and "Japanese CEOs" is likely to support this observation.

So Park's finding makes sense: someone from an East Asian cultural background would find the feet-on-the-desk pose, which is almost entirely about horizontal expansion, to be puzzling and uncomfortable. As Park and her coauthors explained, this pose "was perceived by both Americans and East Asians as the least consistent with East Asian cultural norms of modesty, humility, and restraint...the effects of posture depend on both the type of posture and the symbolic meaning of that posture in a culture."

Expansive postures also reduce anxiety and help us deal with stress. John Riskind found in his research that "people in hunched, threatened physical postures verbally expressed greater stress than those in relaxed positions." When people receive negative feedback while holding an expansive posture, the criticism is less likely to undermine their belief that they — not others — control their own destiny.[13] It's less rattling.

Another example comes from researchers at the University of Auckland, who told participants that they were studying how athletic tape affects physiology, mood, and performance.[14] They then applied tape to participants' backs in patterns that helped hold them in either upright or slumped postures. In these positions, the subjects completed a version of the Trier Social Stress Test, a task you've seen used in several of the experiments in this book: they each prepared five-minute talks on why they were the best candidates for their dream jobs and presented them to a panel of unnervingly impassive judges. But in contrast to those in our power posing studies, these subtle poses were held *during* the actual speech task — i.e., while the participants held expansive or contractive postures, such as sitting erect with shoulders back or slouched with shoulders drooping (see figures 11 and 12). Afterward, they rated their mood, self-esteem, and perceived threat — how scared they thought they'd be in various threatening scenarios.

Compared to the slumped participants, the upright participants felt more enthusiastic and strong and less nervous and sluggish. They reported less fear and greater self-esteem.

The content of their speeches differed as well. Upright speakers used fewer negative and more positive words, consistent with some of the other findings we've seen, but they also used fewer first-person pronouns, such as *I* and *me*. They talked less about themselves, reflecting less self-focused worry and more freedom to engage with what was going on in that challenging present moment. In fact, a series of studies by social psychologists Ewa Kacewicz, James Pennebaker, and their colleagues revealed that the more often people say "I," the less powerful and sure of themselves they are likely to be. As Pennebaker explained in a *Wall Street Journal* interview, "There is a misconception that people who are confident, have power, have high-status tend to use 'I' more than people who are low status . . . .That is completely wrong. The high-status person is looking out at the world and the low-status person is looking at himself."[15]

Upright and Slumped Seated Postures

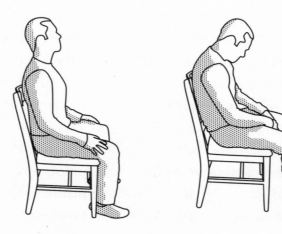

In 2014, psychology professor Johannes Michalak at Witten/Herdecke University, in Germany, conducted a study among thirty clinically depressed inpatients randomly assigned to sit in either a slumped or upright posture.[16] On a computer screen, patients were shown thirty-two words, half of them positive (e.g., *beauty*, *enjoyable*) and half related to depression (e.g., *exhaustion*, *dejected*). Later they completed a memory-recall test of these words. Participants who had been sitting in the slumped pose remembered significantly more depression-related words than positive words. Patients in the upright posture, however, showed no such bias, remembering as many positive words as negative words. Michalak suggests that teaching depressed patients "to change habitual . . . dysfunctional posture or movement patterns . . . might attenuate negatively biased information processing" and that "training depressed patients in mindful body awareness might be useful because it fosters an intuitive understanding of the inter-play of bodily and emotional processes."

Michalak, who had also studied the gait of depressed people — not surprisingly, they exhibited reduced arm swing and head movement and more slumped posture — wondered if that, too, was not only an outcome of mood but also a cause of it. To tackle the question (which is methodologically challenging — after all, how do you get people to walk in a depressed or a happy way?) he teamed up with our collaborator Niko Troje, the biologist who directs the BioMotion Lab at Queen's University in Ontario (see page 154).[17] I'll happily walk you through their study (pun intended).

After the participants arrived at the lab, motion sensors were attached to the most mobile areas of their bodies, such as their joints, feet, and hands. Subjects were then instructed to begin walking on a treadmill, and after six minutes of walking, a monitor in front of each subject displayed a large horizontal scale on which a cursor marked the status of *some quality* of the subject's movement... but the subject wasn't told what that specific quality was. In fact, all she was told was that the study's purpose was to find out if people can adapt their walking styles to real-time feedback, or "biofeedback."

The scale wasn't labeled, but the cursor moved to the right or left as the subject changed how she walked. The experimenter then asked the subject to adapt her walk in a way that made the cursor move as far as possible to either the right or the left without explaining how to do that. What the subject didn't know was that one extreme corresponded with the walking characteristics of happiness (upright and dynamically expansive) and the other corresponded with the walking characteristics of sadness (slumped and dynamically constricted). In addition, because some of us hold biased associations with the concepts of right and left, the sides were counterbalanced so that some people were in a right-happy, left-depressed condition and others were in a right-depressed, left-happy condition.

Within a minute or so, most participants became pretty savvy at moving and holding the cursor all the way to the right or left, as instructed — despite still not knowing what that scale represented. A few minutes later, each subject was asked to read a series of positive and negative words and determine whether each described her, and then she was back to walking for eight more minutes. After all that, she was asked to recall the words — and guess what? If she had been assigned (without knowing it explicitly, of course) to walk in a happy way, she was likely to remember many of the positive words and very few of the negative words, demonstrating an emotional memory bias. The converse, unfortunately, was also true: subjects assigned to walk in a sad way showed a memory bias that favored the negative words, a bias that has been demonstrated many times among people with clinical depression.

Movement, like posture, tells the brain how it feels and even manages what it remembers. As walking becomes more open, upright, and buoyant, our memories about ourselves follow suit.

As I mentioned in chapter 6, when we feel powerful, even our voices spread out and take up more space than they do when we feel powerless. Stanford University psychologists Lucia Guillory and Deborah Gruenfeld refer to this as "a way of claiming social space." We don't rush our words. We're not afraid to pause. We feel deserving of the time we're using. We even make more direct eye contact while we're speaking. Guillory and Gruenfeld suggest that slow speech demonstrates a kind of openness: "When people speak slowly they run the risk of being interrupted by others. In speaking slowly one indicates that he or she has no fear of interruption. People who speak slowly have a higher chance of being heard clearly and understood. They also take up the time of those with whom they're communicating."

The two scientists also predicted that slow speech would have the same kind of body-mind feedback effects as expansive postures, and they conducted studies to test that hypothesis. Subjects read aloud a collection of sentences at various speeds, controlled by the speed at which they were presented in a banner moving across a computer screen, and then answered a series of questions designed to uncover how powerful, confident, and effective they were feeling.[18] For example, participants were asked to rate, on a scale of 1 to 7, their level of agreement with statements such as "I feel like even if I voice them, my views have little sway." Ultimately, participants' speaking rate had an inverse relationship with how powerful they felt. That is, the more slowly they read the sentences, the more powerful, confident, and effective they felt afterward. In a sense, speaking in an unhurried way allows us time to communicate clearly, without runaway social anxieties inhibiting us from presenting our true selves.

Expanding your body language — through posture, movement, and speech — makes you feel more confident and powerful, less anxious and self-absorbed, and generally more positive.

Thinking

Posture not only shapes the way we feel, it also shapes the way we think about ourselves — from our self-descriptions to the certainty and comfort with which we hold them. And those self-concepts can either facilitate or hinder our ability to connect with others, to perform our jobs, and, more simply, to be present.

Jamini Kwon, a graduate student at Seoul National University, became interested in studying the body-mind connection after spending several bedridden months dealing with a rare medication-induced partial paralysis, which happened when she was an undergraduate at Columbia University. She had developed trigeminal neuralgia. The trigeminal nerve communicates sensation from your face to your brain. Damage to it can cause excruciating pain, even in response to the mildest types of stimulation, such as brushing your teeth and applying makeup. "It hurt so much that I could barely drink water," she said. "I lost almost thirty pounds."

She spent a long time in bed. The pain in combination with her abrupt postural change from upright and open to prone and self-protectively closed-off made it hard for her to shut out the creeping, self-destructive thoughts that fed her feelings of hopelessness. "When I stayed in the bed without moving, I felt tired and depressed all the time."

But slowly she reacquired some movement and began to very gingerly stand and do things. She returned to painting, a passion that she'd had to abandon, which forced her out of the contractive posture she'd spent so much time in. "I usually work on huge paintings, so standing up and expanding my arms was necessary when I started painting again," she said.

Moving again not only helped her recover physically, it also aided her psychologically. "For me, this 'cognitive embodiment' gave me a life. I firmly believe that our cognitive processes can be modified through our body." I want to be clear, however, that physical disabilities most certainly do not doom people to a life of depression, hopelessness, and powerlessness. The emotional experience Kwon talks about was unfolding shortly after the onset of the symptoms, which is quite common, and the tremendous ambiguity around her diagnosis and prognosis likely exacerbated those feelings. People with physical disabilities find many ways to adapt and thrive, something I'll return to later in the chapter.

Integrating what she had learned in her courses with her personal experience, she became particularly interested in how posture might affect how we think about ourselves and our abilities and how those thoughts might hinder or facilitate creativity. So she conducted experiments on the effects of the powerless positions she had become so accustomed to occupying, comparing them not to powerful poses but to neutral poses. In her studies, powerless postures significantly undermined people's persistence and creativity when trying to solve complex problems, and these effects were driven by an increase in self-deprecating thoughts, such as "I am useless" and "I lose confidence easily."[19]

In other words, temporarily holding powerless poses increased the negative thoughts people had about themselves, which squashed their drive to face challenges and dulled their creativity. People in neutral poses were not ruminating about all their bad qualities; they were thinking about the tasks at hand. They were in the moment, not trapped in their heads or in an imaginary future ruined by the consequences of their imminent failure.

Other researchers have shown similar effects of posture on our self-image. Erik Peper, a professor of holistic health at San Francisco State University, has been studying the relationship between the body and the mind for more than thirty years. In a study he conducted with sports psychologist Vietta Wilson, subjects adopted two poses — one slumped and one upright — for a minute each while recalling positive memories or events from their own pasts. The vast majority of the subjects — 92 percent — found it easier to recall happy, optimistic thoughts while sitting in the upright posture.[20]

Riskind referred to this "congruence": it's easier to retrieve positive memories when we are in positive postures than it is when we are in negative postures, as Michalak demonstrated in the walking experiment. Positive memories and positive postures fit together. They are — to bring back a word I used in the first chapter — synchronous. And when it's easier to retrieve positive memories about ourselves, it's easier to generalize those self-beliefs to the present and the future. We feel optimistic about ourselves.

Pablo Briñol, a psychology professor at the Autonomous University of Madrid, along with a team of researchers, performed a similar study.[21] They assigned their subjects to either sit up straight and push out their chests or sit slouched forward with their faces looking at their knees. (Try it!) As they held these postures for a few minutes, they were asked to describe themselves with either three positive traits or three negative traits that would be likely to either help or hurt them in their future professional lives. At the end of the study, after they were told they could relax and resume their normal postures, they completed a questionnaire in which they rated their potential to perform well in future jobs.

The researchers found that the way the students rated themselves depended on their postures when they described their traits. Not only did those in the upright position find it easier to think positive, empowering thoughts about themselves, they also believed more strongly in the traits they listed. The slouchers, on the other hand, weren't convinced of their positive or negative traits; they struggled even to know who they were.

As noted in chapter 5, powerful people also find it easier to think abstractly — to extract the gist of a message, to integrate information, and to see patterns and relationships among ideas. The same is true for people who've spent a couple minutes in a power pose. Li Huang, who conducted the pose-versus-role studies, also measured effects on thought abstraction, using a perceptual task that requires people to combine elements from fragmented, ambiguous pictures of items and ultimately form a whole picture that integrates the various pieces. Again, power poses outperformed not only powerless poses and powerless roles but also powerful roles: the power posers showed the greatest agility in abstract thinking.

The concept of abstract thinking is in itself abstract, and the benefits of being a good abstract thinker may not be clear. But let me put this into a social-evaluative context: in a stressful negotiation, you are required to listen to and integrate multiple ideas and opinions, some of which you've never heard before, and to effectively respond to them. Taking in various divergent chunks of information, extracting their essence, and integrating them in a way that makes sense — quickly — is absolutely a fundamental element of presence under pressure, from the classroom to the boardroom and everywhere in between.

Expanding your body causes you to think about yourself in a positive light and to trust in that self-concept. It also clears your head, making space for creativity, cognitive persistence, and abstract thinking.

Acting

Power posing activates the behavioral approach system (see page 111) — the system that makes us more likely to assert ourselves, approach and seize opportunities, take risks, and persist. And that approach orientation goes beyond rolling a die in a lab.

In a study of the effects of body language on leadership ability conducted by psychologists at Coastal Carolina University, people were assigned to sit in an open, upright posture or a slouched seated pose for just one minute. All subjects were then asked to choose where they would sit at a table for a team task. The upright posers consistently chose seats close to the head of the table, while the slouchers chose to avoid sitting near the front. As the authors conclude, "Maintaining an upright position may bolster individual leadership perceptions before important interviews, meetings, tasks, and decisions."[22] Sometimes it's even subtler: Japanese researchers found that schoolchildren who sat with good posture were more productive than their classmates at tasks involving writing.[23] Good posture increases our sense of "being energized," making it easier to do things in general.[24]

Psychologist Jill Allen and her colleagues wondered if expansive postures might help people with eating disorders, conditions in which negative concerns about body image cause people to destructively restrict their caloric intake. In their study, female subjects who had shown symptoms of disordered eating adopted poses that were powerful, neutral, or contractive for just a few minutes. The powerful posers were indeed liberated from concerns about their bodies and proved able to eat in a less restrained manner and consume a more healthful number of calories. In fact, they even found that *spontaneously* expansive postures were associated with less restrained eating among women and that spontaneously contractive postures were related to more restrained eating. They titled their paper "Sit Big to Eat Big."[25]

Pro-social actions — those that are beneficial to others — often require the courage to adopt an approach mind-set. For example, after adopting a high-power or low-power pose, people were asked how willing they'd be to take action in a few pro-social scenarios, including leaving the site of a plane crash to ask for help and joining a movement to free a wrongly imprisoned person. The power posers were significantly more likely to want to help others in these hypothetical scenarios.[26]

As Jamini Kwon — the student who'd started painting after a struggle with temporary paralysis — showed in her research, contractive postures make people less persistent when facing challenges. In fact, powerless, closed postures not only undermine persistence, they also increase learned helplessness — the process whereby people avoid challenges they've previously struggled with, assuming they are not capable of effectively handling them. They may have helped us to hide from predators or to convey submissiveness to dangerous and volatile alphas in primitive times, but it's hard to find evidence that they continue to benefit us today, in the twenty-first century.

Expanding your body frees you to approach, act, and persist.

Body

The body shapes the mind, and the mind shapes behavior. But the body also directs itself.

Presence often begins with the physical — showing up and sticking around. When we're feeling challenged or anxious, we're more likely to want to fight or flee — both of which, in different ways, take us away from the present. Fleeing prevents us from engaging because we're gone in every sense; fighting does the same thing because we're too threatened or riled up to take in and respond to what's actually happening.

Our nonverbal postures prepare our bodies to be present. Hormones constitute one mechanism by which that happens. Also, as I mentioned in chapter 7, the mere act of changing your breathing can significantly alter what your nervous system is doing, attenuating your overactive fight-or-flight response and bolstering your feeling of strength. But these are not the only ways in which power poses prepare our bodies to be strong and grounded in the present.

University of Cambridge psychologists Eun Hee Lee and Simone Schnall had subjects hold some boxes that weighed a few pounds each, both before and after sitting in either high-power or low-power poses. Subjects perceived the boxes as significantly lighter after the expansive posture, likely because they became accustomed to the weight (that is, when the subjects held neither a high-power nor a low-power pose, they also perceived the boxes as lighter the second time around). On the other hand, holding a constrained posture eliminated this habituation effect, and they felt the boxes to be just as heavy afterward as before.[27]

You won't be surprised to learn that sports psychologists are particularly interested in how athletes can use body language to improve their performance. In a 2008 study of body language and success in soccer penalty shoot-outs, sports psychologists Geir Jordet and Esther Hartman looked at all penalty shoot-outs ever held in the World Cup, the European championships, and the Union of European Football Associations Champions League — a total of thirty-six shoot-outs and 359 kicks. Players whose body language immediately preceding the kick was rushed and avoidant (i.e., the player did not make eye contact with the goalkeeper) had a significantly higher rate of unsuccessful shots. The authors conclude that this avoidant nonverbal behavior might cause athletes to wither and choke under pressure.[28]

Expansive body language increases our feelings of physical strength and skill; contractive body language decreases them.

Expanding your body physiologically prepares you to be present; it overrides your instinct to fight or flee, allowing you to be grounded, open, and engaged.

Pain

Power posing can make us feel stronger. Can it enhance our feeling of physical well-being in other ways? Given that pain is as much a psychological experience as it is a physical one (a fact that's been demonstrated in many scientific disciplines), is there a connection between posture and pain?

To find out, psychologists Vanessa Bohns and Scott Wiltermuth calculated changes in people's pain thresholds before and after they adopted a dominant, submissive, or neutral pose. Using an approach known as the tourniquet technique, they were able to capture subjects' thresholds for pain as soon as they arrive at the lab: a blood pressure cuff is wrapped around a subject's arm and inflated at a fixed rate until the subject, who is instructed to indicate when the tightening cuff becomes too uncomfortable to continue, says to stop. Immediately after that first reading, subjects are asked to hold their randomly assigned poses for just twenty seconds, followed by a second measurement of the pain threshold.[29] As predicted, the dominant pose (feet spread and arms straight out to the sides) fortified subjects to endure more pain than the submissive pose (low kneeling with buttocks resting on calves and hands in lap) and the neutral poses (simply standing with arms hanging at sides).

Expanding your body toughens you to physical pain.

Performance and Presence

All these effects of expansive body language — increasing our feelings of power, confidence, and optimism, decreasing our feelings of stress, shoring up the positivity of our self-image, freeing us to be assertive, to take action, and to persist in the face of challenges, and preparing our bodies to be strong and grounded — also facilitate our ability to achieve presence during our biggest challenges.

But is our presence apparent to the people with whom we interact? And does it really improve our performance in a measurable way? I and my collaborators — Caroline Wilmuth, Dana Carney, and Andy Yap — predicted that it would. Specifically, we hypothesized that engaging in preparatory power poses *before* a stressful job interview would improve presence, which would lead to more favorable evaluations of performance and more favorable hiring decisions.[30] Why before? Because, as I've explained, adopting big power poses *during* social interactions often backfires: it's not only strange, it also makes people uncomfortable. Imagine meeting someone for the first time as they stand in the victory pose or sit with their feet on a table and arms akimbo. Now imagine a job candidate doing that while you're interviewing her. . . .

After arriving at the lab, subjects were told they would be participating in an intense mock job interview for their dream jobs. Recall the study I presented in chapter 1? Here we used a similar paradigm. The subjects had a short time to prepare a five-minute response to the question "Why should we hire you?" They were told they'd be presenting their answers as speeches to two trained interviewers who would be evaluating them. They were also informed that they'd be videotaped and judged later by a separate panel of experts. And they were told they could not misrepresent themselves and had to speak for the entire five minutes.

The two judge-researchers, who wore lab coats and held clipboards, were trained to give no feedback of any kind — just neutral expressions. As we've learned from other studies, receiving no feedback from a listener is often more disturbing than getting a negative response.

While preparing their speeches, subjects were assigned to adopt either the high-power or low-power poses that we'd used in earlier studies. They did their posing before the interviews, not during — a critical feature of this study. Each interview was recorded on video, and the recordings were evaluated by three pairs of judges who had no idea what our hypothesis was or anything else about the experiment. This is important.

Two of the judges evaluated the interviewees for performance ("Overall, how good was the interview?") and hireability ("Should this participant be hired for the job?"), two judges evaluated the interviewees for the quality of the verbal content of their answers to questions (intelligent, qualified, structured, and straightforward), and two judges evaluated them for the variable I was most interested in: the applicants' nonverbal presence (confident, enthusiastic, captivating, and not awkward).

As expected, subjects who prepared for the job interview with high-power (versus low-power) poses performed significantly better and were significantly more likely to be "hired" for the mock job. Power poses had no effect on the content of their speeches. But the high-power posers scored much higher on nonverbal presence — and it was nonverbal presence that completely drove the hiring decisions. In other words, judges wanted to hire the high-power posers because of their nonverbal presence.

iPosture

Next time you're in a waiting room, on a train, or in any public space, look around. How many people are hunched over an electronic device? In most places around the world, the answer is "a lot."

It's hard enough to keep track of our posture when we're trying. But our body language is also incidentally influenced by the furniture we sit on, the spaces we reside in, and the technology we use — and that's even harder for us to manage.

New Zealand physiotherapist Steve August has been studying and developing fixes for what he calls the iHunch. I've also heard people call this position text neck, and my colleagues and I have referred to it in our own research as iPosture. Said August when we discussed this, "In someone with perfect posture, the earlobe sits vertically above the point of the shoulder. When I started treating patients more than thirty years ago, certainly we saw dowagers' humps — the upper back frozen into a forward curve — in grandmothers and great-grandmothers. Now I'm seeing the same fixed-flexion thoracic stoop in teenagers. Just observe people from the side — it's not subtle. It's a slouch when they can straighten from it themselves, and it's a hunch when they can't — and this happens fast. The size of the problem is already enormous, and it's exploding."[31]

The average head weighs around twelve pounds (5.4 kilograms), and that's the load on the neck when our heads are balanced directly above the shoulders. But when we bend our necks forward around sixty degrees to use our phones, the effective weight goes up to sixty pounds (27.2 kilograms). August demonstrates this with a broomstick: "Balance a broom vertically on your outstretched palm. Not difficult; doesn't take much effort. Then grasp the nonbristled end of the broomstick and hold the stick out at around sixty degrees." The balancing act takes enormous effort. He explained that when people see him straining to hold a broom out at an angle, they understand. "It's the same as the neck muscles when hunched over a laptop, tablet, or smartphone. Do that for eight hours, and no wonder you're sore!"[32]

August contacted me after watching my TED talk because he had started to wonder about the same thing that worried me: Is it possible that spending hour after hour on our phones, tablets, and laptops is having the same effect on us as powerless postures do? Technology already makes it hard enough to be present. Rather than engage with the people we're sitting next to, we're absorbed in our devices, responding to old e-mails and status updates, transporting ourselves out of the moment, disengaging from the world around us. Our devices are already cognitively stealing our attention away from the moment, but are our devices also contorting us into physical positions that stifle our power and our ability to be present?

Until we corresponded, August said he'd been focused on the musculoskeletal consequences of hunching — "acute pain in the upper back and neck, headaches, and numerous other health-related problems" — rather than the psychological consequences. "I hadn't considered the effects the hunch/cringe position has on self-confidence and projecting submission to others," he said, but these results fit with his clinical experience. "As the devices get smaller, not only does assertiveness [in patients] decrease, but loading on the neck increases (leading immediately or eventually to pain and head-ache) — in exactly the same proportions. It's a perfect (and logical) relationship: smaller device, hunch more to use it, decrease asser-tiveness, increase neck loading, increase pain and headache."[33]

Whoa.

This connection seemed worth studying. Social psychologist Maarten Bos and I devised an experiment that would allow us to actually test the hypothesis that iHunching makes people behave less assertively.[34] We randomly assigned participants to interact with one of four electronic devices that vary in size: an iPod Touch, an iPad, a MacBook Pro laptop computer, or an iMac desktop computer.

Each subject spent five minutes working on his or her assigned device, alone in a room (subjects were being recorded on video, with their consent, so we could be sure they were following the rules). Everyone completed the same "filler" questionnaires — tasks to distract them during the allotted time slot.

But we disguised the critical behavioral measure. After the subjects had interacted with the device for around five minutes by completing some filler tasks (the same tasks were assigned to peo-ple in all conditions), the experimenter returned, retrieved the device, pointed at a clock, and told them, "I will be back in five minutes to debrief you and then pay you so that you can leave. If I am not here, please come get me at the front desk." How long would they wait to assert themselves? This was a way for us to mea-sure the participants' assertiveness — perhaps the central psycho-behavioral component of power. And keep in mind that we had confiscated the subjects' own phones when they arrived at the lab, so they had nothing to do but stare at a clock as they waited for our researcher to return.

As expected, device size significantly affected whether subjects felt comfortable seeking out the experimenter. In the ten minutes before the experimenter returned, only 50 percent of the smartphone users came out to tell experimenters they wanted to leave.

By contrast, 94 percent of the desktop users went to fetch the experimenter. You can see the other results in the figure on the next page: the bigger the device, the more likely subjects were to assert themselves. In fact, not only were the big-device users more likely to interrupt, those who did interrupt did so sooner. We concluded that the smaller the device, the more we must contract our bodies to use it, and the more time we spend in these shrunken, inward postures, the more powerless we feel.

Our findings uncover a cruel irony: while many of us spend hours every day working on small mobile devices, often with the

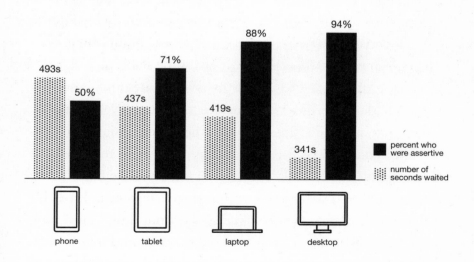

iPosture and Assertiveness

goal of *increasing* our productivity and efficiency, interacting with these tiny objects, even for short periods of time, might reduce assertiveness, potentially *undermining* our productivity and efficiency.

If you must spend long stretches in front of a screen, which many of us do, be sure to choose a device carefully and configure your space to allow for the most upright and expansive posture.

Picturing Powerful Posture (Your Body's in Your Head)

Christine, who works for a nonprofit organization that helps individuals with disabilities to abandon the kinds of beliefs that limit them, wrote to me a short time after my talk was posted. She said:

> My power poses are not actually done physically. No one sees them. No one knows I'm doing them — I'm imagining them. My body is completely nonphysical: I have full sensation but the use of only one finger on one hand, and still I imagine myself using gestures and moving my hands around. When I get ready to give a classroom presentation, I imagine a power pose, because you have to really own it.
>
> I think, when people look at me, the typical judgment is: female, that's one knock against you; disabled and in a wheelchair, that's another one. I could be perceived as quite powerless. But actually I am powerful. It doesn't matter what my body is doing; I'm imagining that I'm moving and owning this whole room right now. I am assertive and competent, sometimes fearless (and maybe a little reckless, but that's all right). I think all that is due to this power I've created. I can express all my gestures and poses, even through my eyes.

I wonder, could we encourage individuals with physical disabilities to actually feel more assertive by using their imaginations?

Christine isn't the only person who wonders. I've heard from many people with disabilities that severely limit how they hold or carry their bodies. And many of them said the same thing: *I imagine myself adopting a powerful pose, and I feel powerful. Have you done any research on that?*

At that point, I had not. But I had reason to believe that merely imagining yourself in a power pose will increase self-confidence. Research conducted over many years has shown that in terms of brain activity and behavioral effects, mental imagery of movement closely resembles actual physical movement. Studies show that going over a sequence of movements in the mind increases one's ability to enact them in the real world. Research also shows that many of the same regions of the brain that become active while executing particular actions — areas in and around the motor cortex — also respond when imagining those same actions. Less direct evidence for the neural overlap of simulated and actual behavior comes from the fact that we take roughly the same amount of time picturing an action as we do performing it and from the fact that Parkinson's disease patients, who move slowly, also slow their mental simulations of movement.[35]

Recent work has shown that using magnetic resonance imaging to assess the brain activity of paralyzed patients during mental imagery exercises can detect what they're thinking about and what they want their limbs to do. One study found that we can tell if a person is imagining walking through a house or playing tennis by looking at functional magnetic resonance imaging (fMRI) scans.[36] (This research is being used to detect whether "locked-in" patients — patients who are mentally aware but unable to move or communicate because of complete paralysis — are conscious by asking them to imagine playing tennis while scanning their brains.[37]) In another study, a quadriplegic patient first was asked to imagine reaching and grasping while his brain was scanned. Devices called microelectrode arrays were then installed in areas of the posterior parietal cortex made active when planning these movements, and the patient used the sensors to control a robot arm as if it were his own.[38] Of course, when you imagine performing an action your body doesn't give you any sensory feedback, but just picturing yourself in a powerful pose might be enough to lead you to behave in a powerful way.

Spurred by e-mails I've received from individuals with physical disabilities, my lab has begun conducting experiments to test the hypothesis that simply imagining oneself in a power pose can confer a sense of power. In our first experiment, we recruited around two hundred subjects online and prompted them, with a vivid description, to imagine themselves in a room, holding a particular high-power or low-power pose, and to continue to imagine that for two minutes. To prevent them from getting bored, we also instructed them to picture a few strangers walking in and out of the room as they were holding the pose and to form impressions of these strangers.[39]

After they had imagined themselves in the poses, we asked them to describe how they felt during the exercise. We did not prompt them with any words, even those that might have been of interest to us, such as *powerful, powerless, present, intimidated,* and so on. Keep in mind also that this was a diverse sample of subjects from all over the country, including a wide range of races, ages, religions, and cultural backgrounds.

Among the people who'd imagined themselves holding high-power poses, 70 percent used words that we called "comfortably confident." What amazed us wasn't only the high percentage of participants who reported feeling this way, it was also the consistency in the way they chose to describe that feeling — many of them used almost exactly the same words. They completed the statement "I felt..." with phrases that reflected their mental image of themselves:

Open and strong
Grounded and confident
Comfortable and poised
Grounded, confident, and solid

The subjects who had imagined themselves in low-power poses had a much less pleasant experience: 72 percent used words we coded as "socially threatened." These also reflected the subjects' mental image of themselves:

Awkward and tense
Scared and lonely
Stupid and embarrassed
Closed off
Threatened and vulnerable
Very, very uncomfortable

Some reported even more extreme descriptions, including "like I was suffocating" and "horrified, like I was tortured."

We also asked subjects to tell us what happened in their imagined scenarios. Again, the question was open-ended, with no specific word prompts or guides. Recall that in order to make the task more engaging, we asked the subjects to imagine that a few strangers had walked in and out of the room in which they were holding their expansive or contractive poses. And that we provided no details about who these people were. If adopting contractive, low-power poses makes us feel threatened and vulnerable, then how do you think it might affect what we remember about random strangers walking all around us?

If you guessed that the subjects imagining low-power poses would be more vigilant when it comes to strangers, you're right. In fact, in response to the open-ended question of what they'd imagined while mentally posing, 82 percent of the low-power posers provided detailed descriptions of those strangers walking around. Their accounts were quite entertaining, as these examples show:

"A male biker, a lady doctor, and a hippie came in."

"There was a cowboy with a hat and boots and a blue plaid shirt. There was a blond girl with a ponytail and a T-shirt that said I HEART NY followed by a brown bear in a Santa hat looking for a handout. There was a big man with a large bag of hamburgers that I could smell from across the room."

"Some tall men came in and stared at me. They asked me what I was doing and I told them yoga. They laughed and tried to push me over, and I fell. I told them that they wouldn't be laughing if they tried it and saw that it works."

"A man who looked like Jack Sparrow, wearing eyeliner and pirate pants, a little girl in a blue dress with pigtails, and an older man with a white short beard. He looked kind of like the guy from the Jose Cuervo commercials."

Even when I am *trying* to get subjects to provide this level of detail in their responses, I can't do it. To elicit it when I wasn't even intending to...and from so many of the subjects — that's rare. Were subjects just messing with us? Apparently not, because high-power posers weren't so concerned about the unspecified strangers: only 16 percent described them in any detail. Instead, when asked to recount their time mentally posing, they stayed serenely focused on their own postures and the environment around them, giving unembellished descriptions without judgment. They were simply *being*:

> "Standing in a room with a wood floor and white walls with my hands on my hips watching strangers walk in and forming impressions of them."
>
> "I was standing in a room with my feet twenty inches apart with hands on my hips and elbows out. I was to imagine the first impressions of the people coming into the room."
>
> "I was at a desk and unknown people came in and walked around."
>
> "I am standing in a small white room; there are wood floors. My hands are on my hips with my elbows out; my feet are twenty inches apart. People are coming into the room."
>
> "I am standing in a room with hands on hips and elbows out. My feet are twenty inches apart. The room is spacious and has a wood floor."

People who are present become less focused on how others might be judging or threatening them. We should be able to attend and respond to others, but focusing on them too much isn't just counterproductive, it's also destructive, undermining our self-confidence and interfering with our ability to notice what's being exchanged in the moment. Even in the imagined power pose condition, people were able to fully inhabit the moment — noticing without judging their environment, feeling neither threatened by nor dominant over the strangers coming in and out of the room.

You might be wondering if these findings square with the findings from the University of Auckland study in which powerless posers used more first-person pronouns in their speeches. The critical difference is that one experiment involved a spoken interaction, the other a written reflection. In the imagination study, participants were not interacting with or being evaluated by others; in the speech study, they were — and in real time, as they were speaking. The powerless posers' use of first-person pronouns more likely reflected a desire to protect themselves from negative evaluation by trying to verbally push judges to see them a certain way as opposed to thoughtfully engaging and allowing the judges come to their own conclusions. When reflecting in writing on a moment that did not involve being socially evaluated, as the imagination subjects were doing, presence would show up as self-awareness — noticing one's own physical and psychological states — which requires the use of more, not fewer, first-person pronouns.

As Christine explained in her e-mail, and as our own and others' research clearly shows, one need not have a fully able body to reap the benefits of power posing. In fact, many of us — with or without disabilities — find ourselves in situations in which we can't find the space or privacy to power pose before walking into a big challenge. But we can always imagine ourselves as Wonder Woman or Superman in our own little thought bubble.

Virtual Posture

The benefits of power posing don't just apply in physical and mental space — they also carry over into virtual space. Even the physical characteristics of your avatar — in a video game or in virtual reality — can change the way you behave in real life. Research has shown that when people perceptually inhabit virtual representations of themselves, they tend to take on their avatars' characteristics. This robust phenomenon has been referred to as the body transfer illusion and even works across genders (e.g., a male participant embodying a female avatar).[40]

Stanford researchers Nick Yee and Jeremy Bailenson investigated how the height of a person's avatar would influence her behavior in a negotiation that took place in a virtual environment.[41] In the physical world, people who occupy more vertical space than those around them are, on average, more likely to acquire social power and status. Yee and Bailenson assigned subjects to a tall, average, or short avatar, and it turns out, sadly, that even in the virtual realm height bestows an advantage. People who'd been assigned to tall avatars negotiated better deals than those who'd been assigned to average or short avatars. In fact, subjects assigned to a short avatar were around twice as likely to accept an unfair deal as those in other conditions. Yee and Bailenson refer to the phenomenon of embodying the characteristics of our avatars as the Proteus effect — named after the Greek god who had the capacity to alter his form.

In one of my favorite experiments designed to test the behavioral effects of immersive virtual reality, people were randomly assigned to one of two virtual experiences in a video game. In one they were given the ability to fly like a superhero (their arm movements were tracked to control their flight), and in the other they rode as a passenger in a helicopter.[42] In addition, half the subjects in each group were randomly assigned to complete a helping task in the video game (getting insulin to a diabetic child), while the other half were assigned a nonhelping task (touring the city from above). So there were four conditions: superpowered helper, helicopter helper, superpowered tourist, and helicopter tourist. When the experiment was supposedly finished, the experimenter "accidentally" knocked over a cup filled with fifteen pens, spilling them onto the floor. The researchers wanted to know who would be most likely to help pick up the pens.

It turned out that the type of task in which subjects engaged — tourism or helping — had no effect on their likelihood of their picking up the pens. But their flying condition did: compared to the helicopter passengers, people who'd been given superhero flying powers were significantly more likely to help the experimenter pick up the pens and were quicker to pitch in to do it. The superhero flyers also reported higher feelings of "presence" during the game — they felt more "real" and engaged during the virtual task.

Stand at Attention

Soldiers are often commanded to "stand at attention," which generally means chin up, chest out, shoulders back, and stomach in. Standing at attention is an upright, grounded, and motionless posture. Not only does it signal respect, it's also the posture most conducive to feelings of alertness and strength. Soldiers are trained to do this for a simple reason: when a commanding officer is communicating information that could influence life-or-death decisions, soldiers must be fully psychologically present. Standing at attention brings them to the present.

When we stop paying attention, we become more susceptible to the potentially destructive outcomes of both expansive *and* contractive postures. We saw how inattentiveness can undermine us when we're hunching over our smartphones or merely slouching in our seats. When we stop looking after our own posture, we are abandoning ourselves.

Moreover, in some temptation-filled situations, failing to attend to our own posture can lead us astray. Because power can be disinhibiting, it's important to keep ourselves in check. When our power is souped up and we're not paying attention, we sometimes loosen our standards, and we can take improper shortcuts to get to where we want to go. For example, in a study led by Andy Yap, my colleagues and I had subjects play a realistic driving video that included a steering wheel and foot pedals. The object of the game was simply to win the race. After a practice round, the subjects were offered an extra ten dollars if they could complete the course in less than five minutes, but there was a catch: they had to do so without committing traffic violations.[43]

What subjects didn't know was that we had designed two different driver's seat areas. One allowed maximal expansion — a high chair and viewing perspective, arms stretched to steering wheel and legs to pedals. The other constricted players in a lower chair and viewing perspective, arms bent to accommodate the steering wheel and legs bent to accommodate the foot pedals. We found that the expansive driver's seat areas led subjects to drive more recklessly in the video game — hitting more objects and failing to pause after accidents as they were supposed to.

These results suggest that awareness of and control over our personal power are vitally important elements of presence and that, in our own civilian way, we need to take care to stand (and sit) at attention.

Starfish Up!

Once, while I was washing my hands in an airport restroom, the woman at the sink next to me turned and said, "I'm really sorry, but are you…" She paused, and rather than finish the question, she stretched her arms out and up. I said, "I think so, yes." (I've become more accustomed to "Are you…" followed by hands on the hips.) Her name was Shannon, and she told me that not only had she incorporated power posing into her own life, she also continues to share it with coworkers, friends, and family. In fact, she and her husband and their four kids have their own name for it: "Starfish up!" When her kids are nervous, she reminds them to "starfish up!"

What I loved was that Shannon and her family had made the practice their own. And it worked. To convince me how much it had affected her, she showed me her favorite piece of jewelry — a delicate diamond-starfish ring that her husband had given her for her birthday to remind her of the personal power that she always has access to.

The activist Maggie Kuhn said (and I think most of us would agree), "Power should not be concentrated in the hands of so few and powerlessness in the hands of so many." This is true of personal power as well as social power. Too many of us suffer from pervasive feelings of personal powerlessness. We have a terrible habit of obstructing our own paths forward, especially at the worst possible moments. Too often we acquiesce to feelings of powerlessness. We consent to them, which does nothing but reinforce them and take us away from the reality of our lives.

But we can use our bodies to get to personal power. A mountain of evidence shows that our bodies are pushing, shaping, even leading our thoughts, feelings, and behaviors.[44] That the body affects the mind is, it's fair to say, incontestable. And it's doing so in ways that either facilitate or impede our ability to bring our authentic best selves to our biggest challenges.

Does this mean that "starfish up!" or standing like Wonder Woman will be effective for every person in every situation? Of course not, as I'm sure you know; there is no intervention that will work for every person in every situation. What I most want you to understand is that your body is continuously and convincingly sending messages to your brain, and *you* get to control the content of those messages. Hundreds (maybe thousands) of studies have examined the body-mind connection, using many different methods — from breathing, to yoga, to lowering vocal pitch, to having people imagine themselves holding an expansive pose, to simply getting people to sit up straight. There are countless ways for us to expand our bodies. And whether the body-mind effect is operating through our vagal tone, our blood pressure, our hormones, or some other mechanism we haven't yet discovered, the outcome is clear: expanding our bodies changes the way we feel about ourselves, creating a virtuous cycle. So what matters to me is that you find the techniques that best suit you. If you don't, you're squandering a precious opportunity.

Ultimately, expanding your body brings you to the present and improves your performance. Although our body language governs the way other people perceive us, our body language also governs how we perceive ourselves and how those perceptions become reinforced through our own behavior, our interactions, and even our physiology.

Why should we not carry ourselves with pride and personal power? When we do, we are able to be present in our most challenging moments. How you carry your body shapes how you carry out your life.

Your body shapes your mind. Your mind shapes your behavior. And your behavior shapes your future. Let your body tell you that you're powerful and deserving, and you become more present, enthusiastic, and authentically yourself. So find your own way to starfish up!

9

How to Pose for Presence

Sit up straight.
— YOUR GRANDMOTHER

WHEN SHOULD WE POWER pose? Most of us would benefit from a power boost before a job interview, a meeting with an authority figure, a class discussion, a difficult conversation, a negotiation, an audition, an athletic event, or a presentation before a group. People have also written to me about how helpful power posing can be

- before entering new situations, meeting new people, or speaking a nonnative language in a foreign country
  - when speaking up for oneself or for someone else,
  - when requesting help,
  - when ending a relationship — professional or personal,
  - when quitting a job, and
  - before receiving — or giving — critical feedback.

We don't all face the same kinds of challenges or feel intimidated by the same experiences. That's why it's important to notice the situations (and people) that trigger powerless body language — so that you know when to apply preparatory power posing. You'll also benefit enormously if you can get in the habit of checking in on your posture, both during challenging situations and generally throughout the day.

Prepare with Big Poses

Use the big poses to speak to yourself before walking into a big challenge. By taking up as much space as you comfortably can in the moments preceding the challenge, you're telling yourself that you're powerful — that you've got this — which emancipates you to bring your boldest, most authentic self *to* the challenge. You're optimizing your brain to be 100 percent present when you walk in. Think of it as a pre-event warm-up.

• In some ways, every day is a challenge. Prepare by power posing first thing in the morning. Get out of bed and practice a couple of your favorite poses for just a couple of minutes.

• In your home, office, and other personal spaces, you're not constrained by cultural norms, stereotypes, or hierarchical status. In other words, you can look as dominant as you'd like. Take advantage of that: pose big in those spaces.

• When you can find it, make the most of privacy in public spaces — pose in an elevator, a bathroom stall, a stairwell.

• Don't *sit* in waiting rooms, hunched over your phone. Stand or walk around instead.

• If you can't strike a pose physically, do it mentally: imagine yourself in the most powerful, expansive pose you can think of. Be a superhero in your own thought bubble.

• If you're about to face a challenging situation and you have no other option but to sit, wrap your arms around the back of your chair and clasp your hands together. This forces you to open your shoulders and chest.

• If you can and when it's advantageous to do so, arrive before your audience arrives. Get comfortable with occupying and expanding in the presentation space. Make the space yours, so your audience is coming to your "home" as opposed to you going to theirs.[1]

Present with Good Posture

As important as it is to adopt bold power poses *before* challenging situations, it's just as important to maintain less bold but still strong, upright, and open postures *during* challenging situations. Power posing is great when you're preparing by yourself for a challenging encounter, but it's not so great in the middle of a meeting. Adopting high-power poses in actual interactions is very likely to backfire — by violating norms, causing others to shrink, and so on, as I explained earlier. It's also not easy to maintain a pose while working at your computer all day. Fortunately there are some subtle things you can do when making like a silverback won't cut it:

• While you're presenting or interacting, sit up or stand up straight.

• Keep your shoulders back and your chest open.

• Breathe slowly and deeply — remember how much proper breathing can center us. (This is hard to do with slouched shoulders and a collapsed chest.)

• Keep your chin up and level, but don't raise it so far up that you're looking down your nose at people.

• When you're stationary, keep your feet grounded (no ankle-wrapping). You should feel solid, not as if you'd lose your balance if someone gently pushed or bumped into you.

• When you can, move around. When it comes to public speaking, one of the biggest trends of the last couple of decades is the move away from the lectern. Why? Because movement is more engaging for the audience. But it's also more energizing and powerful for the speaker. It allows you to occupy more space and inhabit more of the room.

• If the space allows, take a few steps, then pause in one spot as you continue speaking. (Don't pace. Pacing looks nervous and aggravated.) Movements should be neither erratic nor continuous. They should be clear and defined.[2]

• Use props. If your body tends to collapse into powerless poses when you speak, try using props that will force you to stretch out. If you're standing, rest your hand on a table, on the back of a chair, or on a whiteboard. If you're sitting, lean forward and place your hands on a table, or make sure your arms are resting on the arms of the chair rather than knotting up in your lap. If you don't have a big prop, use a little one: hold a glass of water or a laser pointer or a remote control — anything that will prevent you from collapsing your arms and clasping or wringing your hands.

• Adopt open gestures: they're both strong *and* warm. For example, when our arms are outstretched with palms up, it's welcoming and signals trust.

• Avoid "penguin arms." When people feel anxious and powerless they often pin their upper arms — from armpit to elbow — at their sides, gesturing only with the lower halves of their arms. (Try it.) This is just another way in which we contract, but it causes us to feel awkward and anxious and to come across that way.[3] (I learned this helpful piece of advice from some good friends — authors and body language experts John Neffinger and Matt Kohut.)

• Don't just take up physical space, take up temporal space. This advice holds across all the contexts in which you speak (unless you're a contestant on a game show in which you're required to speak very quickly), whether it's during a presentation, a pitch, an interview, a difficult conversation, a discussion with your doctor, or a response to critical feedback at work. When we feel insecure and distracted, we rush, fearful that we're taking too much time, and we seem eager to escape.

• Pause! Terrified of silences, we fail to harness the immense power of pauses.

• Try relaxing the muscles of your throat so that your voice lowers to its natural level.

• If you make a mistake — which we all inevitably do — don't allow yourself to collapse inward. If you feel yourself beginning to collapse, fight it. Pull your shoulders back, unfurl, and power up.

Mind Your Posture Throughout the Day

It's important to avoid falling into the powerless poses we often mindlessly inhabit. How to do this?

• Notice what is happening in the moments when you do begin to contract, collapse, and disappear. What are the situations and stimuli that cause you to shrink? What are the idiosyncratic things that make you feel powerless? This awareness alone will help you resist the urge the next time your find yourself in a similar predicament.

• Set posture reminders for yourself:
   – Make your phone an ally, not an enemy:

- Program your phone to remind you to check your
  posture every hour,
- but don't iHunch over it.
- Place Post-it notes on doors, around your office and
  house, and above your computer screen.
- Enlist the help of trustworthy friends, family, and
  coworkers. Ask them to let you know when you're slouching (and ask if they'd like you to do the same for them).

• Organize the spaces in which you spend time in ways that
facilitate good posture:
  - My collaborator Nico Thornley places his mouse far
    enough from his body that he's forced to expand in order
    to use it.
  - Hang pictures of people and things that make you
    happy high on your walls to entice you to stretch and
    look up.

• If you tend to sleep in the fetal position, stretch in bed before
you fall asleep. If you wake up in the fetal position, stretch
before you get out of bed.

• Combine power posing with daily routines. For example,
my research assistant Anna stands with one hand on her hip while
she brushes her teeth.

• If you spend a lot of time on phone calls, use a headset and
stretch out while you're talking (or listening) rather than pulling
your arms in to hold the phone against your ear.

• We're learning more and more about the many psychological and other health benefits of standing instead of sitting at work,
on your the computer, and so on. If you are able to do that, give it
a try.[4]

• Take breaks to walk around throughout the day. In fact, consider having "walking meetings," which not only improve your mood;

they also lead to better communication, worker engagement, and creative problem-solving.[5]

• You can purchase a wearable device that will monitor and remind you to correct poor posture, although the cost is limiting for many people. This technology is improving at breakneck speed, so I won't recommend any particular device, but there are plenty of options.

• Always cold in your climate-controlled office? Stop swaddling yourself into a fetal ball inside that shawl, scarf, blanket, oversize cardigan, or whatever it is you use. I'm sorry to sound like a mom, but *wear layers!*

• Seize the social opportunities you have to stretch out, such as going to the gym, running, taking a yoga class, and dancing. Don't waste opportunities to expand!

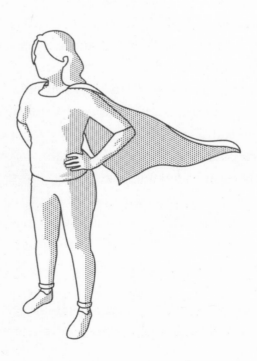

10

Self-Nudging: How Tiny Tweaks Lead to Big Changes

Anyone can carry his burden, however hard, until night-
fall. Anyone can do his work, however hard, for one day.
Anyone can live sweetly, patiently, lovingly, purely, till the
sun goes down. And this is all life really means.
— ROBERT LOUIS STEVENSON

I USED TO PANIC under certain kinds of pressure. For example, if I got a negative review or rejection of a paper I'd submitted for an academic journal, I went into full-blown make-it-better-by-doing-something — *anything* — mode. Without taking a breath, I'd jump right back in, dissecting the editor's and the reviewers' comments ad nauseam, agonizing over them, addressing every single one of them in a "perfect" revision, composing the cleverest, most thorough response letter, and sending the full package back to the editor. Immediately. And doing all this from a place of anxiety and threat.

On many of these occasions, my friend Holly, an unfaltering voice of reason, would remind me, "You don't have to do anything today." And in most cases, she was right: I didn't have to do anything that day. At the very least, I could sleep on it (which, psychologists have demonstrated, often improves the quality of our decisions, something I've written about in the past[1]).

In later years, I realized two things. First, slowing down is a power move. Just as speaking slowly, taking pauses, and occupying space are related to power, so, too, is taking your time to figure out how to respond and slowing down your decision-making process in high-pressure moments. ("Perfectionism," wrote Anne Lamott, "is the voice of the oppressor, the enemy of the people. It will keep you cramped and insane your whole life."[2]) Slowing down is just another kind of expansion. Holly was telling me to take *my* time — to claim the time that was *already mine*.

Because here's the thing about my rushed, panicked response pattern: like making myself physically small, it was an expression of feeling powerless, and it always backfired. Why rush to make what will likely be a poor decision when stress is already preventing me from operating on all cylinders? That's not boldness; it's just reactivity.

A runaway train will keep moving until a force is imposed to stop it, at least according to Isaac Newton. To slow down — to stop the runaway train in my mind — I needed power. To slow down, I had to feel that I was entitled to slow down. My experience of powerlessness in those high-pressure moments was causing me to maddeningly accelerate my decision-making process and to squeeze myself into much less space than I was entitled to — and that just wasn't good for anyone. I had to stop consenting to the feeling of powerlessness and start accessing some of my personal power, which was difficult.

Second, and this may sound kind of weird: doing nothing was doing something. It tempered my feeling of threat. Doing nothing reminded me that I *do* have some power to slow the runaway train. And it freed me to see and respond to the situation with fully functioning cognitive machinery — better working memory, greater clarity, and the ability to adopt several different perspectives. Not only was doing nothing doing something, doing nothing was also much *better* than doing something, at least the kind of something I'd been doing.

When I hastily and nervously tried to "fix" a perceived problem or threat right away, I never felt satisfied with what I'd done. And the outcome was never the one I'd desired. As I explained in the first chapter, presence is not about winning. It cannot be motivated by desire for a certain outcome — although the outcome is likely to be better when you are present. It's about approaching your biggest challenges without dread, executing them without anxiety, and leaving them without regret.

We don't get there by deciding to change *right now*. We do it gently, incrementally, by nudging ourselves — a bit further every time. For me, each time I felt that high-stakes pressure, I actually had to nudge myself toward slowing down and toward fixating less on results. I couldn't change instantaneously, simply by deciding to change. But each time I nudged myself forward, I was creating a memory that I could access the next time I felt a sense of panic. I could say to myself, "I've done this before, so why not do it again?" Slowing down became self-reinforcing. And because I was able to calm down and respond from a place of reason, not threat, my behavior was reinforced by other people as well.

And this, too, is how I "recovered" from a traumatic brain injury — gradually, incrementally, and exasperatingly slowly.[3] When people ask, "How did you recover?" that's really the only answer I have. I nudged myself. I nudged myself through countless sludgy days. Each tiny personal experience of improvement became a new source of both inspiration and information for me — a reminder that I could keep trying. Each time I could make it through a lecture without panicking when I struggled to cognitively process what I was hearing — that was a tiny victory. And as things got easier, other people responded to me as if I were someone who actually *was* competent and strong — even if I didn't yet believe it myself.

I never in a million years thought I'd become a professor at Harvard. In 1992, I just wanted to make it through each week without losing hope. To make it through a class without thinking about dropping out (and I did drop out, more than once, because my brain was just not ready to be back in a classroom). I had no concrete goal in mind. I just wanted to feel a bit more like myself, a bit sharper, a bit less like I was watching from inside a glass bubble and a bit more like a participant in what was happening. I can't even say that I fully, consciously noticed all the changes as they were happening.

That's how it works. In each challenging situation, we nudge ourselves: we encourage ourselves to feel a little more courageous, to act a bit more boldly — to step outside the walls of our own fear, anxiety, and powerlessness. To be a bit more present. And incrementally, over time, we end up where we want to be ... even if we couldn't have said where that was when we started.

Nudges

Around 2005, a group of economists and psychologists began to explore the notion, based on the results of many studies, that the best way to change people's behavior for the better might not be to request or demand big changes in attitudes and preferences but to subtly, almost imperceptibly, nudge people in a healthful direction. The tactics of this approach are neither dramatic nor bold, and the changes produced are, in the beginning, conservative. But over time, the changes spread and fortify. They incrementally build upon themselves, ultimately changing not only behavior but also attitudes and even social norms, which reinforce and extend behavioral changes throughout and across communities. They become the new status quo.

In 2008, University of Chicago economist Richard Thaler and Harvard Law School professor Cass Sunstein published the best-selling book *Nudge*, which inspired policy makers around the world to reexamine their assumptions about human behavior. In 2010, UK prime minister David Cameron commissioned the Behavioural Insights Team, also known as the Nudge Unit, to test and apply this new science to the field of social services: the goal was to improve access to and use of public services and to develop more effective policies. In one application, by simply reminding UK taxpayers that many British citizens pay their taxes on time, the Nudge Unit drastically increased on-time tax payments, resulting in the collection of around £210 million in revenue. Not a bad payoff for a bargain-priced intervention.[4] In 2013, the US government began organizing its own team of behavioral scientists, known as the Nudge Squad, to address social issues such as unhealthy eating, staying in school, and so on.

Consider this true story of how nudging works. Old approaches to reducing household energy consumption commonly encouraged people to make big changes, such as insulating their homes and buying new, energy-saving appliances. What's wrong with this? It's too big an ask. Only a small percentage of people complied, and they tended to be the people whose attitudes and circumstances were already very well aligned with the specific behavior being encouraged. A person, say, who owns (as opposed to rents) a home, identifies as an environmentalist, is interested in renovating her kitchen, and has the money to do so might consider buying a new dishwasher. Although these measures may have yielded impressive energy savings for the few people who took them, most people were not willing to spend a thousand dollars in response to a generic suggestion typed on the back of a utility bill. These big asks were ineffective at changing the attitudes of people who didn't already care about reducing energy consumption.

In 2006, two young guys decided to try an entirely different approach. They started Opower, a company aimed at getting people to consume less energy. Rather than explicitly urging people to make big, expensive changes, they would *nudge* them toward small, incremental changes by simply telling them how their energy usage compared to their neighbors' via feedback in the form of smiley faces. The more smiley faces they got, the better they were performing compared to their neighbors. This tiny intervention led to energy-use reductions of between 1.5 percent and 3.5 percent in 75 percent of households they contacted. Not just in one city or two. But all across the United States and its widely varied demographics. Compare this to the older, heavy-handed approaches, which led to changes in only a tiny percentage of households.[5]

Early nudge researchers, such as psychologist Daniel Kahneman, defined nudges as "nano-sized investments" that lead to "medium-sized gains."[6] The costs are low, and the mechanisms operate through what behavioral economists refer to as "choice architecture" — contexts explicitly designed for good decision making.[7]

Nudges are effective for several reasons. First, *nudges are small and require minimal psychological and physical commitment.* What Opower learned was that even people who didn't identify as environmentalists were willing to slightly reduce their energy use when they learned that their neighbors were doing so.

Second, *nudges operate via psychological shortcuts.* As I've mentioned several times, we have limited cognitive resources, which means that we simply can't attend to all the information provided to us about every decision we make. One shortcut is to just do whatever will cause the least shame or embarrassment, based on what others are doing. In the Opower case, people's behavior was being nudged via *normative influence* (deciding how to behave based on what's socially appropriate) as opposed to *informational influence* (deciding how to behave based on an assessment of objective reality). Human behavior is more often guided by the former than by the latter. We often look at what other people are doing and infer which actions are proper, especially if we identify with the people we're observing. The more similar others are to us, the more influential they are on our behavior. Although many people find it unsettling, the fact is that as much as we like to think of ourselves as unique individuals, we're deeply concerned about fitting in. That's not to say we'd all jump off a cliff if we saw our friends do it; it simply means that when a behavior is not that costly to us, we'd rather fit in than invest a lot of time and cognitive energy trying to figure out precisely the "right" or "best" thing to do.

Third, contrary to most people's assumption that our behaviors follow from our attitudes (e.g., we buy a certain product because we have a positive attitude toward it), the causality between attitudes and behaviors is just as likely to work in the opposite direction — *our attitudes follow from our behaviors* (e.g., we have a positive attitude toward a product because we already bought it — and maybe we bought it because a friend uses it, or because it was on sale, or simply because it was the easiest to grab off the shelf).

Much attention has been given to studies showing how easily we're influenced by others. But what about our influence on ourselves?

In 2013, I began to think about how three principles — *minimal psychological and physical commitments, use of psychological shortcuts, and attitudes following from behaviors* — might apply to self-motivated personal change. Just as organizations can nudge the behavior of large groups of people, individuals can nudge their own behavior toward more healthful, productive habits.[8]

The idea was that incremental changes, based on tiny nudges, would eventually lead not only to professional success but also to confidence, comfort, and improved self-efficacy, relationship quality, health, and well-being. People don't expect nudges to do much at all, so when they feel their effects, when they notice the changes, they're often surprised — "Hey, that really worked!"

Self-nudges, as I began to call them, are minimal modifications to one's own body language and/or mind-set that are intended to produce small psychological and behavioral improvements in the moment. They are tiny tweaks with the potential to, over time, lead to big changes. Unlike more ambitious, programmatic changes, long-term life goals, and forced self-affirmations of things we don't actually believe, self-nudges appeal to our natural, hardwired tendencies. When you give yourself a self-nudge, the gap between reality and goal is narrow; it's not daunting, which means you're less likely to give up. As a result, your behavior change is more authentic, lasting, and self-reinforcing.

Incremental Change — Baby Steps

When it comes to changing the self, no one has done more important psychological research than Carol Dweck and her collaborators. In experiment after experiment, with thousands and thousands of students, Dweck has shown that children thrive in school when they adopt what she calls a growth mind-set — a belief that they can improve in a given area — as opposed to a fixed mind-set, a belief that their abilities are set in stone and can't be changed. When children (and adults) focus on the process, not on the results, their performance remarkably and dramatically improves. In a TEDx talk,[9] Dweck said:

> I heard about a high school in Chicago where students had to pass a certain number of courses to graduate, and if they didn't pass a course, they got the grade "Not Yet." And I thought that was fantastic, because if you get a failing grade, you think, I'm nothing, I'm nowhere. But if you get the grade "Not Yet" you understand that you're on a learning curve. It gives you a path into the future.

Dweck shows that most U S schools are unintentionally set up to foster a doomed, fixed mind-set, directing children's focus to grades, tests, and demonstrations and praising them for their intelligence and talent. She argues that schools should instead be intentionally set up to encourage a growth mind-set, praising students' effort, strategies, focus, perseverance, enthusiasm, and improvement. "This process praise," Dweck explains, "creates kids who are hardy and resilient." It focuses children on process rather than outcome and cultivates the belief that a difficult task is a challenge to attempt rather than an opportunity to demonstrate failure.

This principle isn't limited to academic success. David Scott Yeager of the University of Texas at Austin wanted to find ways to stop the onset of depression in teenagers, which is common in early high school. One of the problems, as he saw it, was that kids believe that personalities are fixed, not mutable, which is pretty demoralizing at a time when many of us are not feeling so great about ourselves and when we are feeling socially categorized and stratified. So he conducted a study of six hundred ninth graders at three high schools. The kids in the treatment condition simply read a passage about the fact that personality is not set in stone, noting that neither bullying nor being bullied results from fixed personal traits. They also read an article about brain plasticity. Afterward they described in their own words how personality can change. Nine months later, kids who had read that passage showed, on average, no increase in signs of depression. However, kids in the control condition (who'd read about the malleability of athletic ability rather than personality) showed around a 39 percent increase in signs of depression — consistent with previous research on rates of depression among adolescents.[10]

Nudges are, in part, about choice architecture — building an environment in which people make good decisions. Self-nudging allows you to be the architect *and* the building. Build a powerful edifice, and you're creating a space for healthful behavior in your own life.

How We Nudge Ourselves from Tiny Tweaks to Big Changes

In a way, simply adjusting our posture is the ultimate tiny tweak. But how do we make sure the effects last? People often ask me that. It's a tricky question, because if we kept subjects alone in our labs with nothing to do and no one to interact with, I'm quite certain any positive effects from power posing would quickly dissipate. For the effects to stick, they need opportunities to take root, grow, and fortify. They need to be reinforced. Here's how that happens:

First, *our behavior reinforces our behavior,* in multiple ways.

As I mentioned earlier, we often derive our attitudes from our behavior as opposed to the reverse — behaving based on our attitudes. This idea is akin to William James's well-supported hypothesis that we acquire our feelings from our expressions.

When we see ourselves doing something with courage or competence once, we can recall that experience the next time we face a similar challenge, making it easier to perform well a second time, a third time, and so on. Our feelings of agency and self-efficacy strengthen, our sense of deservingness increases, and our ability to be in the moment rather than worried about it improves. We start to move away from attributing good outcomes to external causes (e.g., luck, help from others) and toward attributing them to internal causes (e.g., tenacity, intelligence).

When we use nonverbal interventions, such as deep breathing, smiling, sitting up straight, and power posing, we aren't distracted by bewildering in-the-moment self-evaluations of how well we are or are not doing — the "ever-calculating, self-evaluating, seething cauldron of thoughts, predictions, anxieties, judgments, and incessant meta-experiences about experience itself," as Maria Popova described it (see chapter 1). Instead, we're present and performing as well as we can in that moment. We notice our post-intervention performance change later, upon healthy reflection (as opposed to unhealthy rumination). Power posing might incrementally change your set point, which, over time, leads to big behavior changes. It might cause a cascading effect of other changes that reinforce and build upon the initial change.

And physiological changes — such as the hormone changes that accompany power poses — reinforce the behaviors that go with them. For example, our cortisol spikes when we are anxious, which causes us to act from a place of threat, only reinforcing our anxiety the next time we face a similar challenge. But when our testosterone is high, we are more likely to win, which further increases our testosterone.

Body-mind nudges avoid the key psychological obstacles inherent in mind-mind interventions, such as verbal self-affirmations of power (e.g., telling yourself "I am confident!"). Why do those approaches often fail? Because they require you to tell yourself something you don't believe, at least not in the moment. While you're in the throes of doubting yourself, you're certainly not going to trust your own voice to tell you that you're wrong to doubt yourself (even if you are, in fact, wrong to doubt yourself). General self-affirmations can become exercises in self-judgment, particularly when you're already stressed out and extra sensitive to social judgment, in the end reinforcing your mistrust of yourself. Body-mind approaches such as power posing rely on the body, which has a more primitive and direct link to the mind, to tell you

you're confident, thus avoiding these psychological stumbling blocks.

The second way that self-nudges produce lasting effects is through *other people's reinforcement of our behavior.*

Nonverbal expression isn't just a matter of one person "speaking" and another listening. It's a two-way conversation as a person's expression prompts a reply in kind. These interactions reinforce the impressions we have of each other and of ourselves, thus affecting how we will behave not only in the immediate exchange but also the next time we're in a similar situation.

In one of the most famous psychology experiments ever conducted, teachers at an elementary school in California were told at the beginning of a school year that, based on the results of a test that had been administered, experts determined that a particular set of their students were going to experience an academic growth spurt that year.[11] The teachers were given the names of these students. What the teachers didn't know was that the information they'd been given was bogus: although all students did take the test, some of them had been randomly assigned to the "spurters" condition but did not actually differ from the students who'd been randomly assigned to the control condition. (Note that this experiment was conducted in the 1960s and though it complied with the standards of the day, it would not meet the requisite human-subjects ethics standards today. So don't worry — your kids will not be subjected to this kind of study.)

What do you think happened? If you were told that one of your own children was about to experience a significant intellectual growth spurt, would you treat him differently? How about an employee? A friend?

Well, what happened was that the teachers behaved in ways toward the spurters that facilitated greater intellectual growth. They called on them more often, responded to them in more encouraging, affirmative ways, gave them more opportunities to learn, and so on. As a result, by the end of the year, the spurters were outscoring the kids in the control condition on the same test on which they did not actually differ at the beginning of the year. This is how self-fulfilling prophecies work: we have an expectation about who someone is and how she's likely to behave, then we treat her in a way that is likely to elicit those behaviors, thus confirming our initial expectations...and so on.

In a famous 1974 paper, Princeton psychologists presented a pair of experiments on the self-fulfilling power of body language.[12] The researchers wanted to know if white college admissions officers were unconsciously adopting cold, disengaged, and discouraging body postures (e.g., orienting their bodies away from the applicants, crossing their arms, not nodding) when interviewing black applicants, and, if so, how these postures might affect the applicants' interview performance. In the first experiment, white interviewers were randomly assigned to interview either black or white applicants. Indeed, when interviewing the black applicants, white interviewers used cold, disengaged body language, and the black applicants were perceived to have performed more poorly in the interviews than the whites. In the second experiment, trained white job interviewers were split into two groups and instructed to use either cold, disengaged body language or warm, engaged body language. They were then randomly assigned to interview either black or white applicants. The black applicants performed as well as the white applicants when their interviewers exhibited warm, engaged body language. And applicants of both races performed equally poorly when their interviewers behaved in a cold, uninterested way.

Furthermore, in both cases, the applicants' body language matched that of the interviewers; they were unconsciously mimicking what the interviewers did, which is what we usually do in social settings. In short, our body language, which is often based on prejudices, shapes the body language of the people we're interacting with. If we expect others to perform poorly, we adopt body language that is off-putting and discouraging. Naturally, people take the hint and respond as expected — poorly. How could anyone ace an interview under those circumstances?

When our body language is confident and open, other people respond in kind, unconsciously reinforcing not only their perception of us but also our perception of ourselves.

Why Many Popular Self-Change Approaches Fail — And Even Backfire

Why self-nudge? Why not just make a commitment to change your behavior, then follow through? Well, just as early efforts to reduce energy consumption encouraged people to make big changes — such as insulating their homes — we encourage ourselves to make big changes as well. In both cases, the tactic falls short. One of the biggest culprits, at least in the United States, is the repeatedly dispiriting New Year's resolution, which is riddled with psychological traps that work against us.

For one thing, New Year's resolutions are too ambitious. Setting big goals, such as getting straight As in school or working out three times a week, is a positive step in theory, but these goals are not designed in a way that actually allows us to build toward them. They're reliant on the success of hundreds of smaller changes, and they don't come with step-by-step instructions showing us how to get there.

The results we're picturing when we make sweeping

resolutions are also too far away. We can't relate to or really imagine them, which makes it hard to actualize them in our lives. And the long distance to the goal gives us a lot of opportunities to fail along the way — and that means more opportunities to give up. We tell ourselves there's no point because we've already blown it. If we abruptly resolve to go to the gym three times a week, we're likely to fail most weeks, which undermines our self-efficacy, confidence, mood, and tenacity.

As Carol Dweck's work has clearly demonstrated, focusing on process encourages us to keep working, to keep going, and to see challenges as opportunities for growth, not as threats of failure. New Year's resolutions are results-oriented, and too often they loom over us as threats, not encouragements. Nudges, on the other hand, are effective because they focus on the how, not the what.

Big resolutions are also focused on the negative — the bad things we want to rid ourselves of — rather than the positive, the good things that we can improve upon. We don't want to think about what we dislike about ourselves every day. That's unpleasant and can be demotivating, but thinking about the good things that we can make even better gets us excited and ready to go.

Finally, New Year's resolutions can undermine intrinsic motivation — the personal, internal desire to do something — and replace it with external motivators. And decades of research has shown that this can backfire, because extrinsic motivators (e.g., money and avoidance of punishment) won't always be there. In fact, when a goal involves something we really love to do, extrinsic motivators can actually end up killing intrinsic motivation.[13]

For example, I've always wanted to run as a form of exercise. I like the elegance of running — a single graceful movement repeated; minimal gear; no gym; can be done outdoors virtually anywhere... it appealed to me. In the past, almost every New Year, I'd resolve to "become a runner." In my mind, a runner was someone who was self-disciplined, fast, and able to complete marathons. But if you start from scratch, it will be quite a while before you meet those criteria, and I couldn't accept that. By focusing on the outcome — being a runner as I defined it — I was ignoring the reality that there is a whole lot of process in between. Every time I went for a run, it was short, slow, and painful. Every run felt like a failure. And I didn't enjoy the process at first. In fact, every time I resolved to become a runner, I soon started to hate running. That was a real problem. Any intrinsic motivation I had quickly died because the extrinsic motivators were too few and far between. Focused on the unreachable extrinsic incentives, I was forgoing the chance to identify and develop some intrinsic incentives. Every year, I'd quit by the end of January.

Finally I tried something different: I resolved to run just one time. And if I liked it, I'd run another time. I'd run only as fast and as far as was comfortable. I wouldn't try to run through side cramps or keep up with my serious runner friends. I completely dropped the long-term goals, which were far too big and distant. And I figured out a way to turn running into a positive experience, something I'd look forward to. I found my intrinsic motivation by linking running to something I love doing — traveling. I love to travel, but when I travel for work, I'm rushing in and out, taking no time to see or learn anything about the place I'm visiting. By just going for a short run, I could actually experience and see a bit of the place on foot. I also learned that I loved trail-running — running along paths out in nature. I don't run fast when I do this, but I relish spending time in the wilderness, so it's not really about "becoming a runner" at all. Rather than focus on what I couldn't do at that point (i.e., run fast, well, and competitively), I was focusing on what I could do (i.e., enrich my work-travel experiences and get out in nature). I turned every aspect of how I had been trying to honor my New Year's resolutions upside down. Have I run a marathon? No way. I may never run a marathon, and that will be okay. But I haven't quit. And that's something.

Self-Nudges

A body-mind intervention is a powerful way to nudge yourself, but it's not the only way. Researchers around the world are identifying other small tweaks we can make to strengthen our psychological well-being, change our behavior, and improve our follow-through.

In 2014 my colleague Alison Wood Brooks and I organized a symposium called "Self-Nudges: How Intrapersonal Tweaks Change Cognition, Feelings, and Behavior" at the annual meeting of the Society for Personality and Social Psychology.[14]

Brooks, also a professor at Harvard Business School, has a special interest in the psychological hurdles that prevent people from performing well. This stems, in part, from her background as a talented singer who's logged hundreds of hours in front of audiences. Not only is her poise on stage enviable, she also appreciates how that kind of poise can facilitate good leadership, and she realizes that most of us struggle to find it when we're performing. So she set out to find simple interventions that might help people overcome their stage fright.[15]

Warning: if you're a fan of the superviral "keep calm" meme, you will likely be surprised by what she found.

As most of us know, stage fright can feel like a paralyzing overdose of anxiety. And what do people tell us to do when we're anxious? They tell us, with good intentions, to calm down. As it turns out, that might just be the very worst thing they can say. You see, anxiety is what psychologists describe as a high-arousal emotion. As I've explained, when we're anxious, we occupy a heightened state of physiological vigilance. We're hyperalert. Our hearts race, we break out in a sweat, our cortisol may spike — all these reactions are controlled automatically by our nervous system. And it's virtually impossible for most people to shut off that kind of automatic arousal, to abruptly de-escalate it. Not only can we *not* calm down, but when someone *tells* us to calm down, it also reminds us of how calm we are *not*, which stokes our anxiety even more.

But there's another high-arousal emotion that's not so negative. In fact, it's quite positive — excitement. Brooks predicted that we may not be able to extinguish arousal, but we should be able to change the way we interpret it. So rather than fruitlessly trying to change the arousal level of our emotional states from high to low, what if we try to change them from negative to positive? From anxiety to excitement?

To test her prediction, Brooks ran a series of experiments, putting subjects in several situations that elicit stage fright: a singing competition (in which they sang Journey's "Don't Stop Believin'"), a public-speaking contest, and a difficult math exam. In each experiment, subjects were randomly assigned to tell themselves one of three things before their "performance": (1) to keep calm, (2) to get excited, or (3) nothing.

In all three contexts — singing, speaking, and math — the subjects who took a moment to reframe their anxiety as excitement outperformed the others. When you're excited, Brooks explained, "it primes an opportunity mindset, so you think of all of the good things that can happen. You're more likely to make decisions and take actions that will make [good results] likely to occur."[16]

Because I'm lucky enough to work in an office that's around twenty yards down the hall from Alison Wood Brooks's office, we've had quite a few conversations about this work. "Although we haven't studied this phenomenon over long periods of time," she explained, "I suspect that saying 'I am excited' or doing your best to 'get excited' before every anxiety-provoking performance does not have diminishing marginal returns — that is, it doesn't necessarily become less effective over time. On the contrary, the positive effects are likely to compound over time. The more you reframe your anxiety as excitement, the happier and more successful you may become." This is what makes it a self-nudge — by focusing on each new moment in front of you instead of the performance outcome, you slowly, incrementally nudge yourself toward becoming a bolder, more authentic, more effective version of yourself.

"Reframing anxiety as excitement has helped me with singing and playing music in front of crowds, presenting my research, pitching my entrepreneurial ideas, teaching undergraduate, MBA, and executive students, and interacting with my Harvard colleagues every day." When a psychologist is actually able to use her research in her own life, you know you're on to something good.

By simply reframing the meaning of the emotion we're experiencing — by nudging ourselves from anxiety to excitement — we shift our psychological orientation, harnessing the cognitive and physiological resources we need to succeed under pressure. We effectively transform our stage fright into stage presence.

How else can we use tiny tweaks to improve our lives? UCLA professor Hal Hershfield has identified a stunningly simple self-nudge that can help you make better decisions today about how much money you save for tomorrow — or fifty years from tomorrow.

Background: in 2014, Hershfield asked a thousand people from all over the country, "Who is your worst enemy?"[17] Five hundred of them gave the same answer: "Myself."

It turns out that we don't have much more compassion toward ourselves than we do toward a stranger. And that's a big problem when it comes to saving money, because if we can't identify with the person for whom we're saving, then why would we conservatively set aside a big wad of money for him or her? Why not just spend it now, on our present selves?

In order to make good decisions about saving for the future — saving for retirement, in particular — we have to like and respect ourselves. Specifically, we have to like and respect our future selves, the ones who will benefit from having an ample retirement fund. We have to care about them and have a clear picture of who they are. Fund-raisers for organizations that help large causes, for example, are far more effective when their marketing focuses on a specific, nonanonymous victim — one person who is affected by a natural disaster or illness or crime as opposed to a thousand who are affected. Sound counterintuitive? Shouldn't we want to increase the amount we donate if we know it will help thousands of people? Yes, but while we can't easily understand and identify with thousands of people, we can certainly understand and identify with one. And the more vivid that one, the better.[18]

One neuroimaging study conducted by Hershfield and his colleagues showed that when people imagined themselves as they would be ten years in the future, their brain activity looked more like it did when they were thinking about an entirely different person — Matt Damon or Natalie Portman, for example — than when they were thinking of themselves in the present.[19]

Hershfield and his colleagues also found that when they showed their subjects age-advanced photos of themselves, then gave them a hypothetical opportunity to put money into a savings account, the subjects put twice as much money into the account as they did when they were not shown the photos. When they could identify with their future selves, they were far more interested in saving for that person.[20]

Hershfield actually suggests printing an age-progressed image of our future selves,[21] which you can (believe it or not) create online, and posting it in a place where you might be when making important financial decisions about your future. Or he suggests writing a thoughtful letter to your future self before making financial choices. The goal is to decrease the perceived gap between the present self and the distant future self — to bring the future self to the present, so that we can greet him or her and develop a bit of a connection.

Self-nudging can even work at the superficial level of clothing. What we wear can change how we see, feel, think, and behave. For example, in three experiments conducted at Northwestern University, participants were assigned to wear a white lab coat. In the first study, wearing the lab coat improved participants' attention spans — critical to presence in fast-paced, unfamiliar situations. But the results went a step further: when the subjects were told that the coat was a doctor's coat, wearing it improved their attention spans even more. When they were told it was a painter's coat, they did not experience the same benefit.[22]

Reframing an emotion, making friends with a picture of your future self, wearing clothing that fits the role — these are just a few of the ways in which we can change the future by slowly, incrementally changing how we interact with the present. Psychologists are starting to turn their attention toward uncovering other self-nudges. This is only the beginning.

Maria, a woman who'd been struggling with depression that prevented her from fully engaging with her work, wrote me this e-mail:

> I used to identify with my "intelligence" as a great source of confidence. After recurrent bouts of clinical depression, I found myself feeling more and more like an impostor every time I started a new job.
>
> Yesterday, five seconds away from pressing Send on an e-mail I had written to my supervisor explaining why I couldn't accept my new position after all, and forty-five minutes away from my first day on the job, I managed to drag myself out of bed and power pose and "roar" my way into the shower, the car, and the front door of my new office.

It's not as if Maria will never again be daunted by challenges that will cause her self-doubts to flare up. But she will have a new memory, a new self-knowledge, a feeling of self-efficacy and agency, not to mention the reinforcement she'll get from her supervisor and colleagues.

It's about today, the next hour, or just the next moment.

Remember Eve Fairbanks — the journalist who learned to surf — and how she described what happened: "Pleasure built upon pleasure, the certainty of my ability amplifying with each new trial."

With each self-nudge, pleasure builds upon pleasure, power upon power, and presence upon presence.

11

Fake It Till You Become It

*I am larger, better than I thought, I did not know
I held so much goodness.*
— WALT WHITMAN

I WISH I COULD share with you the thousands of stories that people have shared with me. With surprising frequency, they begin with "I want to tell you how you changed my life." But the absolute truth is that I didn't change anyone's lives; *they* changed their *own* lives. They took the simple ideas I presented, then adapted and expanded them in ways that I never could have imagined. I've chosen a handful of their stories to share with you. They come straight from people who, when facing a big challenge or when helping someone else who was facing a big challenge, acted on their new understanding of how the body guides the mind — leading them and the people they were helping to their boldest and most authentic selves. They are stories of people who got there by faking it, in many cases, till they became it.

My hope is that you will recognize yourself somewhere among them. I say this because I believe that the part of my TED talk that had the biggest impact was not the research I presented, it was my confession that I've spent a good part of my life believing "I don't deserve to be here." Although I didn't understand it at the time, I now see why that mattered: it made people feel less alone in the world, knowing that at least one other person has felt this way and has (mostly) overcome that feeling. One true story, one honest confession, can be powerful.

I'll start by telling you about Will, who wrote to me when he was a twenty-one-year-old college student at the University of Oregon and part-time actor.

Will's agent called and told him he'd found a perfect role for him — a long shot, but the kind of opportunity he couldn't refuse. It was a part in a major motion picture that would be filmed in Oregon, and the director and producers were looking for young, outdoorsy male actors. Will thought his agent was crazy. This was way out of his league. He'd done some television commercials, had roles in a couple of small films, and made an appearance on an episode of a TV series, but he really wasn't focused on becoming an actor. He knew he'd be competing against pros.

Will, who considers himself a bit of a risk taker, agreed to go to the audition. But he didn't arrive filled with confidence. Instead he got there, looked around the waiting room, and thought, "What have I gotten myself into?" Suddenly hit by a wave of intense anxiety, he remembered something a friend had told him: if you feel nervous before an interview, you should find some privacy and pose like Wonder Woman for two minutes.

So Will found the men's restroom. "I opened the stall door, laughed at myself for a few seconds, then put my hands on my hips, raised my chin, stuck out my chest, and stood there in silence, smiling, for 120 seconds. Deep breaths." He didn't remember exactly what this was supposed to do, but he admires his friend, whom he describes as someone who "has never let me down when it comes to sharing strange facts or insights into chasing my dreams." Will had enough faith in his advice to at least give it a try.

"I walked back into the waiting room, sat tall in my chair, and waited for my name to be called," Will remembered. When it was, he said, "I walked into the audition room without a care in the world. I had nothing to lose."

The audition went beautifully. Not only did he not feel anxious, he also enjoyed it. He was not the least bit intimidated by the film's famous director. Will had never felt more himself in an audition — more vital, more "on."

When Will walked out, his dad was waiting for him.

"Well?" he asked. "How'd it go?"

Beaming, Will exclaimed, "Great! I nailed it!"

"So you got the part?!"

Will paused. "Oh, no ... I mean, I don't know. But it went great! It was so much fun. I've never felt better during an audition."

Will had nearly forgotten about the role in the film. He was so present during the audition, so engaged with the process, that the outcome became secondary ... or maybe no longer relevant.

By sheer coincidence, Will's surname is Cuddy. (We're not related.) And you will see his name in the credits for the Oscar-nominated film *Wild*, starring Reese Witherspoon. His enthusiasm, confidence, and passion came through during the audition. And his sense of personal power allowed him to unlock and share the competencies he needed to succeed in that situation. The Oregon Cuddys and the Boston Cuddys have stayed in touch. In fact, Will and his father flew to Boston to see *Wild* with my family and me on the night it premiered.

Will's story beautifully captures the ideal effect of presence: you execute with comfortable confidence and synchrony, and you leave with a sense of satisfaction and accomplishment, regardless of the measurable outcome. In Will's case, he nearly forgot there *was* a measurable outcome.

Many of the stories I hear have to do with challenges at work or school, the arenas where we often feel most challenged and where the stakes (and the anxieties) are highest. People find all kinds of ways to apply the science of presence to the job search and interview process. Here's how Melanie did it:

> I had been struggling for months after being laid off from my job, doing the unemployment shuffle, feeling like a perpetual game show contestant. It's been a very demoralizing time. My son pointed me to your video and said, "You need to try this!"
>
> So I did, and I practiced power poses for a few minutes before my next three job interviews. Rather than folding my hands in my lap, I put my elbows on the arms of the chair. I got offers from two out of the three employers I interviewed with. I took the better of the two and start my new job Monday....
>
> When I get to my new job...I will no longer curl up and make myself small. When our minds and insecurities make us feel insignificant, it seems our bodies really can remind us that we are, in fact, made of the stuff of stars.

Thomas brought the science of presence into his business meetings:

I have a commerce company in which I deal with a number of global brands. I've struggled for years with accurately conveying my expertise and delivering my vision to particularly dominant people, and I hadn't realized until your TED talk that in my nonverbal communication, when dealing with business leaders, I have always assumed a powerless role.

For two months I had been working on a huge deal, and the deal had essentially gone stale. Every negotiation had been via video conference calls, and I realized that my posture had always been poor. I would let my shoulders drop and often keep one hand on my chin.

So... today, inspired by your presentation, I stood in my office, arms akimbo, feet spread apart, and I initiated a video call to the key decision makers. I found myself speaking as if I were explaining the deal to a friend in my kitchen.

Moral of the story: for the first time in half a dozen meetings, I was able to accurately display expertise and vision... and I landed the contract. :) I will be implementing power posing as a companywide initiative. We'll be known as the company that meets with their hands on their hips!

As a student from Nigeria, studying in Canada, René felt like he didn't belong.

I never used to participate in class discussions. Like most freshmen, I believe, I was a bit intimidated. I doubted the validity of my opinions. A good friend of mine sent me your TED talk, and I can affirm today that it completely changed my university experience. I started raising my hand in class, attending and speaking at conferences — by choice! Thank you for reminding us that nothing, especially self-doubt, no nothing, should prevent us from realizing our full potential.

René found a way to defeat this doubt to become not only a successful student, but also a leader on campus and an entrepreneur.

I also hear from concerned parents and teachers trying to help their children and students navigate schoolwork, social life, and other important childhood and adolescent issues. For example, a father named Noah helped his daughter use the science of presence to conquer fear:

As an executive coach and author I am very eager to study neuroplasticity and brain research, but your talk went way beyond professional interest for me. After watching it I had my wife and two daughters (ages eight and ten) all watch it as well. Ever since, we have all been doing power poses. Fast-forward a couple of months. In my older daughter's fourth-grade class they have the option to deliver a special presentation on Fridays. This is a thirty-minute presentation by one of the students on any topic of their choice. My daughter Sophie has been... practically petrified of doing this, but for some reason she finally volunteered. Much to my shock (and against my recommendation) she insisted on doing her Expert Friday [presentation] on the brain. In the ten minutes leading up to [it] she started to get nervous and described to me what sounded like precursors to panic attacks. So without anyone there to tell her what to do, she did what you taught her. She power posed in preparation. She said it calmed her down and got her ready to go.

When the time came she said her presentation was "awesome!"

We've spent all year trying to convince her to be willing to say two words from the front of the classroom. Power posing helped get her up there for an entire thirty minutes, and now she wants to do it again.

Rebecca, the mother of a high school freshman, says her daughter used the science of presence to up her academic game:

I loved your TED talk on power poses. By some stroke of fortunate timing, my high-school-freshman daughter was in the room, too, and also watched it. She had been suffering from test anxiety, so partly as a joke and partly out of desperation for a cure, she started power posing before tests, and I swear she hasn't gotten under 100 percent in the past three months! Her friends, who thought she was a kook when she began, are doing it, and their results have also improved. Now it has spread to the girls' soccer team. It's an epidemic of... Wonder Woman look-alikes spreading through the youth of our community! It may be a case of Dumbo's feather, I can't be sure, but even if it's fake (which I don't think it is), it has given my daughter so much confidence in herself and her ability to perform under pressure, it is a miracle to behold. Thank you so much for sharing your wonderful insight.

Here's a message from Barbara, a teacher who brought the science into her classroom:

> I introduced my AP physics students to power posing last spring. One student in particular was always nervous during assessments, and therefore his test scores did not represent his abilities at all. I showed the video of your talk to my class and told them to give it a try. We all know that old saying about correlation and causation, and this was no scientific study, but from that day forward that student power posed before every physics test, and his grades went from high Cs and low Bs to where he belonged — in the middle and low As. He then went on to take the AP exam in early May and earned a 4 [out of 5]. I'm convinced that pp'ing helped him, even if it is difficult to prove.

One of my favorite stories appeared on a wonderful blog called Crazy Mom with Kids, which is the brainchild of C. G. Rawles, a writer, artist, and graphic designer. One of her pieces concerned her six-year-old daughter, Sage, who watched a horror movie on TV that left her with a paralyzing fear. She was convinced that her dolls were going to attack her while she slept, and no amount of comforting could stop her from waking up in the middle of the night, screaming. Even removing all the dolls and stuffed animals from her room didn't help.

Then, Rawles wrote:

> I came across Amy Cuddy's TED talk, "Your Body Language Shapes Who You Are." I was amazed and decided to try the principles with my girls, especially Sage. Going

forward, I told my daughters, we were going to "fake it until we become it," to quote Amy Cuddy.

Every day, I followed the advice Cuddy suggested, which was to tell my girls to find a power position and hold it for two minutes. Sage became a big fan of the Wonder Woman pose, so I made her stand with her hands on her hips, feet at shoulder [width], head held high, before entering a room alone.

It caught on. At times, before fetching things for me from the other side of our home or being alone in her room, Sage would put her hands on her hips and assume the position, or she would raise her arms up high like she'd just crossed the finish line in first place.

Her anxiety began to dissipate, and her confidence returned.

So here we are — a year later . . . and Sage has improved dramatically. She simply needed to tap into her inner Wonder Woman and assume a power pose.

It helps, too, that the dolls are still locked in the closet.

And the e-mail below came from a teacher at an elementary school. He described how he applied the fake-it-till-you-become-it ideas to help a fifth-grade student with selective mutism, a childhood anxiety disorder that blocks children from being able to communicate in certain social situations:

I have been journaling almost daily with [the student] this year, and he's begun to open up a bit in the journal, as well as slightly in the classroom. I watched the last section [of your TED talk], "Fake It Till You Become It," with him and explained how I'd like him to try to do this once each day in the classroom when I'm in there (an hour or so daily). While I watched your talk, I chatted "to" him gently about how I wanted to see him succeed in his future, how smart he is, and how his unspoken leadership skills show by the way others want to work with him on a regular basis. He began to cry at around the same point you did (and I was able to not cry while watching with him, but wasn't able to hold back at home), and since then, he's been answering a question or two daily. Recently I asked him to take charge of a reading response group's first question, and he did so without hesitation.

As we've seen throughout this book, power posing and athletics are a natural match — all the various postures of victory are identical to the positions that have been shown, in the lab, to increase confidence and presence. I've heard from countless athletes and coaches in track and field, ski racing, rowing, baseball, basketball, water polo, soccer, gymnastics, volleyball, even sailing.

In the first month after my TED talk was posted, I heard from an Olympic swimming coach who explained how he'd been using a power posing–type strategy — with great success — for years: encouraging some of his swimmers, beginning on the morning of the race, to physically behave as if they'd won their events. Swimmers, as he pointed out, are notorious for their use of dominant body language in the moments before races, not only to signal their power to their competitors but also to loosen their muscles and pump themselves up. Sometimes they will literally pound their chests, like gorillas. But the approach this coach used — encouraging swimmers to adopt "alpha" nonverbal postures from the minute they wake up on race days — was most helpful to swimmers who'd been thrown off by a poor performance or who were feeling a wave of insecurity and self-doubt.

Kenyon College swimming and diving coach Jess Book happened upon the video of my TED talk by chance and thought it might help his teams' performance. "Power posing reinforces the idea that we want to be powerful, strong, and confident," he told *Swimming World* magazine. "While the whole team did not embrace the idea, many did. And those that drew the most benefit from it were those who typically felt the pressure from their own thoughts. Power posing not only gave them a physiological boost, but provided a tangible connection to the rest of the team — something outside of themselves."

A Kenyon swimmer, Sarah Lloyd, wrote about what happened when the entire team, coaches included, would stand in the X pose before a match:

> You couldn't help but giggle at the sight of it. We all looked pretty silly, but I think it worked for us. We connected as a team in a way that we hadn't the season before. Our energy levels skyrocketed, individuals and relays had mind-blowingly fast swims, and we had a blast on the pool deck.

Here's an e-mail about volleyball from Steve, a high school teacher in the midwestern United States:

> I showed your TED talk to all of my high school classes today. My students were very much engaged and pointed out several power poses throughout the day that just happened without prompting. The coolest part of the story

happened tonight when our volleyball team lost their first game in the regional playoffs and came onto the court to start the second match all in a power pose. They won the next three games to move on to the finals. I think there was some outstanding VB preparation and great coaching involved, but the kids truly believed in YOUR message enough to use it in a tough situation. After the match the girls approached me to ask how proud I was of their "power poses"! I love it. Thanks for a being part of our TED Talk Tuesdays and part of my students' education.

I'm most inspired when I hear from people facing serious difficulties — domestic abuse and violence, homelessness, and other problems that can make life hell — who have managed to regain control over their lives and their futures. I am moved, every time, by these stories.

I've heard from quite a few combat veterans, such as Roberto:

I'm a combat veteran who suffers from PTS issues, and I am currently studying psychology. I stumbled upon your talk video, and to make a long story short, I really took to your information and personal experiences. Since listening to your presentation on power poses, I have become very mindful of my own body language and recognize when I am subconsciously isolating. This information has opened up a previously closed-off existence and has helped me to overcome some of the symptoms of uneasiness and high alert associated with my PTS. Since adding this mindful recognition of body language to my strategies for coping, I have been able to excel in areas I wasn't confident in before.

CJ, outreach coordinator for a domestic violence agency called Turning Point, who teaches classes at a reformatory for women (i.e., a women's prison), shared this story:

I am a survivor of domestic violence. I got a job in a domestic violence shelter after leaving [the abusive relationship]. I have done a lot of self-healing [and] personal growth, and I have continued to do self-education through nonconventional means. I have learned through the years that I am somewhat [of] a geek. I love to read studies and especially love social science.

After twenty years working in the domestic violence field, I began doing educational groups in a women's prison. They soak up the information like sponges, especially when they learn how our bodies kick in with all the chemicals when we are frightened and how old trauma plays into it all.

I have been showing my classes your video. I wish you could see the lightbulbs going on over their heads. We have a discussion afterward, and I ask them how power posing could benefit them.

My students have identified these moments when they can use your power posing.

1. Their judicial hearings before the parole board.
2. Investigation within the prison.
3. Test taking, such as the GED.
4. Interviews after they leave prison.
5. Interviews within the walls for privileged committee seats.

What you have discovered about power posing and the way it takes us back to our true essence really resonated with me. Thank you for saying, "Share the science." I am.

Your work is going [inside] prison walls and being shared with those who need it most.

Mac, who lives in California, confronts daily hardships that many of us have never experienced. He took the time to share these reflections:

I have been homeless since September 2012. It isn't a very interesting story so I won't go into it. What I will tell you is that you and power posing have helped me immensely. No, I didn't turn everything around and get a high-powered job, but I am able to face the myriad difficult and often frightening problems I face as a homeless person in part because while at a warming shelter last winter I watched your TED talk on a tablet I had at the time. Before then I often dealt with intense shame, feelings of marginalization; my lifelong issues of depression and anxiety were hardly helped by becoming homeless either. I was often quite visibly homeless: filthy, unkempt, and I believe I just gave off that air of being homeless.

Right now, even though I will go to sleep on a piece of cardboard tonight, you would never pick me out as homeless. In fact, other homeless people who see me on the street often hit me up for money, to which I reply (with a smile), "I'm out here too." I give quite a bit of credit to [the fact] that I consciously adopted power posing and maximizing my space, and stopping myself when I do the opposite. I do not mean to ramble on, but I was watching something else where you talk about hearing from a violinist and some others and guessed you had never heard from a homeless person before. Well, at least in this case, it works for us too. Thank you very much for your time and I wish you well.

Annike, a recent college graduate from Switzerland, described to me how she found the courage to leave a long-term abusive relationship and begin to recover.

"He took away my self-confidence and all my motivation for having hobbies or any drive for happiness," she wrote. "I was not myself anymore." While visiting a friend in Ireland, she stumbled upon my TED talk, and she and her friend watched it together. Her friend intuited that it might help Annike. Annike describes what happened then:

From that day forward, every day, my friend sent me a message asking for a picture of me in a power position, no matter where I was at that moment. It might sound cheesy, but I think this changed my life. I did it for so long [that], as you said, I faked it until I became it. I slowly changed back to my old self, constantly having your instructions in the back of my head. I managed to break up with my boyfriend, and I started realizing good things about myself. I applied power positions in all kinds of situations as soon as I started to feel insecure.

Now I'm even trying to hop out of my comfort zone regularly because I know this trick to feel good. Yesterday I was doing a presentation in front of the biggest researchers [in my field at my university], even though I started with my PhD only a week ago. Former Annike would have found an excuse not to go, but I did, and it was great. They treated me as an equal, and I could convince them to cooperate with me. I believe in myself again, and I'm proud of myself.

But then came Annike's biggest challenge:

I met my ex-boyfriend two days ago. I haven't seen him since a year and a half ago, and I was terrified of meeting him again. When I saw him walking along the hall of the university, I straightened my back, made myself tall, and approached him myself. For the very first time, it was me leading the conversation, and I could see that he was very surprised about my self-confidence. It's the first time since many years that I'm happy again, and your talk helped me [in] getting there.... It is so easy though so helpful.

I also hear from therapists, clinicians, and physicians who are finding simple ways to use power posing to help their patients. Here's how Myra does it:

I am a clinical psychologist in South Africa who is using [power poses] to enable my patients to change negative belief sets. When they feel trapped by a belief...I get them to stand in a power position. They all report they can no longer hold the negative belief while standing in that posture!

David, a disability instructor in Australia, sent me this message:

I work as a disability instructor, assisting [disabled] people in a supported work environment to gain skills [so that they can] achieve [their] goals of getting work in main-stream employment. Teaching skills to people with dis-abilities is the easy part; assisting them to gain confidence was a little more difficult — before I began to introduce the powerful poses you talked about. The [positive] changes in attitude and the decrease in anxiety are noticeable, and it has assisted a majority of them to successfully obtain full-time employment.

Why stop with humans? Some people are using power posing ideas to help animals. One of the most unusual e-mails I received was from a horse trainer named Kathy, who had been working for years on a project that "encourages horses to find intrinsically motivating behaviors as a means to both physical and mental rehab."

It has been surprisingly successful (though [it] would not be surprising for you, of course). Your TED talk helped put so many things into place, and so I tried a little experiment with one of [my horses]. This horse has always been at the bottom of the herd hierarchy, despite being physically bigger, fitter, stronger than the rest. He is introverted and would not engage in play with the other horses, and never wanted to show off, even in play. Yet he is becoming quite athletic and is very talented.

So, having thought about your work, I devised an exercise that would cause him to physically "act" like a badass (by chasing something as a predator would, trying to strike or attack it, which is what horses do in play or when flirting). It was wildly successful beyond any expectation I had. Within three days, he was acting out those same movements in the pasture and trying to initiate rowdy play with the others. This was entirely new behavior (and has been a little shocking for the other horses). It has not made him more aggressive, but it really does *appear* as though this is precisely what a horse with more testosterone and lower cortisol would demonstrate.

In a follow-up e-mail a few months later, Kathy wrote:

Vafi had been dismissed by almost everyone in our community [of Icelandic horse enthusiasts and trainers] as being "just a family horse," certainly not the kind of horse that belongs in the highest levels of competition, where you find only the most talented, fit, and, above all, *proud* horses.

Last weekend was our annual spring Icelandic horse show. I entered Vafi in the most advanced class, where the current number-one-ranked horse and rider team in the world was competing, along with nine others.

You know where this is going.

We shocked everyone by making it into the finals, where it was five horses — Vafi and four others, who are all qualified for the world championships in Berlin. It was quite a sight, and dozens of people were wondering what magic/voodoo turned Vafi into such a different horse. :)

There were people at this show who had considered buying Vafi before I did, but nobody thought very highly of him as a competition horse...he was just a "kids' trail horse." They saw just how wrong they were, but they are even more shocked by the "mystery" of how this change occurred. Because it was *not* that he is now fitter and more capable, it is that he *wants* to show off...to display his speed and power and general awesomeness, which — in the Icelandic horse world — is a huge part. These are the horses of the Vikings, and spirit matters deeply in this community and to the judges...we show these horses on a racing track. :)

Thank you again — your work led me into something unexpected and wonderful for me and my horses.

And about a year after that, when she began working with a new horse, Draumur, Kathy wrote:

The world championship tryouts for Icelandic horses is happening in ten weeks, and I'm taking *both* my horses to the qualifying. Everyone in the equine world would have thought that absolutely impossible just a few years ago. Meanwhile both Vafi and Draumur have taken the power pose, act-like-a-badass [approach] to new levels. So far, the benefits have not even begun to plateau — [the horses] just keep getting more motivated and much more fit and strong. Equine biomechanics experts are starting to pay attention, and the current world-ranking leader from Iceland flew over to learn how I did this with Draumur. You started something that is taking on a life of its own in the horse world.[1]

And in her most recent e-mail, she wrote:

I've just been talking to our horse community about the fact that this power pose approach seems to have no end to its potential. I've been doing this for several years and the horses are *still* making breakthroughs. If anything, it's such a virtuous cycle that their progress is *accelerating*. They're like Benjamin Button horses with this power pose approach — their behavior is as though they are aging in reverse.

So, NO SLOWING DOWN so far with the power pose progress here!!

In a way, this is the most convincing anecdotal evidence of all — nobody told Vafi or Draumur or any of the other horses what power posing was supposed to do.[2] Kathy and I discovered that trainers have been getting their horses to power pose for a long time — for more than two thousand years, in fact:

> *Let the horse be taught . . . to hold his head high and arch*
> *his neck. . . . By training him to adopt the very airs and*
> *graces which he naturally assumes when showing off to*
> *best advantage, you have . . . a splendid and showy animal,*
> *the joy of all beholders. . . . Under the pleasurable sense of*
> *freedom . . . with stately bearing and legs pliantly moving*
> *he dashes forward in his pride, in every respect imitating*
> *the airs and graces of a horse approaching other horses.*
> — Xenophon (430–354 BCE)

A short time ago, someone shared a story that left me speechless — and in tears. I had just finished giving a talk, and a number of people were waiting to say hello, ask questions, and so on. I noticed a young woman waiting patiently. I've become very sensitive to noticing when people need privacy. I can see an intensity in their eyes. They're letting me know they have something very personal to share, something they're not comfortable saying in front of strangers.

This woman was flanked by two friends, who were gently touching her shoulders, speaking softly to her, comforting and encouraging her. When she reached me, eyes brimming with tears, she at first had trouble speaking. There was quite a long silence — not an uncomfortable one, more like a moment of reorienting, for both of us. Preparing. She gathered herself, took a deep breath, then said, "I came here to meet you because I need you to know how you've changed my life."

The story she told me that night changed my life, too. It

beautifully demonstrated how we connect through our bodies with our authentic best selves, unlock our personal power, and use those things to be present in the midst of our most enormous challenges — freeing others to be present as well. And it illustrated exactly how I'd hoped people would use this research — to find their personal power when they have very little social power or status. To channel courage and generosity. To change the course of their lives. To do well for themselves and good for others.

I asked if she'd be willing to share her story with all of you, and she said, "There's nothing I'd like more than to do that, so other people might feel supported and inspired to do the same."

So we spent the next afternoon talking. Here's Kristin's story:

On a whim, I moved to South America. I got married when I was really young, got divorced when I was thirty, and I felt that I couldn't move on with my life until I saw the world a little bit more. So I made it a point to go there, and I found a place to live with a few other people — we called it the tree house. It was all reclaimed wood and on stilts in completely open air. It was simple and beautiful.

Kristin began working in a local café.

Everything seemed fine, and it wasn't right away, but within a couple of weeks [my boss] started making comments to me about my body. About my chest and about getting better tips because of my chest, and he did that more and more. He made comments all the time, constantly. And my first reaction was disappointment because I thought, he has two small children; he lives very close to me; it's a small town, and I had a different impression of who he was in my head. But I thought, you know, I guess this is what happens... and maybe it's not that bad. Being in a foreign country, I was scared — the sense of needing to belong can be really strong and powerful, and it can make you afraid. You take yourself out of your comfort zone when you move to a foreign country and try to make it. The comforts were completely stripped away.

Every day, the sexual harassment escalated.

So I thought, like, I'm tough, and so I just kept going with it. I just passed it off as "he's being a jerk." But it got worse and worse and worse. I don't think I even realized it then, but I was just feeling smaller and smaller.... And then one day, he just stopped calling me by my name and only referred to me as [a very vulgar name]. From that day forward, that was the only name he used to address me.

I knew how wrong that was, and I hated it, but then again, you sometimes question yourself and wonder, "Is this a big enough deal?" Which sounds ridiculous now.

Shortly thereafter, a small group of her close female and male friends invited her to dinner. She said she was "feeling so small and broken that I almost didn't go." But she did go.

I thought, "I would be so ashamed to tell [my friends] what I've let happen." But then I started thinking about where I had come from, what I'd gone through, and who I am at my core... and so I decided to tell them about what was happening. They were so supportive, the women and the men, and that really propelled my decision: I knew at that point that I had to say something to my boss — I had to stand up for myself and for all the other people who have experienced this. For all the people who were at risk of experiencing it in the future. I had to do it for myself and for them.

My friend had shared your talk with me a few months earlier, and it really struck a nerve then, but I realized that now was the time to put your message into action. I had a couple of days to think about it. I decided to go in early before a morning staff meeting. I remember being alone at the tree house, which was rare. I put on a certain song, and I made sure I dressed up in a way that made me feel good. . . . And then I stood in this house made of stilts, I stood up straight and tall, with my hands on my hips and my shoulders back — and I stood there for more than a couple minutes, because I really wanted to make it stick! When I left the house and as I began to walk into town, I felt myself getting bigger and bigger — in a way I hadn't felt in a long time. I was embodying my own higher self and thinking, "I've got to bring her, I have to do this for myself first and foremost but I also have to do this for everybody else." There was no question about whether I was going to just ignore him or send a note telling him that I quit. I could get out of the situation in other ways, but standing up for myself was a way that elevated me to my own power. . . .

When I got there, I felt strong and I realized that my boss wasn't as big as I thought he was — not as big as he'd been in my mind. He seemed smaller. And I felt myself taking my power back from him. I wasn't taking his power; I was just taking back the power I'd allowed him to take from me. I told him that I was leaving, and I told him why.

I said, "You know that what you've been doing is wrong. You know because you have daughters who you love, and you would never want anyone to treat them as you've been treating me." I told him that I didn't want to hurt him or his business — that I wanted him to change his behavior, to not hurt anyone else, and to be a better and bigger person. He said, "You're right. I'm sorry. I don't know why I did this," and he apologized over and over again. We talked for a good twenty minutes. I felt this incredible generosity. I felt strong, but not dominant in an alpha way. I felt strong enough to be compassionate. And I almost wish I had a tape recorder of what I said because it wasn't me — it was . . . divine.

And I responded to Kristin, "It was divine because it was exactly you. It was the very best you — the strongest most generous you."

As I said at the beginning, this book is about moments. It's about being present in the moments that most challenge us. It's also about trusting that those moments build upon themselves as we nudge ourselves forward, reinforcing our thinking, feelings, and physiology. Ultimately these moments can change our lives.

The most commonly quoted line from my TED talk is "Don't fake it till you make it, fake it till you become it." That's what this is about — incrementally nudging yourself to become the best version of yourself. Being present during challenging moments. It's not about fooling other people to get the things you desire, then having to continue with the charade. It's about fooling yourself, just a little bit, until you feel more powerful, more present — and it's about keeping up the practice, even if it takes time to get there. As one young woman, Monique, wrote to me, "I am still 'faking it until I become it,' but faking it sure is better than avoiding it!" Recall what my academic crush, William James, told us: "Begin to be now what you will be hereafter."

With all these things dancing around in my head, I was reminded of the legendary choreographer and dancer Agnes de Mille, who said: "To dance is to be out of yourself. Larger, more beautiful, more powerful. This is power, it is glory on earth, and it is yours for the taking."

Dance your way to presence. Seize the large, beautiful, powerful parts of yourself — the ones you love and believe. They are, indeed, yours for the taking.

Acknowledgments

Preparing these acknowledgments is daunting — which is mostly a blessing, because it means that many, many people have supported, guided, helped, and challenged me. I am grateful to the countless people who gave so much of their time and wisdom to make the publication of *Presence* possible.

I know it might be unusual to begin an acknowledgments section by quoting someone else's acknowledgments section, but I don't know if I can describe Richard Pine better than Susan Cain described him in *Quiet*: "the smartest, savviest, and menschiest literary agent that any writer could hope to work with." With great clarity, he sees an idea and its potential before other people are fully able to see them. And when he does, he becomes a devoted and stalwart supporter of the idea and its author. I am forever indebted to Richard, and to the whole team at InkWell Management.

At Little Brown, I'm grateful to Reagan Arthur for believing in this project and for giving me a dream team of people to help bring it to life. It's been an honor to work with my extraordinary editor, Tracy Behar, who knew exactly how to help me put all the pieces together, who has given so much of herself to this book, and who has done so with great poise and presence. Thank you for taking me on, Tracy, and not giving up during my many moments of self-doubt. And thanks to my entire, incredibly talented Little, Brown team, including Nicole Dewey, who has walked me through every step of the process of learning how to share with others my own excitement about this book, Jean Garnett, lover of words and incomparable finesser of sentences (I don't know if that's a real word, Jean), and Miriam Parker, who has built a beautiful website. I'm also grateful to Mario Pulice, Julie Ertl, Betsy Uhrig, and Genevieve Nierman — all members of my fantastic Little, Brown dream team. I was fortunate to work with outside editor Bill Tonelli, who has a very special eye for knowing how to tell a story; Matthew Hutson, who meticulously reviewed, challenged, and triple-checked the research I ultimately covered in this book; and Sheri Fink, who wisely spotted the knots that needed to be worked out. Chris Werner, Jeff Gernsheimer, and Jack Gernsheimer, who took my grade-school idea for a jacket and turned it into something I am so proud to be associated with — thank you for your vision and patience.

At Harvard, there are several people who made the publication of *Presence* possible — all of whom are not just incredibly competent, but also kind and generous. My former lab manager Nico Thornley miraculously organized a mess of research projects; recruited, trained, and managed a phenomenal group of undergraduate research assistants; contributed substantively to the development of theory, questions, and methods; and did it all without breaking a sweat. Kailey Anarino *is* my working memory, balancing and organizing the countless moving parts of my work life with grace and professionalism. I truly don't know how she does it. Jack Schultz, my current lab manager, works so hard to efficiently manage my lab group and many research projects, including communicating with collaborators and research assistants; organizing lab meetings, data collection, and analysis; and massive literature reviews; and he is always searching for creative solutions to big challenges. I'm indebted to the many dedicated research assistants and undergraduate students who have assisted with this research over the years. Brian Hall and Joe Navarro, thank you for getting this ball rolling. My kind and clever colleagues in Negotiations, Organizations, and Markets (NOM) unit at HBS — it's an honor to work with all of you. And thank you to my MBA students, doctoral students, executive students, and my students in organizations all around the world.

I am lucky to have been raised by a long line of female teachers and mentors, each of whom fed, watered, and shined sunlight on me before gently passing me along to the next in line. Beginning at my tiny rural Pennsylvania school, Conrad Weiser: Elsa Wertz, my third-grade teacher, brought out my confidence in my ability and deservingness to *think* (and did the same for her two brilliant daughters, Annie and Mary, with whom I now collaborate); Kathy Mohn, my high school English teacher, cultivated my compulsive love of writing; and Barbara O'Connor, my high school history and sociology teacher, showed me how to question the status quo with courage and good humor. When I was an undergraduate at the University of Colorado, Professor Bernadette Park and then-PhD student Jennifer Overbeck introduced me to social psychology, guided me through an honors thesis on a topic I was convinced was important, and then had enough faith in me to pass me along to my graduate school adviser, Susan Fiske. Susan deserves some kind of medal, because I had little more than optimism and chutzpah when I started graduate school. I have never encountered a more devoted and thoughtful doctoral adviser anywhere in my life. Period. I don't know why she took me in, but I am eternally grateful to her for doing so. When I was a junior faculty member at Harvard, other women continued to encourage, support, and challenge me, including Kathleen McGinn, Robin Ely, Teresa Amabile, Jan Hammond, Youngme Moon, Frances Frei, and Rosabeth Moss Kanter. Because of you, I am here. And I will try to do the same for other young women (and men) who are in need of food, water, and sunshine.

Without the research, I most certainly would have a lot less to write about. The list of smart scientists who've contributed to this body of research is very long. But first and foremost, I am enormously and eternally grateful to Dana Carney, a meticulous and devoted scientist and the real brains behind so much of the research in this book; I learned so much from working with you. Andy Yap, you've been a thoughtful and inspiring collaborator; it's been such a pleasure. Susan Fiske and Peter Glick: although our shared research isn't the primary focus of this book, in a way it underpins all of my thinking about social psychology; thank you for including and working with me for more than fifteen years. Lizzie Baily Wolf, you've helped me to think through so many of the details of these ideas, in addition to being an outstanding collaborator. And to all my other collaborators who've significantly contributed to this research, I thank you: Maarten Bos, James Gross, Kelly Hoffman, Elise Holland, Christina Kallitsantsi, Julia Lee, Jennifer Lerner, Christine Looser, Brian Lucas, Chris Oveis, Jonathan Renshon, Jack Schultz, Gary Sherman, Nico Thornley, Niko Troje, Abbie Wazlawek, Annie Wertz, and Caroline Wilmuth.

There's a long list of researchers with whom I haven't directly collaborated but whose outstanding research has been critically important to how I think about presence, power, and the body-mind connection, including (but certainly not limited to): Jessica Tracy, Pamela Smith, Joe Magee, Adam Galinsky, Deb Gruenfeld, Vanessa Bohns, Li Huang, Scott Wiltermuth, Bob Josephs,

Acknowledgments

Pranj Mehta, Lakshmi Balachandra, Leanne ten Brinke, Nancy Etcoff, Dan Cable, Alison Wood Brooks, Francesca Gino, Alison Lenton, Laura Morgan Roberts, Claude Steele, Geoff Cohen, David Sherman, Robert Sapolsky, and Bessel van der Kolk. Thanks to these and to all the other researchers who have contributed their ideas and their studies to this field.

I thank my dear community of writer friends, most of whom listened through panicked phone calls and patiently helped me to find the right words. Many, many thanks to this very special group of people: Susan Cain, Adam Grant, Neil Gaiman, Amanda Palmer, Simon Sinek, Adam Alter, Bill Ury, and Brené Brown. You held the exact sort of calming optimism that I needed.

The support and encouragement of my friends in the field has meant the world to me. Extra special thanks go to Kenworthey Bilz, Molly Crockett, Liz Dunn, Eli Finkel, June Gruber, Elizabeth Haines, Lily Jampol, Michael Morris, Kathy Phillips, Jennifer Richeson, Mindi Rock, and Todd Rose.

Many friends and supporters have helped and encouraged me in different ways before and throughout the book-writing process, including Michael Wheeler, Chantal and Michelle Blais, Marina Mitchell, Monica Lewinsky, Guy Raz, Joanna Coles, Mika Brzezinski, Jane McGonigal, Kelly McGonigal, Ken Cain, David Hochman, Eileen Lorraine, Kristin Vergara, Kendra Lauren "Mayor of Aspen" Gros, Peggy Fitzsimmons, Jason Webley, Wendy Berry Mendes, In Paik, Toni Schmader, David Gergan, Piper Kerman, Sam Sommers, Katie Stewart Sigler, Bret Sigler, Vera Sundström, Olga and Sergei Demidov, Alex and Amy Myles, April Rinne, Laurie and Josh Casselberry, Pat and Jack Casselberry, Christine Getman, Mac McGill, Uyen Nguyen, and so many members of my YGL community.

I owe a very special thanks to the people who helped me find my speaking voice; without you, I may not have had the opportunity to find my writing voice. Liz Dunn, thank you for bringing me as your guest to PopTech in 2010 and for showing me how to give a great psychology talk to a broad audience. Andew Zolli, Erik Hersman, and the PopTech team, thank you for inviting me to speak at PopTech 2011. Bruno Giussani and Chris Anderson, thank you for inviting me to speak at TEDGlobal 2012. I am grateful to the entire TED team, including June Cohen, Ben Lillie, Emily McManus, and many others.

I am forever in debt to the people who gave hours (and hours) of their time to be interviewed for *Presence*, who did so with great generosity (and presence). Their stories and perspectives are essential to this book: Reverend Jeffrey Brown, Pauline Rose Clance, Will Cuddy, Neil Gaiman, Jamini Kwon, Julianne Moore, Mikko Nissinen, Calida Garcia Rawles, Emma Seppälä, and Kathy Sierra.

To the many other wonderful people who allowed me to share their stories throughout the book but whom I cannot name: please know that you have my eternal admiration and gratitude. I have learned so much from you, and I'm honored to be able to share your stories with others who will learn from you.

And to all of you who have courageously shared your stories with me: strange as it seems, you taught me about the very topic I had been studying in the lab. You brought the science to life. You shaped the research questions I now ask. You are on every page of this book. And every day, you fuel my relentless optimism about people, which is truly what keeps me going. You have my deepest gratitude, and I hope that I have adequately honored you in these pages.

Finally: now that I've written a book, I *really* understand why people thank their families — they do it because writing a book is a bit like suddenly adopting and attending to a new family member...'round the clock. If you're not writing, you're thinking about writing. If you're not thinking about writing, you're thinking about how you *should* be thinking about writing. You're listening to your family's stories and thinking about how they relate to the material in the book. Honestly, it takes an enormous amount of love and patience for a family to fully support someone through this process. My husband, Paul Coster, and son, Jonah Cuddy, also deserve some kind of medal for their love, for their patience, and for their complete devotion to and faith in me. I don't know if I could have done what they did. Jonah, you are a wise, gentle soul with a presence that often leaves me awestruck; how did I get so lucky? Paul, you moved halfway around the world to be with me, to bring me adventure and the purest love.... Sheesh, I'm just so glad you got those blue pants! So, from the very bottom of my heart, thank you, Paul and Jonah.

Notes

Chapter 1 What Is Presence?

1. It might have been the fifth floor. It doesn't matter. It felt like the thousandth.

2. Diderot, D. (1830). *Paradoxe sur le comédien: Ouvrage posthume*. Paris: A. Sautelet, 37.

3. As Alan Watts wrote in *The Wisdom of Insecurity*, "Since what we know of the future is made up of purely abstract and logical elements — inferences, guesses, deductions — it cannot be eaten, felt, smelled, seen, heard, or otherwise enjoyed. To pursue it is to pursue a constantly retreating phantom, and the faster you chase it, the faster it runs ahead." Watts, A. (2011). *The wisdom of insecurity: A message for an age of anxiety*. New York: Vintage (original work published 1951), 60.

4. Ibid., 87.

5. Ibid., 61.

6. See Balachandra, L. (2015). *Keep calm and pitch on: Balancing and moderating affect in the entrepreneur's pitch*. Manuscript submitted for publication.

7. In a study of the influence of job applicants' verbal statements on interviewers' ratings of the applicant and on final hiring decisions, Angela Young and Michele Kacmar found that "interpersonal characteristics of enthusiasm, self-confidence and effectiveness had a significant influence on an interviewer's rating of an applicant's overall quality and the ultimate hiring decision." (Young, A. M., & Kacmar, C. M. [1998]. ABCs of the interview: The role of affective, behavioral, and cognitive responses by applicants in the employment interview. *International Journal of Selection and Assessment, 6*, 211–221.)

8. An excellent review of the research on outcomes of entrepreneurial passion for both the entrepreneur and the people working with the entrepreneur is found in Cardon, M. S., Wincent, J., Singh, J., & Drnovsek, M. (2009). The nature and experience of entrepreneurial passion. *Academy of Management*

Review, 34, 511–532. Also see Cardon, M. S., Gregoire, D. A., Stevens, C. E., & Patel, P. C. (2013). Measuring entrepreneurial passion: Conceptual foundations and scale validation. *Journal of Business Venturing, 28,* 373–396.

9. Levine, S. P., & Feldman, R. S. (2002). Women and men's nonverbal behavior and self-monitoring in a job interview setting. *Applied HRM Research, 7,* 1–14; Gudykunst, W. B., & Nishida, T. (2001). Anxiety, uncertainty, and perceived effectiveness of communication across relationships and cultures. *International Journal of Intercultural Relations, 25,* 55–71; McCarthy, J., & Goffin, R. (2004). Measuring job interview anxiety: Beyond weak knees and sweaty palms. *Personnel Psychology, 57,* 607–637.

10. DeGroot, T., & Motowidlo, S. J. (1999). Why visual and vocal interview cues can affect interviewers' judgments and predict job performance. *Journal of Applied Psychology, 84,* 986–993; McGovern, T. V., & Tinsley, H. E. (1978). Interviewer evaluations of interviewee nonverbal behavior. *Journal of Vocational Behavior, 13,* 163–171.

11. Baron, R. A. (1986). Self-presentation in job interviews: When there can be "too much of a good thing." *Journal of Applied Social Psychology, 16,* 16–28.

12. For a review of some of my research on stereotyping, prejudice, and discrimination, see Cuddy, A. J., Fiske, S. T., & Glick, P. (2008). Warmth and competence as universal dimensions of social perception: The stereotype content model and the BIAS map. In M. P. Zanna (Ed.), *Advances in experimental social psychology,* Vol. 40 (pp. 61–149). Waltham, MA: Academic Press; Cuddy, A. J. C., Glick, P., & Beninger, A. (2011). The dynamics of warmth and competence judgments, and their outcomes in organizations. *Research in Organizational Behavior, 31,* 73–98.

13. For privacy reasons, some names have been changed throughout the book.

14. Popova, M. (2014, January 6). An antidote to the age of anxiety. Retrieved from http://www.brainpickings.org/2014/01/06/alan-watts-wisdom -of-insecurity-1/.

15. Haigh, J. (1994). Fear, truth and reality in making presentations. *Management Decision, 32,* 58–60.

16. "Fake it until you become it." I will discuss this phenomenon in detail later in the book. But the essence of that idea is that we sometimes have to trick ourselves into seeing who we are and what we're capable of. We're not tricking others, because they have no reason to believe we're not capable. We're standing in our own way, which is why we have to fake ourselves out from time to time.

17. Cuddy, A. J. C., Wilmuth, C. A., & Thornley, N. Nonverbal presence signals believability in job interviews. Working manuscript.

18. If you're interested in learning more about introversion, I urge you to read Susan Cain's 2013 bestseller *Quiet: The Power of Introverts in a World*

That Can't Stop Talking. New York: Crown. Quotes were taken from an August 24, 2015, *Wall Street Journal* article by Elizabeth Bernstein, "Why Introverts Make Great Entrepreneurs": http://www.wsj.com/articles/why -introverts-make-great-entrepreneurs-1440381699.

19. If you'd like to know more about how impression-management techniques affect job interview outcomes, see Barrick, M. R., Shaffer, J. A., & DeGrassi, S. W. (2009). What you see may not be what you get: Relationships among self-presentation tactics and ratings of interview and job performance. *Journal of Applied Psychology, 94,* 1394–1411; Tsai, W. C., Chen, C. C., & Chiu, S. F. (2005). Exploring boundaries of the effects of applicant impression management tactics in job interviews. *Journal of Management, 31,* 108–125; Gilmore, D. C., & Ferris, G. R. (1989). The effects of applicant impression management tactics on interviewer judgments. *Journal of Management, 15,* 557–564; Stevens, C. K., & Kristof, A. L. (1995). Making the right impression: A field study of applicant impression management during job interviews. *Journal of Applied Psychology, 80,* 587–606; Howard, J. L., & Ferris, G. R. (1996). The employment interview context: Social and situational influences on interviewer decisions. *Journal of Applied Social Psychology, 26,* 112–136; Baron, R. A. (1986). Self-presentation in job interviews: When there can be "too much of a good thing." *Journal of Applied Social Psychology, 16,* 16–28; Baron, R. A. (1989). Impression management by applicants during employment interviews: The "too much of a good thing effect." In R. W. Eder & G. R. Ferris (Eds.), *The employment interview: Theory, research, and practice.* Newbury Park, CA: Sage Publications.

20. Marr, J. C., & Cable, D. M. (2014). Do interviewers sell themselves short? The effects of selling orientation on interviewers' judgments. *Academy of Management Journal, 57,* 624–651.

21. For a review, see Kernis, M. H. (2003). Toward a conceptualization of optimal self-esteem. *Psychological Inquiry, 14,* 1–26.

22. For a review, see Perkins, A. M., & Corr, P. J. (2014). Anxiety as an adaptive emotion. In G. Parrott (Ed.), *The positive side of negative emotions.* New York: Guilford Press.

23. Todd, A. R., Forstmann, M., Burgmer, P., Brooks, A. W., & Galinsky, A. D. (2015). Anxious and egocentric: How specific emotions influence perspective taking. *Journal of Experimental Psychology: General, 144,* 374–391.

24. Jung, C. G. (1962). *An analysis of a prelude to a case of schizophrenia.* Vol. 2 of *Symbols of transformation.* (R. F. C. Hull, Trans.). New York: Harper & Brothers.

25. For a review of stereotypes about liars, see Hartwig, M., & Bond, C. F., Jr. (2011). Why do lie-catchers fail? A lens model meta-analysis of human lie judgments. *Psychological Bulletin, 137,* 643–659.

26. Henig, R. M. (2006, February 5). Looking for the lie. *The New York Times Magazine*, 47–53.

27. That said, using thermography, a team of researchers from the University of Granada have shown some initial evidence that the temperature around the nose rises when we are telling a lie. Of course this is not visible to the naked eye, so it really can't be seen as a "Pinocchio effect." See University of Granada. (2012, December 3). *Researchers confirm the "Pinocchio Effect": When you lie, your nose temperature raises*. Retrieved from http://canalugr.es /index.php/social-economic-and-legal-sciences/item/61182-researchers -confirm-the-"pinocchio-effect"-when-you-lie-your-nose-temperature-raises.

28. Darwin, C. (1872). *The expression of the emotions in man and animals*. Chicago: University of Chicago Press. (As cited in ten Brinke, Leanne; Mac-Donald, Sarah; Porter, Stephen; O' Connor, Brian. [2012]. Crocodile tears: Facial, verbal and body language behaviours associated with genuine and fabricated remorse. *Law and Human Behavior, 36*, 51–59.)

29. Ormerod, T. C., & Dando, C. J. (2014). Finding a needle in a haystack: Toward a psychologically informed method for aviation security screening. *Journal of Experimental Psychology: General 144*, 76–84.

30. Ten Brinke et al., Crocodile tears, 52.

31. Ekman, P. (2009). *Telling lies: Clues to deceit in the marketplace, politics, and marriage* (Revised ed.). New York: W. W. Norton & Company.

32. Ten Brinke et al., Crocodile tears, 51.

33. Charles Bond and Bella DePaulo analyzed responses from nearly twenty-five thousand subjects and found that people accurately distinguish a lie from a truth about 54 percent of the time, which is barely better than the flip of a coin. This is consistent with many previous findings. See Bond, C. F., & DePaulo, B. M. (2006). Accuracy of deception judgments. *Personality and Social Psychology Review, 10*, 214–234.

34. Etcoff, N. L., Ekman, P., Magee, J. J., & Frank, M. G. (2000). Lie detection and language comprehension. *Nature, 405*, 139.

35. Ten Brinke, L., Stimson, D., & Carney, D. R. (2014). Some evidence for unconscious lie detection. *Psychological Science, 25*, 1098–1105.

36. Repp, B. H., & Su, Y. H. (2013). Sensorimotor synchronization: A review of recent research (2006–2012). *Psychonomic Bulletin & Review, 20*, 403–452.

Chapter 2 Believing and Owning Your Story

1. If you are interested in learning more about the psychology of the self, I strongly recommend Deci, E. L. (with Flaste, R.) (1995). *Why we do what we do: The dynamics of personal autonomy*. New York: Putnam.

2. More on academic theories of the authentic self and personal authenticity: Kernis and Goldman say that an authentic person possesses the following: awareness of and motivation to know his or her own goals, feelings, and self-beliefs, even if contradictory; unbiased processing of his or her own attributes, emotions, experiences, and knowledge; behavior in accord with personal needs, desires, and values; and a relational orientation toward honesty and openness to others. Wood says that to be authentic, one's actions must align with the personal values, preferences, beliefs, and motivations of which one is aware. Maslow, A. H. (1965). Some basic propositions of a growth and self-actualization psychology. In G. Lindzey and L. Hall (Eds.), *Theories of personality: Primary sources and research* (pp. 307–316). New York: John Wiley; Rogers, C. R. (1963). The concept of the fully functioning person. *Psychotherapy: Theory, Research & Practice, 1*, 17–23; Kernis, M. H., & Goldman, B. M. (2006). A multicomponent conceptualization of authenticity: Theory and research. In M. P. Zanna (Ed.), *Advances in experimental social psychology*, Vol. 38 (pp. 283–357). Waltham, MA: Academic Press; Wood, A. M., Linley, P. A., Maltby, J., Baliousis, M., & Joseph, S. (2008). The authentic personality: A theoretical and empirical conceptualization and the development of the Authenticity Scale. *Journal of Counseling Psychology, 55*, 385–399. Cable, D. M., Gino, F., & Staats, B. R. (2013). Breaking them in or eliciting their best? Reframing socialization around newcomers' authentic self-expression. *Administrative Science Quarterly, 58*, 1–36.

3. Lenton, A. P., Bruder, M., Slabu, L., & Sedikides, C. (2013). How does "being real" feel? The experience of state authenticity. *Journal of Personality, 81*, 276–289.

4. Lenton, A. (n.d.) Social Psychology Network profile. Retrieved from http://lenton.socialpsychology.org.

5. Sherman, D. K., & Cohen, G. L. (2006). The psychology of self-defense: Self-affirmation theory. In M. P. Zanna (Ed.), *Advances in experimental social psychology*, Vol. 38 (pp. 183–242). Waltham, MA: Academic Press.

6. Roberts, L. M., Dutton, J. E., Spreitzer, G. M., Heaphy, E. D., & Quinn, R. E. (2005). Composing the reflected best-self portrait: Building pathways for becoming extraordinary in work organizations. *Academy of Management Review, 30*, 712–736.

7. Roberts, L. M. (2010, September 30). *Your reflected best self.* Retrieved from http://positiveorgs.bus.umich.edu/news/your-reflected-best-self/.

8. Roberts et al., Composing the reflected best-self portrait.

9. Cohen, G. L., & Sherman, D. K. (2014). The psychology of change: Self-affirmation and social psychological intervention. *Annual Review of Psychology, 65*, 333–371. For support they cite Steele, C. M. (1988). The psychol-

ogy of self-affirmation: Sustaining the integrity of the self. *Advances in Experimental Social Psychology, 21*, 261–302.

10. Cohen & Sherman, The psychology of change. This article provides a thorough and very accessible review of this vast literature. I highly recommend it to anyone who's interested in learning more about this method and its applications.

11. Creswell, J. D., Welch, W. T., Taylor, S. E., Sherman, D. K., Gruenewald, T. L., & Mann, T. (2005). Affirmation of personal values buffers neuroendocrine and psychological stress responses. *Psychological Science, 16*, 846–851.

12. Kirschbaum, C., Pirke, K. M., & Hellhammer, D. H. (1993). The Trier Social Stress Test — a tool for investigating psychobiological stress responses in a laboratory setting. *Neuropsychobiology, 28*, 76–81.

13. For a review of how acute stressors affect the cortisol response and what that means for psychological well-being, see Dickerson, S. S., & Kemeny, M. E. (2004). Acute stressors and cortisol responses: a theoretical integration and synthesis of laboratory research. *Psychological Bulletin, 130*, 355–391.

14. Sherman, D. K., Bunyan, D. P., Creswell, J. D., & Jaremka, L. M. (2009). Psychological vulnerability and stress: The effects of self-affirmation on sympathetic nervous system responses to naturalistic stressors. *Health Psychology, 28*, 554–562.

15. Cohen & Sherman, The psychology of change. Kang, S.; Galinsky, A.; Kray, L.; and Shirako, A. (2015). Power affects performance when the pressure is on: Evidence for low-power threat and high-power lift. *Personality and Social Psychology Bulletin, 41*, 726–735.

16. Creswell, J. D., Dutcher, J. M., Klein, W. M., Harris, P. R., & Levine, J. M. (2013). Self-affirmation improves problem-solving under stress. *PLoS ONE, 8*, e62593.

17. Schlegel, R. J., Hicks, J. A., Arndt, J., & King, L. A. (2009). Thine own self: True self-concept accessibility and meaning in life. *Journal of Personality and Social Psychology, 96*, 473–490.

18. As is true for all correlational studies, we cannot know with certainty the direction of causation among the variables — only that they are associated. That said, because of the authors' thoroughly prepared theoretical foundation and careful statistical analyses, we can more comfortably infer that these narrative identities do indeed influence mental health trajectories, even if the trajectories then reinforce the narrative identities or if there are additional contributing variables. See Adler, J. M., Turner, A. F., Brookshier, K. M., Monahan, C., Walder-Biesanz, I., Harmeling, L. H., Albaugh, M., McAdams, D. P., & Oltmans, T. F. (2015). Variation in narrative identity is associated with trajectories of mental health over several years. *Journal of Personality and Social Psychology, 108*, 476–496.

19. Kahn, W. A. (1992). To be fully there: Psychological presence at work. *Human Relations, 45*, 321–349.

20. Ibid., 322.

21. Ibid., 325.

22. Cable, D. M., Gino, F., & Staats, B. R. (2013). Breaking them in or eliciting their best? Reframing socialization around newcomers' authentic self-expression. *Administrative Science Quarterly*, 58, 1–36.

23. You know how disappointing it is when you learn that your favorite celebrity is a jerk? That's especially disappointing when your favorite celebrity is someone you see as having depth, sensitivity, wisdom — someone who has created something that is meaningful to you, such as a song, a piece of writing, or a character in a film. Because it's meaningful to you, you want to believe that it's meaningful to that person, so learning that he or she is a jerk makes that impossible. Now imagine the opposite. Your favorite celebrity has more depth, sensitivity, and wisdom than you could reasonably expect any one person to possess. And she is so easy to be around — so seamlessly in tune and accommodating — that you feel you just might have been best friends for a year at summer camp. And then you have the revelation that everyone who has ever interviewed her has probably felt the same way. This is Julianne Moore.

24. Corliss, R. (2014, December 12). Review: Still Alice: Julianne Moore reveals Alzheimer's from the inside. *Time*. Retrieved from http://time.com/3628020/still-alice-julianne-moore-movie-review/.

25. Waterman, L. (n.d.). The most honest actress in Hollywood. *DuJour*. Retrieved from http://dujour.com/news/julianne-moore-interview-carrie-movie/.

26. Wurtz, J. (Producer). (2002, December 22). *Inside the actors studio* [Television broadcast]. New York: Bravo.

27. Dillon, K. (2015, August 28). What you should (and shouldn't) focus on before a job interview. *Harvard Business Review*. Retrieved from https://hbr.org/2015/08/what-you-should-and-shouldnt-focus-on-before-a-job-interview.

Chapter 3 Stop Preaching, Start Listening: How Presence Begets Presence

1. For more on our own and others' research on warmth and competence judgments, see Cuddy, A. J. C., Fiske, S. T., & Glick, P. (2008). Warmth and competence as universal dimensions of social perception: The Stereotype Content Model and the BIAS Map. In M. P. Zanna (Ed.), *Advances in experimental social psychology*, Vol. 40 (pp. 61–149). Waltham, MA: Academic Press; Cuddy, A. J. C., Fiske, S. T., & Glick, P. (2007). The BIAS Map: Behaviors from intergroup affect and stereotypes. *Journal of Personality and Social Psychology*, 92, 631–648; Cuddy, A. J. C., Glick, P., & Beninger, A. (2011). The dynamics of warmth and competence judgments, and their outcomes in organizations. *Research in Organizational Behavior*, 31, 73–98; Fiske, S. T.,

Cuddy, A. J. C., & Glick, P. (2007). Universal dimensions of social cognition: Warmth, then competence. *Trends in Cognitive Sciences, 11*, 77–83.

2. Casciaro, T., & Lobo, M. S. (2005). Competent jerks, lovable fools, and the formation of social networks. *Harvard Business Review, 83*, 92–99.

3. Ybarra, O., Chan, E., & Park, D. (2001). Young and old adults' concerns about morality and competence. *Motivation and Emotion, 25*, 85–100.

4. For related work, see Wojciszke, B., Baryla, W., Parzuchowski, M., Szymkow, A., & Abele, A. E. (2011). Self-esteem is dominated by agentic over communal information. *European Journal of Social Psychology, 41*, 617–627.

5. Cuddy, A. J., Kohut, M., & Neffinger, J. (2013). Connect, then lead. *Harvard Business Review, 91*, 54–61.

6. Zenger, J., & Folkman, J. (2013, May 2). I'm the boss! Why should I care if you like me? *Harvard Business Review.* Retrieved from https://hbr.org/2013/05/im-the-boss-why-should-i-care.

7. Lombardo, M. M., & McCall, M. W. J. (1984). *Coping with an intolerable boss.* Greensboro, NC: Center for Creative Leadership.

8. All quotes: Ury, W. L. (2015). *Getting to yes with yourself: And other worthy opponents.* New York: HarperOne, 90–93.

9. For more on the role of shared goals in reducing intergroup conflict, see Gaertner, S. L., Dovidio, J. F., Anastasio, P. A., Bachman, B. A., & Rust, M. C. (1993). The common ingroup identity model: Recategorization and the reduction of intergroup bias. *European Review of Social Psychology, 4*, 1–26.

10. For a closer look at procedural justice, see, among other reports, Tyler, T. R., & Blader, S. L. (2003). The group engagement model: Procedural justice, social identity, and cooperative behavior. *Personality and Social Psychology Review, 7*(4), 349–361, and Bagdadli, S., Roberson, Q., & Paoletti, F. (2006). The mediating role of procedural justice in responses to promotion decisions. *Journal of Business and Psychology, 21*, 83–102.

11. Lloyd, K. J., Boer, D., Kluger, A. N., & Voelpel, S. C. (2015). Building trust and feeling well: Examining intraindividual and interpersonal outcomes and underlying mechanisms of listening. *International Journal of Listening 29*(1), 12–29.

12. Because this wasn't a controlled experiment, it's not possible to rule out other variables that might have contributed to this drop in youth violence — and it's likely that other variables *did* contribute. However, a detailed analysis by researcher Anthony A. Braga, formerly of the John F. Kennedy School of Government at Harvard, and his colleagues clearly concludes that the work of the TenPoint Coalition played an enormous and unique causal role in bringing about the change. See Braga, A. A., Kennedy, D. M.,

Waring, E. J., & Piehl, A. M. (2001). Problem-oriented policing, deterrence, and youth violence: An evaluation of Boston's Operation Ceasefire. *Journal of Research in Crime and Delinquency, 38*(3), 195–225.

Chapter 4 *I Don't Deserve to Be Here*

1. Clance, P. R., & Imes, S. A. (1978). The imposter phenomenon in high achieving women: Dynamics and therapeutic intervention. *Psychotherapy: Theory, Research & Practice, 15,* 241–247.

2. Izadi, E. (2015, May 28). At Harvard, Natalie Portman acknowledges what many of us feel: Impostor syndrome. The *Washington Post.* Retrieved from http://www.washingtonpost.com/news/grade-point/wp/2015/05/28/natalie -portmans-harvard-speech-reminds-us-how-we-all-can-feel-we -arent-smart-enough/.

3. Clance, P. R. (1985). *The impostor phenomenon: When success makes you feel like a fake.* New York: Bantam Books, 20–22. You can see the entire scale at http://paulineroseclance.com/pdf/IPTestandscoring.pdf.

4. Clance & Imes, The imposter phenomenon in high achieving women, 241.

5. Ibid.

6. Ibid., 242.

7. I can't cite the thousands of scientific studies that support this statement, so I will refer you to one particularly well-conducted (and troubling) study: Moss-Racusin, C. A., Dovidio, J. F., Brescoll, V. L., Graham, M. J., & Handelsman, J. (2012). Science faculty's subtle gender biases favor male students. *Proceedings of the National Academy of Sciences, 109,* 16474–16479.

8. Langford, J., & Clance, P. R. (1993). The imposter phenomenon: Recent research findings regarding dynamics, personality and family patterns and their implications for treatment. *Psychotherapy: Theory, Research, Practice, Training, 30,* 495–501; Castro, D. M., Jones, R. A., & Mirsalimi, H. (2004). Parentification and the impostor phenomenon: An empirical investigation. *The American Journal of Family Therapy, 32,* 205–216; Vergauwe, J., Wille, B., Feys, M., De Fruyt, F., & Anseel, F. (2015). Fear of being exposed: The trait-relatedness of the impostor phenomenon and its relevance in the work context. *Journal of Business and Psychology, 30*(3), 565–581.

9. McGregor, L. N., Gee, D. E., & Posey, K. E. (2008). I feel like a fraud and it depresses me: The relation between the imposter phenomenon and depression. *Social Behavior and Personality: An International Journal, 36,* 43–48; Jöstl, G., Bergsmann, E., Lüftenegger, M., Schober, B., & Spiel, C. (2012). When will they blow my cover? The impostor phenomenon among Austrian doctoral students. *Zeitschrift für Psychologie, 220,* 109–120.

10. Rudman, L. A., & Fairchild, K. (2004). Reactions to counterstereotypic behavior: The role of backlash in cultural stereotype maintenance. *Journal of Personality and Social Psychology, 87,* 157–176.

11. For an excellent discussion of the research on stereotype backlash against women, see Rudman, L. A., & Phelan, J. E. (2008). Backlash effects for disconfirming gender stereotypes in organizations. *Research in organizational behavior, 28,* 61–79.

12. Many of the citations for impostorism studies involving these demographics can be found in the reference list compiled by Pauline Rose Clance at this link: http://paulineroseclance.com/pdf/IP%20Ref%20List-MOST%20RECENT-8-2-13.doc.

13. Matthews, G., & Clance, P. R. (1985). Treatment of the impostor phenomenon in psychotherapy clients. *Psychotherapy in Private Practice, 3,* 71–81.

14. Friedman, A. (2013, October 22). Not qualified for your job? Wait, you probably are. *Pacific Standard.* Retrieved from http://www.psmag.com/business-economics/qualified-job-wait-probably-imposter-syndrome-psychology-68700.

15. Bernard, N. S., Dollinger, S. J., & Ramaniah, N. V. (2002). Applying the big five personality factors to the impostor phenomenon. *Journal of Personality Assessment, 78,* 321–333; Castro et al., Parentification and the impostor phenomenon; Clance & Imes, The imposter phenomenon in high achieving women.

16. That said, psychologists have found that *many* personality traits correlate with impostorism, including perfectionism and performance anxiety (Thompson, T., Foreman, P., & Martin, F. [2000]. Impostor fears and perfectionistic concern over mistakes. *Personality and Individual Differences, 29,* 629–647), low self-acceptance and sense of mastery over the environment (September, A. N., McCarrey, M., Baranowsky, A., Parent, C., & Schindler, D. [2001]. The relation between well-being, impostor feelings, and gender role orientation among Canadian university students. *The Journal of Social Psychology, 141,* 218–232), high neuroticism and low conscientiousness (Bernard et al., Applying the big five personality factors to the impostor phenomenon), low self-esteem (Cozzarelli, C., & Major, B. [1990]. Exploring the validity of the impostor phenomenon. *Journal of Social and Clinical Psychology, 9,* 401–417), and introversion (Lawler, N. K. [1985]. The impostor phenomenon in high achieving persons and Jungian personality variables. [Doctoral dissertation, Georgia State University, 1984]. *Dissertation Abstracts International, 45,* 86; Prince, T. J. [1989]. The impostor phenomenon revisited: A validity study of Clance's IP Scale. Unpublished master's thesis, Georgia State University, Atlanta). There is certainly a pattern of traits and tendencies correlated with impostorism; however, in most cases, it is unclear

which direction these traits go in relation to impostorism — that is, whether these things *cause* impostorism or whether they are *caused by* impostorism. It seems likely that impostorism and these traits feed off each other, exacerbating the problem. Impostorism is as much a product of the given situation as it is a product of personality traits (McElwee, R., & Yurak, T. J. [2010]. The phenomenology of the Impostor Phenomenon. *Individual Differences Research*, 8, 184–197).

17. Kumar, S., & Jagacinski, C. M. (2006). Imposters have goals too: The imposter phenomenon and its relationship to achievement goal theory. *Personality and Individual Differences, 40,* 147–157; September et al., The relation between well-being, impostor feelings, and gender role orientation among Canadian university students; Clance & Imes, The imposter phenomenon in high achieving women.

18. Thompson, T., Davis, H., & Davidson, J. (1998). Attributional and affective responses of impostors to academic success and failure outcomes. *Personality and Individual Differences, 25,* 381–396.

19. The name, locations, and several other details of this story have been changed to protect the e-mail writer's privacy.

20. Thompson, T., Foreman, P., & Martin, F. (2000). Impostor fears and perfectionistic concern over mistakes. *Personality and Individual Differences, 29,* 629–647.

21. Cozzarelli & Major, Exploring the validity of the impostor phenomenon; Thompson et al., Impostor fears and perfectionistic concern over mistakes.

22. Kim, Y. H., Chiu, C. Y., & Zou, Z. (2010). Know thyself: Misperceptions of actual performance undermine achievement motivation, future performance, and subjective well-being. *Journal of Personality and Social Psychology, 99,* 395–409.

23. Schmader, T., Johns, M., & Forbes, C. (2008). An integrated process model of stereotype threat effects on performance. *Psychological Review, 115,* 336–356.

24. O'Reilly, J., Robinson, S. L., Berdahl, J. L., & Banki, S. (2014). Is negative attention better than no attention? The comparative effects of ostracism and harassment at work. *Organization Science, 26,* 776–793.

25. Eisenberger, N. I., Lieberman, M. D., & Williams, K. D. (2003). Does rejection hurt? An fMRI study of social exclusion. *Science, 302,* 290–292.

26. Sanford, A. A., Ross, E. M., Blake, S. J., & Cambiano, R. L. (2015). Finding courage and confirmation: Resisting impostor feelings through relationships with mentors, romantic partners, and other women in leadership. *Advancing Women in Leadership, 35,* 33–43.

Chapter 5 How Powerlessness Shackles the Self (and How Power Sets It Free)

1. The name and minor details of this story have been changed to protect the e-mail writer's privacy.

2. Keltner, D., Gruenfeld, D. H., & Anderson, C. (2003). Power, approach, and inhibition. *Psychological Review, 110,* 265–284.

3. Ibid., 268.

4. This theory — regulatory focus theory, developed by E. Tori Higgins — is one of the most influential theories in modern psychology. If you delve into the literature about it, you will soon learn that hundreds of researchers and thousands of studies have explored it. Consider starting with Brockner, J., & Higgins, E. T. (2001). Regulatory focus theory: Implications for the study of emotions at work. *Organizational Behavior and Human Decision Processes, 86,* 35–66. As the authors explain:

> Previous theory and research have shown that people have two distinct self-regulatory foci. When promotion focused, people are motivated by growth and development needs in which they attempt to bring their actual selves (their behaviors and self-conceptions) in alignment with their ideal selves (self-standards based on wishes and aspirations of how they would like to be). When prevention focused, people are responsive to security needs in which they try to match their actual selves with their ought selves (self-standards based on felt duties and responsibilities). Strategically, eagerness or ensuring gains predominate for promotion-focused persons, whereas vigilance or ensuring nonlosses predominate for prevention-focused persons. People's regulatory focus influences the nature and magnitude of their emotional experience. Promotion-focused people's emotions vary along a cheerful-dejected dimension, whereas prevention-focused people's emotions vary along a quiescent-agitated dimension.

5. Thurman, H. (1953). *Meditations of the heart.* Boston: Beacon Press.

6. For an enthralling read that examines this vast research on social power — specifically, how and when to use it — read a book written by two of the foremost experts on the topic, Columbia Business School professor Adam Galinsky and Wharton professor Maurice Schweitzer: *Friend and foe: When to cooperate, when to compete, and how to succeed at both* (New York: Crown).

7. Magee, J. C., & Galinsky, A. D. (2008). Social hierarchy: The self-reinforcing nature of power and status. *The Academy of Management Annals, 2,* 351–398, 351.

8. Smith, P. K., & Galinsky, A. D. (2010). The nonconscious nature of power: Cues and consequences. *Social and Personality Psychology Compass, 4,* 918–938.

9. Nearly all the research described in this chapter is about social power, but I believe much of it can be applied to personal power, because both types of power give you a sense of control.

10. Tomaka, J., Blascovich, J., Kelsey, R. M., & Leitten, C. L. (1993). Subjective, physiological, and behavioral effects of threat and challenge appraisal. *Journal of Personality and Social Psychology, 65*(2), 248.

11. Qin, S., Hermans, E. J., van Marle, H. J., Luo, J., & Fernández, G. (2009). Acute psychological stress reduces working memory-related activity in the dorsolateral prefrontal cortex. *Biological Psychiatry, 66,* 25–32; Liston, C., McEwen, B. S., & Casey, B. J. (2009). Psychosocial stress reversibly disrupts prefrontal processing and attentional control. *Proceedings of the National Academy of Sciences, 106,* 912–917.

12. Derakshan, N., & Eysenck, M. W. (2009). Anxiety, processing efficiency, and cognitive performance: New developments from attentional control theory. *European Psychologist, 14,* 168–176.

13. Smith, P. K., Jostmann, N. B., Galinsky, A. D., & van Dijk, W. W. (2008). Lacking power impairs executive functions. *Psychological Science, 19,* 441–447.

14. Stroop, J. R. (1935). Studies of interference in serial verbal reactions. *Journal of Experimental Psychology 18*(6), 643–662.

15. Todd, A. R., Forstmann, M., Burgmer, P., Brooks, A. W., & Galinsky, A. D. (2015). Anxious and egocentric: How specific emotions influence perspective taking. *Journal of Experimental Psychology: General, 144,* 374–391.

16. Mor, N., & Winquist, J. (2002). Self-focused attention and negative affect: A meta-analysis. *Psychological Bulletin, 128,* 638–662.

17. Gendolla, G. E., Abele, A. E., Andrei, A., Spurk, D., & Richter, M. (2005). Negative mood, self-focused attention, and the experience of physical symptoms: The joint impact hypothesis. *Emotion, 5,* 131–144.

18. Gilovich, T., Medvec, V. H., & Savitsky, K. (2000). The spotlight effect in social judgment: An egocentric bias in estimates of the salience of one's own actions and appearance. *Journal of Personality and Social Psychology, 78,* 211–222.

19. Gaydukevych, D., & Kocovski, N. L. (2012). Effect of self-focused attention on post-event processing in social anxiety. *Behaviour Research and Therapy, 50,* 47–55.

20. Kuehn, M. M., Chen, S., & Gordon, A. M. (2015). Having a thicker skin: Social power buffers the negative effects of social rejection. *Social Psychological and Personality Science, 6,* 701–709.

21. Carney, D. R., Yap, A. J., Lucas, B. J., Mehta, P. H., McGee, J., & Wilmuth, C. (working paper). Power buffers stress — for better and for worse. Retrieved from http://faculty.haas.berkeley.edu/dana_carney/vita.html.

22. Schmid Mast, M., Jonas, K., & Hall, J. A. (2009). Give a person power and he or she will show interpersonal sensitivity: The phenomenon and its why and when. *Journal of Personality and Social Psychology, 97,* 835–850.

23. Karremans, J. C., & Smith, P. K. (2010). Having the power to forgive: When the experience of power increases interpersonal forgiveness. *Personality and Social Psychology Bulletin, 36,* 1010–1023.

24. Shepherd, S. V., Deaner, R. O., & Platt, M. L. (2006). Social status gates social attention in monkeys. *Current Biology, 16,* R119–R120.

25. Anderson, C., & Berdahl, J. L. (2002). The experience of power: Examining the effects of power on approach and inhibition tendencies. *Journal of Personality and Social Psychology, 83,* 1362–1377.

26. Goodstadt, B. E., & Hjelle, L. A. (1973). Power to the powerless: Locus of control and the use of power. *Journal of Personality and Social Psychology, 27,* 190–196.

27. Fast, N. J., Burris, E. R., & Bartel, C. A. (2014). Managing to stay in the dark: Managerial self-efficacy, ego defensiveness, and the aversion to employee voice. *Academy of Management Journal, 57,* 1013–1034.

28. Smith, P. K., Dijksterhuis, A., & Wigboldus, D. H. (2008). Powerful people make good decisions even when they consciously think. *Psychological Science, 19,* 1258–1259, 1258.

29. Galinsky, A. D., Magee, J. C., Gruenfeld, D. H., Whitson, J., & Liljenquist, K. A. (2008). Power reduces the press of the situation: Implications for creativity, conformity, and dissonance. *Journal of Personality and Social Psychology, 95,* 1450–1466.

30. Hecht, M. A., & LaFrance, M. (1998). License or obligation to smile: The effect of power and sex on amount and type of smiling. *Personality and Social Psychology Bulletin, 24,* 1332–1342.

31. Keltner, D., Gruenfeld, D. H., & Anderson, C. (2003). Power, approach, and inhibition. *Psychological Review, 110,* 265–284.

32. Galinsky, A. D., Gruenfeld, D. H., & Magee, J. C. (2003). From power to action. *Journal of Personality and Social Psychology, 85,* 453–466.

33. Magee, J. C., Galinsky, A. D., & Gruenfeld, D. H. (2007). Power, propensity to negotiate, and moving first in competitive interactions. *Personality and Social Psychology Bulletin, 33,* 200–212.

34. Ibid.

35. Guinote, A. (2007). Power and goal pursuit. *Personality and Social Psychology Bulletin, 33,* 1076–1087.

36. Van der Toorn, J., Feinberg, M., Jost, J. T., Kay, A. C., Tyler, T. R., Willer, R., & Wilmuth, C. (2015). A sense of powerlessness fosters system jus-

tification: Implications for the legitimation of authority, hierarchy, and government. *Political Psychology, 36*, 93–110.

37. Kang, S. K., Galinsky, A. D., Kray, L. J., & Shirako, A. (2015). Power affects performance when the pressure is on: Evidence for low-power threat and high-power lift. *Personality and Social Psychology Bulletin, 41*, 726–735.

38. Nickols, R.A. (2013) *The relationship between self-confidence and interpretation of competitive anxiety before and after competition* (Doctoral dissertation). Retrieved from ProQuest. (Dissertation number 3560269.)

39. Stajkovic, A. D., & Luthans, F. (1998). Self-efficacy and work-related performance: A meta-analysis. *Psychological Bulletin, 124*, 240–261.

40. A couple more facts: Testosterone levels are around seven or eight times higher in males than they are in females, but testosterone affects males and females similarly. Small amounts of testosterone are also secreted by the adrenal cortex.

41. To learn more about the behaviors that correlate with testosterone and cortisol in various species, see Mehta, P. H., & Josephs, R. A. (2010). Testosterone and cortisol jointly regulate dominance: Evidence for a dual-hormone hypothesis. *Hormones and Behavior, 58*(5), 898–906.

42. Sapolsky, R. M. (1991). Testicular function, social rank and personality among wild baboons. *Psychoneuroendocrinology, 16*(4), 281–293.

43. For more information, see Hamilton, L. D., Carré, J. M., Mehta, P. H., Olmstead, N., & Whitaker, J. D. (2015). Social neuroendocrinology of status: A review and future directions. *Adaptive Human Behavior and Physiology, 1*(2), 202–230; Mehta & Josephs, Testosterone and cortisol jointly regulate dominance.

44. Sherman, G. D., Lee, J. J., Cuddy, A. J. C., Renshon, J., Oveis, C., Gross, J. J., & Lerner, J. S. (2012). Leadership is associated with lower levels of stress. *Proceedings of the National Academy of Sciences, 109*, 17903–17907.

45. For a review of this and related research on stress and performance, see LeBlanc, V. R. (2009). The effects of acute stress on performance: Implications for health professions education. *Academic Medicine, 84*(10), S25–S33.

46. Mehta & Josephs, Testosterone and cortisol jointly regulate dominance.

47. Sherman, G. D., Lerner, J. S., Josephs, R. A., Renshon, J., & Gross, J. J. (2015). The interaction of testosterone and cortisol is associated with attained status in male executives. *Journal of Personality and Social Psychology*. Retrieved from http://scholar.harvard.edu/files/jenniferlerner/files/sherman_lerner_et_al._in_press_testosterone_cortisol_and_attained_status_jpsp.pdf.

48. Mehta, P. H., & Prasad, S. (2015). The dual-hormone hypothesis: A brief review and future research agenda. *Current Opinion in Behavioral Sciences, 3,* 163–168.

49. Jiménez, M., Aguilar, R., & Alvero-Cruz, J. R. (2012). Effects of victory and defeat on testosterone and cortisol response to competition: Evidence for same response patterns in men and women. *Psychoneuroendocrinology, 37,* 1577–1581.

50. Edwards, D. A., & Casto, K. V. (2015). Baseline cortisol moderates testosterone reactivity to women's intercollegiate athletic competition. *Physiology & Behavior, 142,* 48–51.

51. Edwards, D. A., & Casto, K. V. (2013). Women's intercollegiate athletic competition: Cortisol, testosterone, and the dual-hormone hypothesis as it relates to status among teammates. *Hormones and Behavior, 64,* 153–160.

52. Lee, J. J., Gino, F., Jin, E. S., Rice, L. K., & Josephs, R. A. (2015). Hormones and ethics: Understanding the biological basis of unethical conduct. *Journal of Experimental Psychology: General,* doi: 10.1037/xge0000099; *Science Daily* (2015, July 28). Hormones influence ethical behavior, experts say. Retrieved from http://www.sciencedaily.com/releases/2015/07/150728110809.htm.

53. Fiske, S. T. (1993). Controlling other people: The impact of power on stereotyping. *American Psychologist, 48,* 621–628.

54. Ibid.

55. Goodwin, S. A., Gubin, A., Fiske, S. T., & Yzerbyt, V. Y. (2000). Power can bias impression processes: Stereotyping subordinates by default and by design. *Group Processes & Intergroup Relations, 3,* 227–256.

56. Overbeck, J. R., & Park, B. (2006). Powerful perceivers, powerless objects: Flexibility of powerholders' social attention. *Organizational Behavior and Human Decision Processes, 99,* 227–243; Fiske, S. T. (1993). Controlling other people: The impact of power on stereotyping. *American Psychologist, 48,* 621–628; Goodwin et al., Power can bias impression processes.

57. Azzam, T. I., Beaulieu, D. A., & Bugental, D. B. (2007). Anxiety and hostility to an "outsider," as moderated by low perceived power. *Emotion, 7,* 660–667.

58. McGreal, C. (2012, June 9). Robert Caro: A life with LBJ and the pursuit of power. *The Guardian.* Retrieved from http://www.theguardian.com/world/2012/jun/10/lyndon-b-johnson-robert-caro-biography.

Chapter 6 Slouching, Steepling, and the Language of the Body

1. The All Blacks have won 76 percent of their test matches (a game between international teams), are the holders of the 2014 men's Rugby World Cup, and are the 2014 World Rugby Team of the Year. Since the introduction

of the World Rugby rankings in October of 2003, New Zealand has been ranked first longer than all other teams combined. They also became the first team to win four hundred test matches and since 2005 have been named the World Rugby Team of the Year seven times. See New Zealand national rugby union team. (n.d.) In Wikipedia. Retrieved July 17, 2015, from https://en.wiki pedia.org/wiki/New_Zealand_national_rugby_union_team.

2. Others include Asians, Pacific Islanders, and people of Middle Eastern, Latin American, and African heritage. See Statistics New Zealand Tatauranga Aotearoa. (2014, April 15). *2013 Census QuickStats about culture and identity.* Retrieved from http://www.stats.govt.nz/Census/2013-census/profile -and-summary-reports/quickstats-culture-identity/ethnic-groups-NZ.aspx.

3. For the lyrics to the ka mate see: Haka (sports) (n.d.) in Wikipedia. Retrieved July 17, 2015, from https://en.wikipedia.org/wiki/Haka (sports); All Blacks. (n.d.); The Haka. Retrieved from http://allblacks.com/Teams/Haka; Wikipedia, New Zealand national rugby union team. Both Wikipedia articles contain numerous links to reliable outside sources.

4. Lewis, P. (2006, July 15). NZRU spin puts the 'ha' into new haka. *The New Zealand Herald.* Retrieved from http://www.nzherald.co.nz/opinion /news/article.cfm?c_id=466&objectid=10391465.

5. Here's a good one: https://www.youtube.com/watch?v=HcMO2NqntHA.

6. American International Group (2014, October 6). Haka: History. Retrieved from https://www.youtube.com/watch?v=AnlFocaA64M.

7. De Waal, F. (2008). *The ape and the sushi master: Reflections of a primatologist.* New York: Basic Books, 310.

8. For more on primate body language, read de Waal, F. (2007). *Chimpanzee politics: Power and sex among apes* (25th anniversary ed.). Baltimore: Johns Hopkins University Press.

9. Carney, D. R., Hall, J. A., & LeBeau, L. S. (2005). Beliefs about the nonverbal expression of social power. *Journal of Nonverbal Behavior, 29,* 105–123.

10. J. Navarro, personal communication (July 9, 2015). For more, see Navarro, J., & Karlins, M. (2008). *What every body is saying.* New York: HarperCollins.

11. In study 1, feelings of power or powerlessness were induced through recall manipulation (i.e., subjects wrote about a time when they had or lacked power); in study 2, power and powerlessness were induced through role assignments (i.e., subjects were randomly assigned to a powerful or powerless role based on the results of a bogus leadership test). Yap, A. J., Mason, M. F., & Ames, D. R. (2013). The powerful size others down: The link between power and estimates of others' size. *Journal of Experimental Social Psychology, 49,* 591–594. Https://www.researchgate.net/publication/256752593_The_powerful

_size_others_down_The_link_between_power_and_estimates_of
_others%27_size.

12. Charles Darwin (1872). *The expression of the emotions in man and animals.* London: John Murray.

13. Martens, J. P., Tracy, J. L., & Shariff, A. F. (2012). Status signals: Adaptive benefits of displaying and observing the nonverbal expressions of pride and shame. *Cognition & Emotion, 26,* 390–406, 391.

14. Tracy, J. L., & Robins, R. W. (2004). Show your pride: Evidence for a discrete emotion expression. *Psychological Science, 15,* 194–197.

15. Tracy, J. L., & Matsumoto, D. (2008). The spontaneous expression of pride and shame: Evidence for biologically innate nonverbal displays. *Proceedings of the National Academy of Sciences, 105,* 11655–11660.

16. Ibid.

17. Martens, Tracy, & Shariff, Status signals.

18. Martens, J. P., & Tracy, J. L. (2013). The emotional origins of a social learning bias: Does the pride expression cue copying? *Social Psychological and Personality Science, 4,* 492–499.

19. Shariff, A. F., Tracy, J. L., & Markusoff, J. L. (2012). (Implicitly) judging a book by its cover: The power of pride and shame expressions in shaping judgments of social status. *Personality and Social Psychology Bulletin, 38,* 1178–1193.

20. Motion data is collected using the same varieties of advanced technology used by movie studios to capture the movement of a human and apply it to an animated figure. Simple markers are placed on the body at the joints (and other key points, such as the head, hands, and feet), and an array of cameras feeds video data into software that can triangulate the location of each marker in 3-D. This data can be replayed as an animation or analyzed.

21. Cuddy, A. J. C., Troje, N., & Schultz, S. (2015). Kinematics of powerful versus powerless movement: Do the powerful walk with a swagger? Working manuscript. The perceived kinematics of power were highly correlated with the perceived kinematics of the gender of the walker. (That is, the more male the figure appeared in arm movement, head movement, and stride, for example, the more powerful it looked to the participants. The size and structure of the walkers did not vary; the dots represent only movement.) In our final analysis, we removed the gender-kinematics information in order to clearly see which characteristics were related to power and to create gender-neutral powerful and powerless walkers for future studies. Note that the figures presented are based on the raw data (i.e., gender information has not been removed).

22. See http://www.biomotionlab.ca/walking.php.

23. Stel, M., van Dijk, E., Smith, P. K., van Dijk, W. W., & Djalal, F. M. (2012). Lowering the pitch of your voice makes you feel more powerful and think more abstractly. *Social Psychological and Personality Science, 3,* 497–502; Puts, D. A., Hodges, C. R., Cárdenas, R. A., & Gaulin, S. J. (2007). Men's voices as dominance signals: Vocal fundamental and formant frequencies influence dominance attributions among men. *Evolution and Human Behavior, 28,* 340–344; Puts, D. A., Gaulin, S. J., & Verdolini, K. (2006). Dominance and the evolution of sexual dimorphism in human voice pitch. *Evolution and Human Behavior, 27,* 283–296.

24. Ellyson, S. L., & Dovidio, J. F. (Eds.). (1985). *Power, dominance, and nonverbal behavior.* New York: Springer-Verlag; Holtgraves, T., & Lasky, B. (1999). Linguistic power and persuasion. *Journal of Language and Social Psychology, 18,* 196–205; Hosman, L. A. (1989). The evaluative consequences of hedges, hesitations and intensifiers. *Human Communication Research, 1,* 383–406; Keltner, D., & Harker, L. A. (1998). The forms and functions of the nonverbal display of shame. In P. Gilbert & B. Andrews (Eds.), *Interpersonal approaches to shame* (pp. 78–98). Oxford: Oxford University Press.

25. Elizabeth Baily Wolf, unpublished manuscript.

26. Leaper, C., & Ayres, M. M. (2007). A meta-analytic review of gender variations in adults' language use: Talkativeness, affiliative speech, and assertive speech. *Personality and Social Psychology Review, 11,* 328–363.

27. La France, M., & Mayo, C. (1979). A review of nonverbal behaviors of women and men. *Western Journal of Communication, 43,* 96–107.

28. Cuddy et al., Kinematics of powerful versus powerless movement.

29. For an excellent discussion of this work, see Adam Galinsky and Maurice Schweitzer's 2015 book, *Friend and foe: When to cooperate, when to compete, and how to succeed at both* (New York: Crown).

30. Holland, E., Baily Wolf, E., Looser, C., Cuddy, A. J. C. (2015). Visual attention to powerful postures: People reflexively avert their gaze from nonverbal dominance displays. Working manuscript.

31. Q&A with Jessica Tracy: *New York Times.* (2009, April 6). *Questioning pride.* Retrieved from http://consults.blogs.nytimes.com/2009/04/06/questioning-pride/.

For a short review of Jessica Tracy's research on pride displays, see her open-access article, Tracy, J. L., Randles, D., & Steckler, C. M. (2015). The nonverbal communication of emotions. *Current Opinion in Behavioral Sciences, 3,* 25–30. Retrieved from http://www.sciencedirect.com/science/journal/23521546/3.

32. Tiedens, L. Z., & Fragale, A. R. (2003). Power moves: Complementarity in dominant and submissive nonverbal behavior. *Journal of Personality and Social Psychology, 84,* 558–568.

33. Barrick, M. R., Shaffer, J. A., & DeGrassi, S. W. (2009). What you see may not be what you get: Relationships among self-presentation tactics and ratings of interview and job performance. *Journal of Applied Psychology, 94,* 1394–1411. Examination of various impression management (IM) tactics has revealed significant effects for some verbal tactics (e.g., the use of positive self-descriptive terms and the telling of personal success stories) but not for non-verbal tactics (e.g., frequent eye contact and smiling; see Gilmore, D. C., & Ferris, G. R. [1989]. The effects of applicant impression management tactics on interviewer judgments. *Journal of Management, 15,* 557–564; Stevens, C. K., & Kristof, A. L. [1995]. Making the right impression: A field study of applicant impression management during job interviews. *Journal of Applied Psychology,* 80, 587–606). However, these effects are attenuated or disappear as interviews become longer (see Tsai, W. C., Chen, C. C., & Chiu, S. F. [2005]. Exploring boundaries of the effects of applicant impression management tactics in job interviews. *Journal of Management, 31,* 108–125), are more structured or standardized (see Barrick, M. R., Shaffer, J. A., & DeGrassi, S. W. [2009]. What you see may not be what you get: Relationships among self-presentation tactics and ratings of interview and job performance. *Journal of Applied Psychology,* 94, 1394–1411), and involve more highly trained interviewers (see Howard, J. L., & Ferris, G. R. [1996]. The employment interview context: Social and situational influences on interviewer decisions. *Journal of Applied Social Psychology, 26,* 112–136). Many other variables moderate the extent to which IM tactics lead to positive versus negative hiring decisions, such as the gender of both candidate and interviewer (see Baron, R. A. [1986]. Self-presentation in job interviews: When there can be "too much of a good thing." *Journal of Applied Social Psychology, 16,* 16–28; Rudman, L. A. [1998]. Self-promotion as a risk factor for women: The costs and benefits of counterstereotypical impression management. *Journal of Personality and Social Psychology, 74,* 629–645; Von Baeyer, C. L., Sherk, D. L., & Zanna, M. P. [1981]. Impression management in the job interview when the female applicant meets the male (chauvinist) interviewer. *Personality and Social Psychology Bulletin, 7,* 45–51), the valence of the interviewer's affective state (see Baron, R. A. [1987]. Interviewer's moods and reactions to job applicants: The influence of affective states on applied social judgments. *Journal of Applied Social Psychology, 17,* 911–926), and the perceived similarity of the candidate to the interviewer (see Judge, T. A., Cable, D. M., & Higgins, C. A. [2001]. The employment interview: A review of recent research and recommendations for future research. *Human Resource Management Review, 10,* 383–406). And, perhaps most important, as candidates increase their use of nonverbal IM tactics, interview-

ers begin to perceive them as inauthentic and manipulative, leading to negative evaluations and hiring decisions (see Baron, Self-presentation in job interviews).

34. Semnani-Azad, Z., & Adair, W. L. (2011). The display of "dominant" nonverbal cues in negotiation: The role of culture and gender. *International Negotiation, 16*, 451–479.

35. American International Group, Haka: History.

Chapter 7 *Surfing, Smiling, and Singing Ourselves to Happiness*

1. Fairbanks, E. (2015, February 25). How surfing taught me to make choices. The *Washington Post*. Retrieved from http://www.washingtonpost.com/posteverything/wp/2015/02/25/how-surfing-taught-me-to-make-choices/.

2. As cited in Brower, V. (2006). Mind-body research moves towards the mainstream. *EMBO Reports, 7*, 358–361.

3. James, W. (1884). What is an emotion? *Mind, 9*, 188–205, 194.

4. Note, however, that around the same time, Danish physician Carl Georg Lange was independently developing a similar theory that emotions are responses to physical sensations. As a result, the idea that nonverbal expressions are causes, not outcomes, of emotions, is often referred to as the James-Lange theory.

5. James, What is an emotion?, 190.

6. Critchley, H. D., Mathias, C. J., & Dolan, R. J. (2001). Neuroanatomical basis for first- and second-order representations of bodily states. *Nature Neuroscience, 4*, 207–212; Critchley, H. D., Mathias, C. J., & Dolan, R. J. (2002). Fear conditioning in humans: The influence of awareness and autonomic arousal on functional neuroanatomy, *Neuron, 33*, 653–663.

7. Laird, J. D. (1974). Self-attribution of emotion: The effects of expressive behavior on the quality of emotional experience. *Journal of Personality and Social Psychology, 29*, 475–486.

8. Strack, F., Martin, L. L., & Stepper, S. (1988). Inhibiting and facilitating conditions of the human smile: A nonobtrusive test of the facial feedback hypothesis. *Journal of Personality and Social Psychology, 54*, 768–777. This study in fact closely resembles a cartoon-rating experiment in Laird's 1974 paper.

9. Dzokoto, V., Wallace, D. S., Peters, L., & Bentsi-Enchill, E. (2014). Attention to emotion and non-western faces: Revisiting the facial feedback hypothesis. *The Journal of General Psychology, 141*, 151–168; Mori, K., & Mori, H. (2009). Another test of the passive facial feedback hypothesis: When your face smiles, you feel happy. *Perceptual and Motor Skills, 109*, 76–78.

10. Ito, T. A., Chiao, K. W., Devine, P. G., Lorig, T. S., & Cacioppo, J. T. (2006). The influence of facial feedback on race bias. *Psychological Science, 17,* 256–261.

11. Mori, H., & Mori, K. (2007). A test of the passive facial feedback hypothesis: We feel sorry because we cry. *Perceptual and Motor Skills, 105,* 1242–1244.

12. Mori, K., & Mori, H. (2010). Examination of the passive facial feedback hypothesis using an implicit measure: With a furrowed brow, neutral objects with pleasant primes look less appealing. *Perceptual and Motor Skills, 111,* 785–789; Larsen, R. J., Kasimatis, M., & Frey, K. (1992). Facilitating the furrowed brow: An unobtrusive test of the facial feedback hypothesis applied to unpleasant affect. *Cognition & Emotion, 6,* 321–338; Duclos, S. E., & Laird, J. D. (2001). The deliberate control of emotional experience through control of expressions. *Cognition & Emotion, 15,* 27–56.

13. Lewis, M. B., & Bowler, P. J. (2009). Botulinum toxin cosmetic therapy correlates with a more positive mood. *Journal of Cosmetic Dermatology, 8,* 24–26.

14. Wollmer, M. A., de Boer, C., Kalak, N., Beck, J., Götz, T., Schmidt, T., . . . & Kruger, T. H. (2012). Facing depression with botulinum toxin: A randomized controlled trial. *Journal of Psychiatric Research, 46,* 574–581.

15. Neal, D. T., & Chartrand, T. L. (2011). Embodied emotion perception amplifying and dampening facial feedback modulates emotion perception accuracy. *Social Psychological and Personality Science, 2,* 673–678.

16. Dimberg, U., Thunberg, M., & Elmehed, K. (2000). Unconscious facial reactions to emotional facial expressions. *Psychological Science, 11,* 86–89.

17. North-Hager, E. (2011, April 22). Botox impairs ability to understand emotions of others. Retrieved from https://pressroom.usc.edu/botox-impairs -ability-to-understand-emotions-of-others/.

18. Ibid.

19. Laird, J. D., & Lacasse, K. (2014). Bodily influences on emotional feelings: Accumulating evidence and extensions of William James's theory of emotion. *Emotion Review, 6,* 27–34, 31–32. For a more complete review of the research on facial feedback, see Laird, J. D. (2006). *Feelings: The perception of self.* Oxford: Oxford University Press.

20. Some people advocate dropping the D from PTS to remove the stigma of the word *disorder.* See Thompson, M. (2011, June 5). *The disappearing "disorder": Why PTS is becoming PTS.* Retrieved from http://nation.time .com/2011/06/05/the-disappearing-disorder-why-PTS-is-becoming-pts/.

21. Van der Kolk, B. A. (2014). *The body keeps the score.* New York: Viking, 213.

22. Interlandi, J. (2014, May 22). A revolutionary approach to treating PTS. The *New York Times Magazine*. Retrieved from http://www.nytimes.com/2014/05/25/magazine/a-revolutionary-approach-to-treating-PTS.html.

23. Seppälä, E. M., Nitschke, J. B., Tudorascu, D. L., Hayes, A., Goldstein, M. R., Nguyen, D. T. H., Perlman, D., & Davidson, R. J. (2014). Breathing-based meditation decreases posttraumatic stress disorder symptoms in U.S. military veterans: A randomized controlled longitudinal study. *Journal of Traumatic Stress, 27,* 397–405.

24. As cited in ibid.

25. McGonigal, K. (2009). *Yoga for pain relief: Simple practices to calm your mind and heal your chronic pain.* Oakland, CA: New Harbinger Publications.

26. Van der Kolk, *The body keeps the score,* 214.

27. Ibid., 208. In this book I'm focusing on only breathing and movement, but rhythm and chanting can also be helpful in achieving presence. For more, see van der Kolk's book.

28. Van der Kolk, B. A., Stone, L., West, J., Rhodes, A., Emerson, D., Suvak, M., & Spinazzola, J. (2014). Yoga as an adjunctive treatment for posttraumatic stress disorder: A randomized controlled trial. *The Journal of Clinical Psychiatry, 75,* 559–565.

29. Melville, G. W., Chang, D., Colagiuri, B., Marshall, P. W., & Cheema, B. S. (2012). Fifteen minutes of chair-based yoga postures or guided meditation performed in the office can elicit a relaxation response. *Evidence-Based Complementary and Alternative Medicine, 2012.*

30. For a recent overview, see Muhtadie, L., Koslov, K., Akinola, M., & Mendes, W. B. (2015). Vagal flexibility: A physiological predictor of social sensitivity. *Journal of Personality and Social Psychology, 109,* 106–120.

31. Van der Kolk, *The body keeps the score,* 201.

32. Seppälä et al., Breathing-based meditation; Bhasin, M. K., Dusek, J. A., Chang, B. H., Joseph, M. G., Denninger, J. W., Fricchione, G. L., Benson, H., & Libermann, T. A. (2013). Relaxation response induces temporal transcriptome changes in energy metabolism, insulin secretion and inflammatory pathways. *PLoS ONE, 8,* e62817–e62825; Peters, R. K., Benson, H., & Porter, D. (1977). Daily relaxation response breaks in a working population: I. Effects on self-reported measures of health, performance, and well-being. *American Journal of Public Health, 67,* 946–953; Benson, H., Wilcher, M., Greenberg, B., Huggins, E., Ennis, M., Zuttermeister, P. C., Myers, P., & Friedman, R. (2000). Academic performance among middle school students after exposure to a relaxation response curriculum. *Journal of Research and Development in Education, 33,* 156–165; Tyson, P. D. (1998). Physiological arousal, reactive

aggression, and the induction of an incompatible relaxation response. *Aggression and Violent Behavior*, 3, 143–158; Marchand, W. R. (2013). Mindfulness meditation practices as adjunctive treatments for psychiatric disorders. *Psychiatric Clinics of North America*, 36, 141–152; Marchand, W. R. (2012). Mindfulness-based stress reduction, mindfulness-based cognitive therapy, and Zen meditation for depression, anxiety, pain, and psychological distress. *Journal of Psychiatric Practice*, 18, 233–252.

33. Philippot, P., Chapelle, G., & Blairy, S. (2002). Respiratory feedback in the generation of emotion. *Cognition & Emotion*, 16, 605–627.

34. Terathongkum, S., & Pickler, R. H. (2004). Relationships among heart rate variability, hypertension, and relaxation techniques. *Journal of Vascular Nursing*, 22, 78–82; Bhasin et al., Relaxation response induces temporal transcriptome changes; West, J., Otte, C., Geher, K., Johnson, J., & Mohr, D. C. (2004). Effects of Hatha yoga and African dance on perceived stress, affect, and salivary cortisol. *Annals of Behavioral Medicine*, 28, 114–118; Kim, S. H., Schneider, S. M., Bevans, M., Kravitz, L., Mermier, C., Qualls, C., & Burge, M. R. (2013). PTSD symptom reduction with mindfulness-based stretching and deep breathing exercise: Randomized controlled clinical trial of efficacy. *The Journal of Clinical Endocrinology & Metabolism*, 98, 2984–2992; Nater, U. M., & Rohleder, N. (2009). Salivary alpha-amylase as a non-invasive biomarker for the sympathetic nervous system: Current state of research. *Psychoneuroendocrinology*, 34, 486–496.

35. Fairbanks, How surfing taught me to make choices.

Chapter 8 The Body Shapes the Mind (So Starfish Up!)

1. Until I was in kindergarten and we moved back to Pennsylvania, where my parents were born and raised, my dad was a park ranger in Washington State. The park I describe here is called Ginkgo Petrified Forest State Park in Vantage, Washington. By the year 2000, the population of Vantage had dropped to seventy, but the tiny stone house still sits there, right in the middle of the park.

2. Carney, D., Cuddy, A. J. C., & Yap, A. (2010). Power posing: Brief nonverbal displays affect neuroendocrine levels and risk tolerance. *Psychological Science*, 21, 1363–1368. Note that both experiments are reported in the article. However, in response to editorial feedback, we had to omit most of the methodological details about the first experiment. If you search for it in the original paper, go to the "General Discussion," where you'll find it summarized in a single paragraph. I'm providing more details here in the book.

3. Minvaleev, R. S., Nozdrachev, A. D., Kir'yanova, V. V., & Ivanov, A. I. (2004). Postural influences on the hormone level in healthy subjects: I. The cobra posture and steroid hormones. *Human Physiology*, 30, 452–456.

4. They also looked at dehydroepiandrosterone (DHEA) and aldosterone (which plays a central role in the regulation of blood pressure), but results were mixed, with some subjects experiencing changes and others not.

5. Even in the simplest yoga disciplines, most postures are fairly complex. There are numerous moving parts, all of which must be properly aligned. The postures must be held for a certain amount of time, and there are breathing and mindfulness components as well. And as a practical strategy for quick results, yoga may not be the easiest option for most of us in most situations.

6. Hormone levels are typically measured in blood or saliva samples. Although the former may allow for a more conservative test, social psychologists very rarely collect blood samples, so saliva samples are standard. To accurately measure changes in salivary levels of testosterone and cortisol in response to a stimulus, such as power posing, (1) the study should be conducted and samples collected in the afternoon (because of normal diurnal changes in these hormone levels), (2) the experimenter should wait at least ten minutes after the subjects have arrived at the lab before taking the first saliva sample, thereby allowing hormones to return to baseline levels, and (3) the experimenter should wait fifteen to twenty minutes after the onset of the stimulus to take the second saliva sample.

7. Riskind, J. H., & Gotay, C. C. (1982). Physical posture: Could it have regulatory or feedback effects on motivation and emotion? *Motivation and Emotion, 6*, 273–298; Riskind, J. H. (1984). They stoop to conquer: Guiding and self-regulatory functions of physical posture after success and failure. *Journal of Personality and Social Psychology, 47*, 479–493.

8. Stepper, S., & Strack, F. (1993). Proprioceptive determinants of emotional and nonemotional feelings. *Journal of Personality and Social Psychology, 64*, 211–220.

9. The concept of "idea stickiness" is quite interesting, especially in the context of marketing. To learn more about the research into why some ideas stick and others don't, read Heath, C., & Heath, D. (2007). *Made to stick*. New York: Random House.

10. For a brief summary of these many studies, see Carney, D. R., Cuddy, A. J., & Yap, A. J. (2015). Review and summary of research on the embodied effects of expansive (vs. contractive) nonverbal displays. *Psychological Science, 26*, 657–663.

11. Huang, L., Galinsky, A. D., Gruenfeld, D. H., & Guillory, L. E. (2011). Powerful postures versus powerful roles: Which is the proximate correlate of thought and behavior? *Psychological Science, 22*, 95–102.

12. Thein, S. M. (2013). *Embodied foundations of the self: Food, grooming, and cultural pathways of human development in Burma-Myanmar and the*

United States (UCLA: psychology dissertation 0780). Retrieved from https://escholarship.org/uc/item/6n09v64m.

13. Riskind, They stoop to conquer.

14. Nair, S., Sagar, M., Sollers III, J., Consedine, N., & Broadbent, E. (2015). Do slumped and upright postures affect stress responses? A randomized trial. *Health Psychology, 34,* 632–641.

15. Kacewicz, E., Pennebaker, J. W., Davis, M., Jeon, M., & Graesser, A. C. (2014). Pronoun use reflects standings in social hierarchies. *Journal of Language and Social Psychology, 33*(2), 125–143; Bernstein, E. (2013, October 7). A tiny pronoun says a lot about you: How often you say "I" says a lot more than you realize. *Wall Street Journal.* Retrieved from http://www.wsj.com/articles/SB10001424052702304626104579121371885556170.

16. Michalak, J., Mischnat, J., & Teismann, T. (2014). Sitting posture makes a difference — Embodiment effects on depressive memory bias. *Clinical Psychology & Psychotherapy, 21,* 519–524.

17. Michalak, J., Rohde, K., & Troje, N. F. (2015). How we walk affects what we remember: Gait modifications through biofeedback change negative affective memory bias. *Journal of Behavior Therapy and Experimental Psychiatry, 46,* 121–125.

18. Guillory, L. E., & Gruenfeld, D. H. (2010). Fake it till you make it: How acting powerful leads to feeling empowered. Manuscript in preparation.

19. Kwon, J., & Kim, S. Y. (2015). The effect of posture on stress and self-esteem: Comparing contractive and neutral postures. Unpublished manuscript.

20. Wilson, V. E., & Peper, E. (2004). The effects of upright and slumped postures on the recall of positive and negative thoughts. *Applied Psychophysiology and Biofeedback, 29,* 189–195.

21. Briñol, P., Petty, R. E., & Wagner, B. (2009). Body posture effects on self-evaluation: A self-validation approach. *European Journal of Social Psychology, 39,* 1053–1064.

22. Arnette, S. L., & Pettijohn II, T. F. (2012). The effects of posture on self-perceived leadership. *International Journal of Business and Social Science, 3,* 8–13.

23. Noda, W., & Tanaka-Matsumi, J. (2009). Effect of a classroom-based behavioral intervention package on the improvement of children's sitting posture in Japan. *Behavior Modification, 33,* 263–273.

24. Peper, E., & Lin, I. M. (2012). Increase or decrease depression: How body postures influence your energy level. *Biofeedback, 40,* 125–130.

25. Allen, J., Gervais, S. J., & Smith, J. (2013). Sit big to eat big: The interaction of body posture and body concern on restrained eating. *Psychology of Women Quarterly, 37,* 325–336.

26. Park, L. E., Streamer, L., Huang, L., & Galinsky, A. D. (2013). Stand tall, but don't put your feet up: Universal and culturally-specific effects of expansive postures on power. *Journal of Experimental Social Psychology, 49*, 965–971.

27. Lee, E. H., & Schnall, S. (2014). The influence of social power on weight perception. *Journal of Experimental Psychology: General, 143*, 1719–1725.

28. Jordet, G., & Hartman, E. (2008). Avoidance motivation and choking under pressure in soccer penalty shootouts. *Journal of Sport and Exercise Psychology, 30*(4), 450–457.

29. Bohns, V. K., & Wiltermuth, S. S. (2012). It hurts when I do this (or you do that): Posture and pain tolerance. *Journal of Experimental Social Psychology, 48*, 341–345.

30. Cuddy, A. C., Wilmuth, C. A., Yap, A. J., & Carney, D. R. (2015). Preparatory power posing affects nonverbal presence and job interview performance. *Journal of Applied Psychology, 100*, 1286–1295.

31. For more information on this, see Fejer, R., Kyvik, K. O., & Hartvigsen, J. (2006). The prevalence of neck pain in the world population: A systematic critical review of the literature. *European Spine Journal, 15*, 834–848.

32. S. August, personal communication.

33. In an e-mail to me, Steve August continues:

> Very briefly, here's what happens:
> (1) Hunch-over heaps. Eventually the upper-back hinges, which allow this movement, will freeze up in that flexed position, and the tough collagen around the spine will shorten up around the immobile joints. When this gets tight enough, no one can straighten the hinges themselves — you have to use sufficient external force. It's a matter of leverage.
> (2) The muscles down the back of the neck work several times harder to hold the head up, just to look ahead or at a small screen. So these strain, then scar (adhesive fibrosis) as part of the repair of that strain, then shorten because of the scarring.
> (3) The muscles around the front of the neck work less and weaken, so the chin pokes out.
> (4) This hunched, poked-chin posture compresses every joint in the neck, and sooner or later some will lock acutely, causing neck pain, referred pain, and headache....

According to conservative estimates, right now, as you read this, around one adult in six in the computer-using world has acute pain in the upper back or neck or headaches arising from the neck. That means sixty million Europeans, forty-five million Americans, and 3.3 million Aussies. Those figures are probably already out of date. A good single overview is found in a paper by René Fejer, Kirsten Ohm Kyvik, and Jan Hartvigsen called "The prevalence of neck pain in the world population: A systematic critical review of the literature," published in the *European Spine Journal* of June 2006 (15[6], pages 834–848).

34. Bos, M. W., & Cuddy, A. J. (2013). iPosture: The size of electronic consumer devices affects our behavior. Harvard Business School working paper. In a separate study with 100 participants we showed that the smaller the device, the more contractive our posture — hands are closer together, shoulders are more slumped, and we're generally less expansive.

35. Sharma, N., & Baron, J. C. (2013). Does motor imagery share neural networks with executed movement: A multivariate fMRI analysis. *Frontiers in Human Neuroscience, 7,* 564; Nyberg, L., Eriksson, J., Larsson, A., & Marklund, P. (2006). Learning by doing versus learning by thinking: An fMRI study of motor and mental training. *Neuropsychologia, 44,* 711–717; Jeannerod, M., & Frak, V. (1999). Mental imaging of motor activity in humans. *Current Opinion in Neurobiology, 9,* 735–739.

36. Boly, M., Coleman, M. R., Davis, M. H., Hampshire, A., Bor, D., Moonen, G., Maquet, P. A., Pickard, J. D., Laureys, S., & Owen, A. M. (2007). When thoughts become action: An fMRI paradigm to study volitional brain activity in non-communicative brain injured patients. *NeuroImage, 36,* 979–992.

37. Cyranoski, D. (2012, June 13). Neuroscience: The mind reader. *Nature.* Retrieved from http://www.nature.com/news/neuroscience-the-mind-reader-1.10816.

38. Aflalo, T., Kellis, S., Klaes, C., Lee, B., Shi, Y., Pejsa, K., Shanfield, K., Hayes-Jackson, S., Aisen, M. Heck, C., Liu, C., & Andersen, R. A. (2015). Decoding motor imagery from the posterior parietal cortex of a tetraplegic human. *Science, 348,* 906–910.

39. Cuddy, A. J. C., & Thornley, N. The body in the brain: Imagining oneself in a powerful posture increases confidence and decreases social threat. Working manuscript.

40. Lanier, J. (2001). Virtually there. *Scientific American, 284,* 66–75; Slater, M., Spanlang, B., Sanchez-Vives, M. V., Blanke, O. (2010). First person experience of body transfer in virtual reality. *PLoS ONE, 5,* e10564; Kilteni, K., Normand, J.-M., Sanchez-Vives, M. V., Slater, M. (2012). Extending body space in immersive virtual reality: A very long arm illusion. *PLoS ONE 7,* e40867.

41. Yee, N., & Bailenson, J. (2007). The Proteus effect: The effect of transformed self-representation on behavior. *Human Communication Research*, 33, 271–290.

42. Rosenberg, R. S., Baughman, S. L., & Bailenson, J. N. (2013). Virtual superheroes: Using superpowers in virtual reality to encourage prosocial behavior. *PLoS ONE*, 8, e55003.

43. Yap, A. J., Wazlawek, A. S., Lucas, B. J., Cuddy, A. C., & Carney, D. R. (2013). The ergonomics of dishonesty: The effect of incidental posture on stealing, cheating, and traffic violations. *Psychological Science*, 24, 2281–2289.

44. As with any psychological phenomenon, there are variables that amplify or dampen the effects of expansive postures. Most important, context matters. For example, one study showed that adopting expansive postures did not increase risk tolerance when people were asked to imagine that they were being frisked by a police officer. Engaging in social tasks — such as looking at photos of faces — while holding poses seems to increase the strength of the effects, perhaps because power is so often considered a social construct. Another factor that needs further examination is the duration of time one holds a pose. Because I discussed our first study, in which people held the two poses for a total of two minutes, in my TED talk, "two minutes" took on some kind of magical quality as news of the talk and research spread throughout popular culture. Yes, two minutes worked in that study, but across the fifty or more studies on the effects of adopting expansive postures, subjects have held postures anywhere from thirty seconds to more than five minutes. And in yoga classes, people are moving through a series of poses for an hour or more. Two minutes isn't a rigid prescription. In fact, it seems that holding a single pose for more than a minute or two (outside of a yoga studio) becomes uncomfortable and awkward, making people too self-aware and perhaps diluting some of the effects of power posing. In some pilot studies we've done with children, holding a pose for more than twenty seconds becomes awkward. If you'd like to read more about some of the possible moderators, see Carney, D. R., Cuddy, A. J., & Yap, A. J. (2015). Review and summary of research on the embodied effects of expansive (vs. contractive) nonverbal displays. *Psychological Science*, 26(5), 657–663.

Chapter 9 How to Pose for Presence

1. Finkel, E. J., & Eastwick, P. W. (2009). Arbitrary social norms influence sex differences in romantic selectivity. *Psychological Science*, 20, 1290–1295.

2. For more great advice about effective body language during presentations, read Neffinger, J., & Kohut, M. (2014). *Compelling People*. New York: Plume.

3. Ibid.

4. Merchant, N. Sitting is the new smoking of our generation (January 14, 2013). *Harvard Business Review.* Retrieved from https://hbr.org/2013/01/sitting-is-the-smoking-of-our-generation/.

5. For more on walking meetings, watch Nilofer Merchant's TED talk, "Got a meeting? Take a walk," retrieved from: https://www.ted.com/talks/nilofer_merchant_got_a_meeting_take_a_walk. Also, see this *Inc.* article that describes some of the scientific findings on the benefits of walking meetings: Economy, P. (2015, April 6). 7 powerful reasons to take your next meeting for a walk. *Inc.* Retrieved from http://www.inc.com/peter-economy/7-powerful-reasons-to-take-your-next-meeting-for-a-walk.html.

Chapter 10 Self-Nudging: How Tiny Tweaks Lead to Big Changes

1. Bos, M. & Cuddy, A. (2011, May 16). A counter-intuitive approach to making complex decisions. *Harvard Business Review.* Retrieved from https://hbr.org/2011/05/a-counter-intuitive-approach-t/.

2. Lamott, A. (1995). *Bird by bird: Some instructions on writing and life* (p. 28). New York: Anchor.

3. I don't think I know of anyone who ever completely recovers from a traumatic brain injury; everyone inevitably changes as a result of it. I process information in a different way and continue to deal with non-life-threatening but annoying TBI-related issues, such as vision problems.

4. Jachimowicz, J. M., & McNerney, S. (2015, August 13). Should governments nudge us to make good choices? *Scientific American.* Retrieved from http://www.scientificamerican.com/article/should-governments-nudge-us-to-make-good-choices/.

5. For more on Opower, see Cuddy, A. J. C., Doherty, K., & Bos, M. W. OPOWER: Increasing energy efficiency through normative influence (A). Harvard Business School Case 911-016 (2010, Revised 2011); Bos, M. W., Cuddy, A. J. C., & Doherty, K. OPOWER: Increasing energy efficiency through normative influence (B). Harvard Business School Case 911-061 (2011); Navigant Consulting. Evaluation Report: OPOWER SMUD pilot year2. (February 20, 2011). Retrieved from http://opower.com/company/library/verification-reports?year=2011; Allcott, H. (2011). Social norms and energy conservation. *Journal of Public Economics, 95,* 1082–1095; Ayres, I., Raseman, S., & Shih, I. (2009). Evidence from two large field experiments that peer comparison feedback can reduce residential energy usage. (July 16, 2009). Fifth Annual Conference on Empirical Legal Studies Paper. Retrieved from http://papers.ssrn.com/sol3/papers.cfm?abstract_id=1434950.

6. Singal, J. (2013, April 26). Daniel Kahneman's gripe with behavioral economics. *The Daily Beast.* Retrieved from http://www.thedailybeast.com /articles/2013/04/26/daniel-kahneman-s-gripe-with-behavioral-economics.html.

7. Thaler, R. H., Sunstein, C. R., & Balz, J. P. (2012). Choice architecture. In E. Shafir (Ed.), *The behavioral foundations of public policy* (pp. 245–263). Princeton, NJ: Princeton University Press.

8. I started noticing that a lot of the small self-interventions people were devising, including power posing, relied on at least two or three principles underlying the classic nudges. I coined the term *self-nudge* and then co-organized a symposium on the topic for the annual meeting of the Society for Personality and Social Psychology (SPSP).

9. Dweck, C. (2014, December). The power of believing that you can improve. *TED.* Retrieved from https://www.ted.com/talks/carol_dweck_the _power_of_believing_that_you_can_improve/transcript.

10. Miu, A. S., & Yeager, D. S. (2015). Preventing symptoms of depression by teaching adolescents that people can change: Effects of a brief incremental theory of personality intervention at 9-month follow-up. *Clinical Psychological Science.* DOI: 10.1177/2167702614548317.

11. Rosenthal, R., & Jacobson, L. (1968). Pygmalion in the classroom. *The Urban Review, 3,* 16–20.

12. Word, C. O., Zanna, M. P., & Cooper, J. (1974). The nonverbal mediation of self-fulfilling prophecies in interracial interaction. *Journal of Experimental Social Psychology, 10,* 109–120.

13. See, for example, Lepper, M. P., Greene, D., & Nisbett, R. E. (1973). Undermining children's intrinsic interest with extrinsic reward: A test of the "overjustification" hypothesis. *Journal of Personality and Social Psychology, 28,* 129–137.

14. Cuddy, A. J. C., & Brooks, A. W. (Chairs). (2014). Self-nudges: How intrapersonal tweaks change cognition, feelings, and behavior. Symposium conducted at the fifteenth annual meeting of the Society for Personality and Social Psychology, Austin, TX.

15. Brooks, A. W. (2014). Get excited: Reappraising pre-performance anxiety as excitement. *Journal of Experimental Psychology: General, 143,* 1144–1158.

16. Baer, D. (2013, November 26). Feeling anxious? Why trying to "keep calm" is a terrible idea. *Fast Company.* Retrieved from http://www.fast company.com/3022177/leadership-now/feeling-anxious-why-trying-to-keep -calm-is-a-terrible-idea.

17. Hershfield, H. (2014, September 9). How can we help our future selves? (TEDxEast talk). *YouTube.* Retrieved from https://www.youtube.com /watch?v=tJotBbd7MwQ.

18. Kogut, T., & Ritov, I. (2005). The "identified victim" effect: An identified group, or just a single individual? *Journal of Behavioral Decision Making,* 18, 157–167; Loewenstein, G., Small, D., & Strnad, J. (2006). Statistical, identifiable, and iconic victims. In E. J. McCaffery & J. Slemrod (Eds.), *Behavioral public finance* (pp. 32–46). New York: Russell Sage Foundation.

19. Ersner-Hershfield, H., Wimmer, G. E., & Knutson, B. (2009). Saving for the future self: Neural measures of future self-continuity predict temporal discounting. *Social Cognitive and Affective Neuroscience, 4,* 85–92.

20. Hershfield, H. E., Goldstein, D. G., Sharpe, W. F., Fox, J., Yeykelis, L., Carstensen, L. L., & Bailenson, J. N. (2011). Increasing saving behavior through age-progressed renderings of the future self. *Journal of Marketing Research, 48,* S23–S37.

21. Learn more about age-progression technology at http://www.modiface .com/news.php?story=210.

22. Adam, H., & Galinsky, A. D. (2012). Enclothed cognition. *Journal of Experimental Social Psychology, 48,* 918–925.

Chapter 11 Fake It Till You Become It

1. To watch a video about Vafi, go to https://www.youtube.com/watch?v =1Kzftoa2WAE. To watch a video about Draumur, go to https://vimeo .com/104160336.

2. Humans and horses are not alone: the same holds true for dogs, particularly in social situations, such as one would find at a dog park — hunched and "lowering" postures in dogs have been linked to elevated cortisol levels and apparent stress; open postures, on the other hand, are not. See Carrier, L. O., Cyr, A., Anderson, R. E., & Walsh, C. J. (2013). Exploring the dog park: Relationships between social behaviours, personality and cortisol in companion dogs. *Applied Animal Behaviour Science, 146,* 96–106; Beerda, B., Schilder, M. B., van Hooff, J. A., de Vries, H. W., & Mol, J. A. (1998). Behavioural, saliva cortisol and heart rate responses to different types of stimuli in dogs. *Applied Animal Behaviour Science, 58,* 365–381.

Index

Index

Index

Index

Index

Index